FINDING THE ENEMY WITHIN

BLASPHEMY ACCUSATIONS
AND SUBSEQUENT VIOLENCE
IN PAKISTAN

FINDING THE ENEMY WITHIN

BLASPHEMY ACCUSATIONS
AND SUBSEQUENT VIOLENCE
IN PAKISTAN

SANA ASHRAF

PRESS

For Mashal Khan and many others who have lost their lives after being accused of blasphemy

Published by ANU Press
The Australian National University
Acton ACT 2601, Australia
Email: anupress@anu.edu.au

Available to download for free at press.anu.edu.au

ISBN (print): 9781760464547
ISBN (online): 9781760464554

WorldCat (print): 1264380427
WorldCat (online): 1264380445

DOI: 10.22459/FEW.2021

This title is published under a Creative Commons Attribution-NonCommercial-NoDerivatives 4.0 International (CC BY-NC-ND 4.0).

The full licence terms are available at
creativecommons.org/licenses/by-nc-nd/4.0/legalcode

This publication was awarded a College of Arts and Social Sciences PhD Publication Prize in 2020. The prize contributes to the cost of professional copyediting.

Cover design and layout by ANU Press

This edition © 2021 ANU Press

Contents

Acknowledgements	ix
Abbreviations	xi
Glossary	xiii
Prologue	xv
Introduction	1

Part I

1. Historical roots of anti-blasphemy violence in Pakistan: Formation of self, community and the state — 31
2. Religious discourse concerning blasphemy: Politics of uncertainty and legitimacy — 61

Part II

3. Blasphemy accusations: Power, purity and the enemy within — 97
4. Violence in the making: The politics of escalation from accusation to punishment — 117

Part III

5. Legitimate punishment of blasphemy: Contestation between the legal system and popular justice — 147
6. At the nexus of state and society: Continuities and discontinuities between the legal system and popular justice — 171

Conclusion	201
Appendix: Text of offences relating to religion (Pakistan Penal Code, 1860)	207
Bibliography	211
Index	233

Acknowledgements

This book started life as a PhD thesis and I owe my thanks to many people who contributed to this project over the years, not all of whom can be listed here. Particular thanks go to my PhD supervisor, Dr Patrick Guinness, who has been remarkably supportive throughout my journey. From reading my drafts promptly, to giving me constant, constructive feedback, he has been an incredible mentor. He pushed me to think critically about every aspect of this work and has offered endless theoretical and analytical insights that have shaped my arguments in this book. His vast knowledge of modern states, social movements and conflict in societies has significantly enriched my understanding of my research topic. It is because of Dr Guinness's exceptional confidence in me that I have been able to revise my PhD thesis into a book and win the CASS PhD Publishing Prize for 2020. I am grateful to the College of Arts and Social Sciences (CASS) at The Australian National University for funding the editing and final production of this book. I would also like to extend my gratitude to the rest of my supervisory panel—Professor Francesca Merlan, Professor Chris Gregory and Dr Joyce Das—who shared their expertise and critical insights, which were vital to refining my PhD thesis. In revising my thesis into this book, I was guided by the remarkably detailed and valuable reviews by my three anonymous examiners to whom I shall always remain indebted. I am fortunate to have had the opportunity to learn from incredible academic mentors and improve my work under their guidance. Any errors, omissions and inadequacies remaining are entirely my own.

This book would not have been possible without the trust of the people who shared their lives and experiences with me. Many of these people cannot be identified but have my absolute gratitude; I am eternally obliged to them. Many organisations and individuals facilitated my access to the research participants and archival materials. In particular, I would like to thank Engage Pakistan, Pakistan for All, Centre for Legal Aid Assistance and Settlement Pakistan (CLAAS), Centre for Justice and Peace (CJP) and Voice Society Pakistan for their cooperation. I would specifically like to mention Joseph Francis, Peter Jacob and Napoleon Qayyum for their unending support. I would further like to acknowledge the assistance of lawyers from both sides who generously let me study their cases and interact with their clients. Additionally, several people at my alma mater, Lahore University of Management Sciences (LUMS), have aided my research by providing patronage, support and facilities. I am grateful to all of them.

The process of writing my PhD thesis was made bearable (and sometimes even enjoyable) by my colleagues and friends at The Australian National University and beyond. The anthropology thesis writing group was a source of moral support and intellectual enhancement throughout 2017. Dr Caroline Schuster, the convener of our thesis writing group, provided immense encouragement and invaluable mentorship to kickstart the long journey of writing that culminated in this book. Since 2017, I have been a part of many other writing groups that made writing on evenings, and even weekends, fun in a positive community environment. I would especially like to thank my constant writing companions and affectionate friends, Lina Koleilat and Joowhee Lee, for enriching my PhD journey with their love and care. I would also like to thank my friends Areeba Nabeel, Farhana Bashar, Becky Gidley and Bec Heland, who have been constant pillars of support over the past few years. I am thankful to them all for having been there for me whenever I needed them and for keeping me sane.

In the end, I would like to thank my family and my partner for their unshaking faith and confidence in me even when I was steeped in self-doubt and could not see myself ever crossing the finish line (of the PhD and then of the book). My parents and my siblings have stood by my side (and put up with me) while I prioritised my research over their important life events. It was their trust and unconditional love that kept me going. I can never thank my parents enough for encouraging me to follow my dreams even in the face of criticism from people around them who deemed my pursuit of a PhD a useless venture. Finally, I owe infinite gratitude to my husband, William Baldwinson, who has played multiple roles in bringing this book to fruition. In addition to providing unswerving emotional support, he has read and edited several drafts of this book, helped me get through mind blocks by patiently listening to me and advised me on how to organise and structure my ideas. I could not have asked for a better companion through the most crucial years of my life as a researcher.

Abbreviations

AIML	All India Muslim League
CIA	Central Intelligence Agency (US)
FIR	first information report
ISI	Inter-Services Intelligence
JI	Jamaat-e-Islami
KNLF	Khatm-e-Nabuwwat Lawyers' Forum
NGO	non-governmental organisation
PAT	Pakistan Awami Tehreek
PBUH	peace be upon him
PMLN	Pakistan Muslim League
PPC	Pakistan Penal Code
PTI	Pakistan Tehreek-e-Insaf
SSP	Sipah-e-Sahaba Pakistan
TLP	Tehreek-e-Labbaik Pakistan

Glossary

bey-hurmati	sacrilege
dhimmi	non-Mulsim minority
fatwa	religious verdict
fiqh	Islamic jurisprudence
gustaakhi	irreverence
hadd	mandatorily enforced law
hadith	transmitted knowledge of the Prophet
maarifat	inner knowledge or gnosis
madrasah	educational institute
na'at	song in praise of the Prophet
pir	spiritual leader
sunnah	the prophetic traditions
tauheen-e-risaalat	insult to the Prophet
tazeer	discretionary law

Prologue

Masjid dha de, Mandir dha de, dha de jo kuch dhainda
Ik banday da dil na dhaawiin, rabb Dillan wich rehnda.
[Tear down the mosque, demolish the temple; Break whatever you like,
But do not break a person's heart; That is where the God resides.]

This couplet from a famous Punjabi Sufi poet, Bulleh Shah (1680–1757), speaks of the intrinsic value of every person regardless of their religion and conveys the message that God is found not in mosques or temples but in people's hearts. This is just one example of the much wider ethos of Sufi poetry, which I started reading and listening to in my undergraduate years. It provided me with solace and hope in the face of sectarian tensions that had defined my identity until that point.

I grew up in a lower-middle-class, mixed-sect family in Pakistan. My father's family are Shia Muslims and my mother's family are Sunni Muslims. The mix was even more muddled by the fact that my father's father had converted from Sunni Islam to Shi'ism in his midlife, effectively causing his wife and children to convert as well. Therefore, my father's cousins (and their children) are Sunni Muslims. I grew up in an environment where tensions related to right or wrong religious practices and beliefs were a part of everyday life. There were conflicts and ruptures, but there were also reconciliations and bridges. There were judgements and disapproval, but there was also tolerance and acceptance. Impassioned arguments about Shia versus Sunni religious practices were common, but so was joint participation by Sunni and Shia members of the family in each other's rituals. Regardless, I grew up tremendously confused about my religious identity.

I spent my teenage years trying to figure out the 'right path' for myself by reading religious books from both sects. As I navigated the journey, I swung different ways at different points in my life. At one point,

I became more religious than anyone else in my family, including in ways of which they did not approve. In my early undergraduate years, I started praying regularly, fully covering my head and body and adopted many other religious practices that were not common in my family. In my early twenties, I gave up most of the outwardly religious practices I had adopted so fiercely only a few years earlier.

There were several factors that influenced the changes I went through and the practices I adopted at different points along my journey. Sufism has been one of the strongest and longest-lasting influences on my life. In fact, my earliest introduction to the values of inclusivity, pluralism, tolerance, coexistence and humanism was not through Western philosophy or anthropology. It was through Sufi poetry that I first learnt the idea of transcending the boundaries of religion, sect or caste. Ironically, however, as I would learn later, the followers of Sufism are the ones who are at the forefront of anti-blasphemy campaigns in Pakistan, promoting violence and hatred instead of the message of peace that Sufism enshrines. Bulleh Shah, the highly revered Sufi poet quoted above, would have been persecuted for his blasphemous views and writings in present-day Pakistan. I have written this book from a place of deep sorrow and pain because I see the ideas I once admired and found comfort in being used to spread hatred and violence instead of love and peace.

This book is deeply personal for me. It is a product of the complex emotional and ethical journey in which I have searched myself as much as I have searched other people in the quest for answers to questions that have perplexed me for a long time. Questions of sameness and difference, boundaries and transgressions, the self and the other are central to my life as well as to this book. It is therefore not merely an academic inquiry into a topic I find interesting, but also an important dimension of my life as I have *lived* it.

Growing up in Pakistan, I felt I was constantly being measured against certain religious and cultural moral standards by people around me. The standards changed depending on the people, but there was always a sense of insufficiency and the need to prove one's 'goodness' as a woman, as a Pakistani and as a Muslim. As a young person, I constantly tried changing myself to fit the ever-elusive moral standards and to carve out my own ideals at the same time. In the process, I was not only being measured by others, but also participating in measuring others. I was not only being judged with respect to my faith but also judging others'

Muslim-ness. I was not only the recipient of everyday moral policing, I was also policing others' moral goodness. From my experience of growing up in Pakistani society, I have learnt that the constant struggle to achieve moral and religious correctness and to police other people's moral and religious behaviour is an ingrained aspect of life in Pakistan. This perspective shapes my arguments in this book and is rooted in my own subjective experiences and position in that society.

As an academic inquiry, this book is based on more than seven years of research of blasphemy accusations and subsequent violence in Pakistan, conducted as part of my Masters and PhD degrees (2012–19). I first went to Pakistan explicitly as a 'researcher' in 2014 to conduct three months of fieldwork for my Masters thesis. It was after those three months that I first realised I had hardly scratched the surface of an extremely complex issue and started building a PhD proposal while writing my dissertation. The three months of fieldwork for my Masters thesis were also helpful in facilitating my re-entry into the field to conduct my doctoral research from March 2016 to February 2017.

I was based in Lahore for the duration of my research. Lahore, the capital of Punjab, is a metropolitan city with a population of 11.1 million, according to the 2017 census (PBS 2017). While Lahore is the second-most populous city in Pakistan, after Karachi, it has seen the most cases of blasphemy accusations in the country since 1987 (Jacob 2018). Lahore is a hub for religious organisations and political parties that have been actively engaged in campaigning against alleged blasphemers. During my fieldwork, there were tens of protests, religious gatherings and conferences that took place in Lahore with the explicit aim of protecting the honour of the Prophet and punishing alleged blasphemers. Lahore has multiple shrines central to the religious beliefs and practices of the Barelwis, who are most active in anti-blasphemy activities and campaigns. Most of the Muslim population in Lahore belongs to the Barelwi sect of Sunni Islam, according to unofficial estimates; the state does not identify sectarian affiliations in the official census (Ramzan 2015). Moreover, Lahore has a host of non-governmental organisations (NGOs) and other civil society organisations that have been at the forefront of advocacy and relief activities for those affected by blasphemy accusations. Lahore's session and high courts hear multiple cases of blasphemy every day. For all these reasons, I chose Lahore as the primary site for my research. It was also convenient for me because I had lived in Lahore for four years during my undergraduate studies and my parents also now live in the city. Thus, it was a familiar place, with friends and family, who were crucial to making my fieldwork emotionally and practically viable.

Despite Lahore being the primary site of my research, I describe my research as multi-sited for two reasons. First, within Lahore, I was constantly moving between different spaces, including NGO offices, the houses and neighbourhoods of those affected by blasphemy accusations, courts, shrines and religious centres. Given these spaces are all quite different to one another and often contradictory in what they represent, I find it more useful to see them as multiple sites than as parts of the same big site— the city of Lahore. Second, while based in Lahore, I also visited other towns and cities within Punjab and Islamabad Capital Territory to follow certain cases, meet certain people and see certain places (for example, the shrine of Mumtaz Qadri in Bara Kahu, Islamabad). The towns and cities I visited to understand and follow specific cases included Gujrat, Bhera, Jehlum, Mandi Bahauddin and Rawalpindi.

Ethnography is understood as the classic methodology of anthropology, traditionally defined as a prolonged period of research in which the researcher lives with and observes a community closely to understand their point of view (Spradley 1980: 3). Since the 1980s, however, anthropologists have questioned the traditional understandings of a defined field and bounded community as the objects of ethnographic research (Appadurai 1990; Clifford 1997; Marcus 1996). Such critiques have pointed out that the field no longer operates in fixed localities due to the changing nature of a globalised world. It has also been argued that the traditional notion of ethnography creates false dichotomies, such as home versus the field and insider versus outsider (see, for example, Gupta and Ferguson 1997; Olwig and Hastrup 1997). The ethnographic field is thus seen no longer as a fixed site but as a set of 'shifting locations' defined by the topic of interest (Clifford 1997).

Given the shifting locations of my research, I used the methodology of multi-sited ethnographic research developed in response to critiques of traditional ethnography. The earliest concepts of multi-sited ethnography emerged in 1986 with *Writing Culture* (Clifford and Marcus 1986) and were later developed into a more elaborate theory by Marcus (1995). According to this theory, the researcher follows ideas, people, narratives, connections and objects in time and place. Multi-sited ethnography is:

designed around chains, paths, threads, conjunctions, or juxtapositions of locations in which the ethnographer establishes some form of literal, physical presence, with an explicit, posited logic of association or connection among sites that in fact define the argument of the ethnography. (Marcus 1995: 105)

Adopting multi-sited research methods, I followed cases, stories and people as I moved between different sites and groups of people.

My research participants, as varied as they were, often belonged to opposing schools of thought—for example, those who supported violent punishment of blasphemy and those who did not. I conducted my research, on the one hand, with people who were accused of blasphemy (regardless of whether or not the case was taken to the state legal system), their lawyers, their families, friends and neighbours, activists, social workers, NGO professionals, journalists and some government and police officers. On the other hand, my research participants also included the accusers, their friends, supporters and witnesses, their lawyers, religious clerics, scholars and members of religious parties who either mobilised for violent punishment of the accused in specific cases of blasphemy or wrote, preached or campaigned against blasphemers in general.

Apart from the clearly identified 'research participants', my analysis and insights are also drawn from my experiences and interactions while growing up in Pakistan for the better part of my life. These insights are based on my interactions with my own family, friends, colleagues, neighbours and many other people from whom I have learnt. Sometimes even brief conversations with taxi drivers, shopkeepers and so on provided a window on to the sensibilities of certain sections of Pakistani society. Whether or not these interactions form a part of my 'research' is a tricky question. As Ceja-Zamarripa (2007: 11) asked: '[W]hat does it mean to anthropology that the anthropologist's whole life could be characterized as one continuous participant-observation?' There has been a tendency in traditional anthropology to draw absolute distinctions between experiences of *living in a society* and *doing fieldwork* such that the former is not an accepted basis of knowledge. However, these distinctions have been challenged, as Gupta and Ferguson (1997: 32) write:

> A discipline in which 'experience' is so central has been surprisingly unfriendly to the notion that 'experience' is constantly reconfigured by memory. If an anthropologist can 'write up' an ethnography based on data collected during doctoral fieldwork twenty or thirty

years ago, why should it not be possible for 'natives' to 'write up' an ethnography based on their lives? In what sense might we think of one's 'background'—growing up, as it were, in 'the field'— as a kind of extended participant observation?

In my research, I find it impossible to separate the insights I have gained through explicitly *doing fieldwork* from those I gained by *living* in Pakistani society for an extended period. I draw on these insights to make sense of the knowledge I gained during my fieldwork. I do not quote or use specific information provided by those with whom I casually interacted and learnt from over the years. However, at a broader level, I recognise that the pool of my research participants is much larger than those who appear in this book.

There were two major concerns that guided me as I moved between different sites and groups of people while doing my research: the logic of my topic and the safety of my participants and myself. In terms of the logic of my topic, I wanted to understand the perspectives of various parties to the conflict and how they were opposed but connected to each other. The lack of significant ethnographic work on the issue of blasphemy in Pakistan meant there was a lot of potential in almost every dimension of the topic. Each of my 'sites' could have been a focus for the whole dissertation in itself: the courtrooms, the NGOs, the neighbourhoods, the shrines and so on. However, I was guided by my curiosity to gain a broader understanding of the issue by studying its multiple aspects. On the flip side, it required sacrificing the depth of each aspect to some extent. At such an early stage in research, it made more sense to get a wide understanding of the issue; future research can delve deeper into each of the dimensions.

The second guiding concern was safety. Spending too much time with the accused and their families—specifically those who were living in hiding— could have compromised their and possibly my own safety. On the other hand, there were groups and individuals whose perspective was important to me, but I would have had to risk my safety to access them. For example, towards the end of my fieldwork, I was offered an opportunity by a group of lawyers—who were supporting and representing the killers of alleged blasphemers in court—to go on a countrywide tour with them to meet those who had killed for the love of the Prophet Muhammad, and their families. It was an extremely tempting offer because it would have provided me with a wealth of information about the lives of those who engage in anti-blasphemy violence. However, I was warned by concerned people not to take the risk and I decided to let go of that opportunity. Thus, my decisions regarding my field sites and participants were guided—and limited—by safety concerns.

There are two aspects of my research methodology that I would like to discuss in more detail: the methods that I used to identify and approach my research participants and my methods of data collection. In terms of approaching the research participants, for my initial entry into the field during my Masters research, I began with some publicly available contacts with NGOs—because it appeared the safest option at the time. Some of those who responded positively to my research aims and intentions helped me get in touch with others, within the NGO sector and among those affected by blasphemy accusations. When I later returned for my doctoral research, some of my previous contacts were extremely helpful in letting me back into their circles and introducing me to even more people.

During my PhD fieldwork, I began expanding the scope of my research and used publicly available phone numbers to contact some religious scholars and leaders. Some of them agreed to meet me in person; for others, I had to use family contacts (for example, an uncle of mine who is a member of Jamaat-e-Islami put me in touch with some people in that organisation). Once I had established some key contacts, they were happy to refer me to more people within their circles. Some of my academic friends and mentors at the Lahore University of Management Sciences (where I studied for my undergraduate degree) were also of great help in connecting me with relevant people such as lawyers and journalists. One defence lawyer gave me the contact details of prosecution lawyers, which is how I ended up studying a specific group of prosecution lawyers representing the accusers in court. The prosecution lawyers put me in touch with their clients (the accusers), who then let me talk to their witnesses, their spiritual and religious leaders, and so on. Hence, for most of my research, I used the snowball sampling or chain-referral methods to identify and approach my research participants. Of course, there were many referred persons who never responded; there were also some who promised collaboration that did not materialise. Nevertheless, I found a wealth of connections and information through my initial contacts and their referrals.

As for the data collection, I used a range of different methods, including participant observation, structured and semi-structured interviews and content analysis. For most of my participants, I started with formal interviews and continued to see them regularly such that the relationships grew into more informal interactions over time, allowing me to engage in casual conversations and participant observation. Since I was not based at one fixed site, among one group or community, I kept moving between different groups and individuals depending on their availability and my schedule. However, I actively tried to dedicate weeks (and sometimes even months) to specific groups to develop deeper connections and understanding. For example, with the Khatm-e-Nabuwwat Lawyers' Forum (the group of prosecution lawyers I studied), I spent several days a week over four months to understand their perspective. Similarly, I maintained connections with the accused and their families, trying to see them as many times as they were willing to see me. Some of them kept calling and inviting me to their homes to talk about their experiences. However, I was cautious not to put pressure on any of them to maintain contact because of their safety concerns. I also collected a lot of published data, mostly from the religious organisations and scholars whom I met. They gave me or referred me to dozens of religious publications (mostly in Urdu). I acquired as many of those books and other publications as I could and used them for content analysis. I also followed the social media accounts of religious organisations that were active in anti-blasphemy campaigning during my fieldwork. Some of the major organisations used Twitter to organise their regular protests and gatherings. While I was not able to participate in those protests and gatherings because they were male-only, familiarising myself with the language of mobilisation helped me gain a deeper understanding of the issue. I also kept an eye on their social media content to understand the religious and political narratives being generated and promoted.

My interactions with my research participants—particularly while using ethnographic research methods—were shaped by my own identity and social position in the society. Kirin Narayan's 1993 essay first dispelled the myth of insider versus outsider anthropologists and argued that a multiplex of identities shapes any anthropological research (pp. 673–76). It has since been widely recognised in anthropology that the positions we occupy in society, including class, gender and education, define how we interact with and are perceived by our research participants. More importantly, these social loci also define our own subjectivities and determine how we look at, understand and write about people. I believe various markers of my identity—including my being an educated Pakistani woman from a lower-middle-class, mixed-sect (Sunni–Shia) Muslim family—are crucial to my research.

PROLOGUE

I was the first woman from my entire family (both mother's and father's sides) to go to university and live alone in a different city.[1] I went to a private university—considered the most expensive and most prestigious in Pakistan—which my parents were certainly not able to afford. I was selected for university through a national outreach program that gave scholarships to deserving students with insufficient financial means to pay their fees. At university, I attended a class on the ethnography of Pakistan in my first year because of the university's requirements to take out-group courses (that is, courses from different streams and disciplines). That is where I was first drawn to anthropology and eventually changed my major to anthropology from economics. My parents were not happy with that choice because they wanted me to study something that would get me a well-paying job. They did not know much about anthropology; in fact, they had never even heard of the subject before. What they knew was that 'social science subjects' were not an economically viable option for people with modest economic backgrounds such as ours.

The pursuit of social sciences (and anthropology) has in fact been a luxury for most scholars of Pakistani origin—at least those who have been writing for an international academic audience. There have been brilliant anthropologists—including women—from Pakistan who are highly regarded in the international academic community, but most come from privileged backgrounds. For those from lower-middle-class backgrounds like mine, education is usually a means to attain social prestige and upward economic mobility. Therefore, studying anthropology is an act of going against the grain.[2] My place in the social and economic setup of society is important because it defines my experiences of living in Pakistani society, which may be different from most other scholars, who come from higher socioeconomic backgrounds than mine. These experiences shape who I am as a researcher, how I approach and am perceived by my research participants and how I understand the experiences of those about whom I am writing.

---

1   One of my female cousins had started university a year before me, but she went to an all-female university, studied medicine and lived with her relatives during her studies. I, on the other hand, went to a coed university, did not study medicine (the expected and most prestigious profession for women in our social circle at the time) and lived by myself in a hostel.
2   This is changing now, as increasing numbers of students from backgrounds similar to mine are studying these subjects due to rising awareness about scholarships and career opportunities. However, it remains to be seen how many of those without the privilege and social capital that comes with it are able to make it as successful academics and scholars.

My gender is also an important part of my identity that affects every aspect of my life, from education to personal relationships. What is most important to highlight here are the ways in which my gender impacts my research. Most of my research participants were male and many of them came from backgrounds where it was not common for women to be educated, independent and able to freely mix with men, let alone do research among men. Having said that, even though many of my research participants would not allow women from their families to do what I was doing, they were moving in public spaces where women *were* present as lawyers, religious scholars, NGO workers, farmers, labourers, and so on. Thus, I was not an entirely unusual sight for them. Most of them were extremely respectful in their dealings with me, and perhaps even more respectful because of my gender. I realise that male researchers may not be able to get as favourable a response from some groups of participants as I did. This is partly due to the culture of special treatment of women (pampering, protecting, looking after them) and partly because, as a woman, I was less threatening to them than male researchers.

There were some unfortunate incidents of sexual harassment as well, which cut across the varied groups of my research participants. I am not the first woman to have experienced sexual harassment in the field; it is recognised as a widespread problem for which anthropology students are insufficiently prepared (see, for example, Johansson 2015; Berry et al. 2017; Kloß 2017). Thus, while my gender enabled my entry into certain circles, it became a barrier to participating in others. There were situations in which I had to turn down valuable opportunities to learn simply because I felt vulnerable as a woman and had to look after my safety first. There were potential spaces for research that I could not access because of my gender. For example, most of the religious and political gatherings concerning disrespect of the Prophet are male-only and I could not attend them to enrich my research.

It is not only the researcher's identity that is complex; every research participant also brings a multiplex of identities to interactions. It is precisely because of this complexity of interaction between people occupying different positions in society that anthropological research is considered subjective. Our different social positions determine what type of connections we establish with our research participants. As researchers, 'there will inevitably be certain facets of self that join us up with the people we study, other facets that emphasize our difference' (Narayan 1993: 680).

There are certain aspects of my identity that the participants themselves chose to emphasise because they could relate to them. Most of my research participants from religious minorities related to my minority status as a Shia Muslim. They often took me to be 'one of their own'—the persecuted minorities of Pakistan. There were a few exceptions—for example, a Christian woman I interviewed expressed her deep anger for Muslims by addressing me as 'You, Muslim people!' I was a face of both (rare) Muslim compassion and Muslim brutality for her. To my Muslim participants who were accused (or their friends/families), I was a sympathiser, a comrade, who understood their experiences when their own relatives had abandoned them. To the accusers and their supporters (witnesses, lawyers, religious scholars and so on), I was someone suspicious whose ideas and aims were unclear. Sometimes they took me to be a journalist; at other times, I was regarded as someone who did not know much about religion and needed guidance. I was cautious about revealing my Shia identity to my Sunni participants in the beginning, but soon realised that Sunni Barelwis also relate to Shias on many levels—in their reverence for holy personalities (many of whom are common to both sects), devotional practices and shrine culture. Both Barelwis and Shias have been criticised by the Deobandis and other sects in Pakistan for their Sufism-inspired devotional practices and reverence of shrines and saints. Thus, after I had disclosed my Shia identity to the Barelwi participants, they discussed their devotional Sufi ideas and practices with me much more openly.

I also chose to intentionally highlight or suppress certain facets of myself depending on with whom I was interacting. For example, to the accusers and supporters of anti-blasphemy violence, I did not divulge my religious views or my opinions on the issue of punishment for blasphemers. They were of course suspicious of me and kept asking me for my opinion on specific cases or the issue in general. I presented myself as someone without much religious knowledge, seeking to learn from them to build my own opinions. When they asked me how I felt someone should be punished after they had allegedly committed blasphemy, I told them I was not an expert on religious or legal matters, so I was not able to issue a verdict. I did in fact want to learn from them and understand their point of view. Some of my research participants expressed on multiple occasions their hope that I would use my pen to write for Islam, for the Prophet Muhammad and his honour. They expected me to write what they thought I should write, but I never made any promises to them.

Class differences (perceived and real) also played a significant role in determining my relationships with my participants. A majority of my research participants had lower socioeconomic backgrounds (workers, manual labourers and so on). Many of them saw me as a member of the elite class because of my education and physical attributes such as my clothing and the vehicle I used. I always felt a little uneasy because of my privileges compared with these people. The uneasiness was compounded by the fact that many of them went out of their way to entertain me. They would cook meals with multiple dishes including meat for me despite my insistence on not visiting them during mealtimes. I knew that many of those families could not afford meat as a part of their everyday diet. They cooked those meals to match what they thought of as *my* status. I was often left in situations where I could not say no to them because they had already gone out of their way to arrange something for me, but taking those favours made me extremely embarrassed. I tried to dress as plainly as possible when visiting these people and to underplay any other physical or perceived attributes of my socioeconomic status.

On other occasions, I decided to highlight certain aspects of myself that would join me with the people with whom I was interacting. There were times when people expressed what they thought of as differences in our socioeconomic backgrounds. I took some of those occasions as opportunities to put them (and myself) at ease by talking about things that joined us. For example, when visiting one family, I was left to sit with their three teenage daughters for quite some time. They were brilliant girls, all going to a nearby public school, and talked to me about their education and studies. They talked to me about how they dreamt of being 'as educated as me' but had no hope due to their limited means. I told them that I had been in a similar position because my parents were unable to pay for higher education in a good university, and that I had received all my education without paying a single rupee because of the scholarships I won. They were inspired and motivated and felt a lot more connected to me.

There was also an element of people's expectations of me when they went out of their way to treat me nicely. In some cases, they dropped subtle hints that they were expecting financial and/or material help from me. In other cases, they explicitly asked me for help (material, political, strategic and so on). Once again, I felt I was betraying them by turning their pains and woes into the objects of my study and not returning any favours to them. Due to various constraints, I could not provide direct financial or material help to anyone, but I did put them in touch with relevant NGOs and other sources that could help.

Despite being a Pakistani Muslim woman, or a so-called insider/native anthropologist, the challenges of connecting with people and developing respectful relationships with them defined my research. In some ways, being an 'insider' comes with a much higher degree of moral responsibility as people put certain expectations (such as to abide by local norms) on the researcher. It was due to my insider/native status (as a Pakistani Muslim) that some of my research participants hoped I would write to defend Islam and the Prophet Muhammad. It was also because of my insider status that I was rebuked by others for my lack of 'proper knowledge of Islam'. My native status thus made me more vulnerable to moral policing within familiar settings. As an insider, I posed a different kind of threat, as 'the enemy within', for some of my research participants, who criticised me for tarnishing the image of Pakistan or presenting a dark side of Pakistan to the world. For them, I was a misguided, Westernised person at best and a traitor of the nation at worst. To them, I represented the much dreaded 'Western agenda' of undermining the national image of Pakistan.

These perceptions joined me with those who have been, or are likely to be, accused of blasphemy—as they are also often seen as the enemy within, the dreaded face of Western, anti-Islam or anti-Pakistan forces, the uncanny face of the other. Concerns about the enemy within, group boundaries, individual and collective identities and the self and the other form central themes of this book. However, as I will show, these concerns are not unique to Pakistani Muslims, and blasphemy accusations are not the only form in which they are expressed. On the contrary, my focus on these concerns shows that the issue of blasphemy in Pakistan—while embedded in a specific historical and political context—is a part of the struggle that many societies across the globe have experienced in the past and continue to deal with in the contemporary world. I draw on anthropological studies to show how blasphemy accusations and subsequent violence in Pakistan are similar to other forms of violence targeted at those deemed transgressive or misfits within communities; parallels can be drawn with witchcraft accusations in Indonesia, anti-Muslim violence in India, lynching of African-Americans, among a plenitude of other examples. This book, therefore, deals with ever-pertinent questions surrounding violent conflict in societies through a detailed study of blasphemy-related violence in Pakistan.

Introduction

On 13 April 2017, I was in California for a conference titled 'Public Life of Injury in South Asia' at Stanford University. I had flown in from Australia the previous day and the next day I was going to present my paper on the public understanding of nonstate violence against those accused of blasphemy in Pakistan. As I sat in my accommodation making some last-minute changes to my presentation and ruminating over the Stanford University campus that I had visited earlier that day, I heard the terrible news that would forever mark my memory of that trip. At another university campus, in the north of Pakistan, a 23-year-old student had been lynched by his fellow students in broad daylight. Not only that, the lynching was filmed by the participants and videos of it were circulating on social media. I watched one of the videos, despite the graphic content warning. The image of Mashal Khan's lifeless body being kicked, stoned and lynched as the crowd cheered and chanted slogans made me forget about my presentation. I could not work any further, and I could not sleep that night.

Mashal Khan was a journalism student at Abdul Wali Khan University in Mardan, Pakistan. He was lynched after allegations were made against him of 'publishing blasphemous content online' (Akbar 2017a). Just before the incident, the university had announced on its online notice board that Khan along with two other students was under investigation for 'blasphemous activities carried out' by them and was banned from entering the university premises (Akbar 2017a). A month earlier, the Government of Pakistan had started a crackdown on blasphemous online content following an order issued by the Islamabad High Court (HRW 2017). However, nothing had been reported to police prior to Mashal Khan's lynching. After the incident, some screenshots of Facebook comments on a profile displaying Khan's picture were circulated that were considered insulting towards the Prophet Muhammad and Islam. The Judicial Inquiry Committee that was formed after the incident found that the said profile did not belong to Mashal Khan and no evidence of blasphemy was found against him (Firdous 2017). The committee also reported that Mashal Khan's murder was premeditated by leaders of the student union, who were threatened by Khan's critique of the university's administration (Firdous 2017). In an interview with a local TV channel only a few days before his lynching, Khan had spoken up against the corruption within the university administration and highlighted the illegal activities carried out on campus (Akbar 2017b). Thus, the judicial inquiry report concluded that Khan's murder was a result of the malicious intentions and rivalry of his fellow students and the university administration (Firdous 2017).

The findings of the report in Khan's case reflect what many analysts, academics and human rights organisations have already pointed out: the instrumental use of Pakistan's blasphemy laws to settle personal scores (for example, Amnesty International 2016; Gregory 2012; HRW 2018; Julius 2016; Siddique and Hayat 2008). However, in Khan's case, the state's blasphemy laws were not even mobilised; instead, members of the public took it on themselves to execute 'justice'. If we ignore state law for the moment and look at blasphemy accusations themselves as a means of settling personal scores, we need to explain why Khan's rivals chose such accusations as *the method* by which to be rid of him. One explanation is that blasphemy accusations are an *effective method* to get rid of one's rivals. Spreading rumours of blasphemy against Khan was indeed effective in mobilising a crowd big enough that the 20 policemen present at the scene could not prevent the lynching (Akbar 2017a). It was efficacious in keeping clerics from leading Mashal Khan's funeral prayers and his neighbours from participating in his funeral (Dawn News 2017). It was also successful in ensuring that the perpetrators of the lynching had support and were later hailed as heroes and lovers of the Prophet (Bibi 2018; Khan and Constable 2018). However, what rendered the blasphemy accusations effective, what enthused the crowd, what inhibited local residents from participating in Khan's funeral and what led to glorification of the perpetrators of violence remain unexplained. It is the power of blasphemy accusations to incite and exalt violence against the accused that I aim to address in this book.

Mashal Khan's case is not the first nor will it be the last of its kind. There were more than 1,500 reported cases of blasphemy accusations and 75 incidents of nonstate killings following blasphemy accusations between 1987 and 2017 (Ahmed 2018). The effectiveness of such accusations in putting an end to the normal life of the accused, in glorifying the perpetrators of violence and in permitting the disregard of the courts of law when it comes to punishing the perpetrators is a common trend in cases of blasphemy accusations (see, for example, Rumi 2018; Shakir 2015). Even if the accused manages to escape vigilante action, they may spend the rest of their lives in hiding or languishing in prison, afraid that anyone, including the police supposedly responsible for their safety, may kill them at any time (ICJ 2015: 7). Some of the killers of those accused of blasphemy have been turned into saints, have shrines erected in their memory and are revered by masses of devotees (Hashim 2017b). Even if the perpetrators of nonstate violence against those accused of blasphemy are tried and found guilty in court, they are glorified by large sections of the public (Khan 2011: 51–52; Philippon 2014: 290; Suleman 2018: 9). And even when an alleged blasphemer has been proved innocent in court, they will be punished by the public (Amnesty International 2016: 42). There is thus a symbolic power associated with blasphemy accusations in Pakistan that is beyond that of the law. This book explores the meanings that blasphemy accusations and subsequent violent action hold for the perpetrators, their supporters and society in general. More specifically, I am looking for the sources of legitimacy, authority and morality that render blasphemy accusations and subsequent violence not only effective, but also sacrosanct in the eyes of the people.

I argue that blasphemy accusations and subsequent violence are not only strategic means to achieve malicious ends, but also *meaningful* phenomena for the social actors involved. By focusing on interpersonal relationships between the accused and the accusers, I contend that such accusations are triggered by perceived transgressions of social hierarchies and religious-cultural notions of purity among people known to each other. Through ethnographic examples, I demonstrate that most accusations are motivated simultaneously by religious-cultural ideals, emotion and personal rivalries. However, once accusations of blasphemy have been made, regardless of the initial motives of the accusers, they quickly escalate into a shared religious concern, inciting passionate responses from a much wider audience of believers living with anxieties about their faith, their religious and national identities and the purity of their society. To the mobilised crowds, the accused becomes a symbolic figure, 'the impure other', who threatens national, communal and individual purity. The violent punishment of 'the impure other' that follows is, however, not inevitable; rather, it is orchestrated and enabled by various actors motivated by both reason and passion.

Some of these actors are key proponents of ideas of popular justice. By promoting nonstate punishment of alleged blasphemers, the agents of popular justice contest the state's sole authority over legitimate violence and its sovereignty in representing Islamic ideals. I argue that blasphemy-related violence is political contestation through which the state's interpretation and implementation of justice are challenged by those competing with the state in the shared religious-political sphere. The state and nonstate proponents of justice draw on the same sources of legitimacy and sovereignty in claiming to represent Islamic principles of justice. Consequently, the assertions by proponents of nonstate violence become enshrined in the state's foundations and its laws. This book thus reworks accepted analytical dichotomies of reason/emotion, culture/religion, traditional/Western, state/nonstate and legal/extralegal to extend our understanding of the upsurge of blasphemy-related violence in Pakistan.

Background and context

To fully grasp the meanings associated with blasphemy accusations and subsequent violent action, it is pertinent to first understand what it means to blaspheme in Pakistan, who is offended and what are the characteristics of those who offend. I therefore begin by explaining these key concepts below.

What is blasphemy in Pakistan?

Blasphemy—the English word—does not correspond to any of the local language words or terms used to describe religious offences; neither is the word blasphemy used in the legislation concerning religious offences. It is, however, used by lawyers in their discourse and by judges in their official judgements, which are often in English—one of Pakistan's official languages. The word blasphemy is also commonly used by local and international media and human rights organisations. Consequently, this word has become popular among the English-speaking sections of Pakistani society. Nevertheless, given there is no local term that accurately corresponds to the word blasphemy, we must ask: exactly what phenomenon is being referred to when we say 'blasphemy in Pakistan'? To answer this question, I will look at two aspects of the problem: the offence according to the legislation and public understandings of it. Before I discuss the differences between the two, it must be noted that both state and nonstate understandings of the offence are extensions of each other as the legislation has evolved in response to public demands and has in turn shaped public understanding.

The offence according to the legislation

The offence according to state law is enshrined in the Pakistan Penal Code (1860) under Chapter XV, titled 'Offences relating to religion'. This chapter comprises Sections 295 to 298; Sections 295 and 298 have three subsections each. Some of the clauses (295, 295-A, 296, 297, 298) were part of British colonial legislation. First codified in 1860 by Lord Macaulay, they were meant to control what were thought to be the emotional and irrational masses of the Indian Subcontinent (Ahmed 2009). Section 295 and Subsection 295-A prohibit *acts* of defiling places of worship and injuring the religious feelings of any person belonging to any religion. Section 296 forbids disturbing religious assembly and Section 297 criminalises trespassing on burial sites. Section 298 criminalises *words* that hurt the religious feelings of others. These clauses were aimed to prevent discord between different religious communities and are seen by analysts as a tool of governance devised to 'reserve the right for the colonial state to demarcate and govern the boundaries' between different social groups on the Subcontinent (Saeed 2013: 245). Of these clauses, 295-A was added in 1927 in response to a major controversy after a Hindu publisher published a book allegedly insulting the Prophet Muhammad (Stephens 2014).

The remaining clauses (295-B, 295-C, 298-A, 298-B, 298-C) were added after the creation of Pakistan, by military ruler General Zia-ul-Haq between 1980 and 1986. These clauses are more specific and protect the religious feelings of Muslims exclusively. They prohibit defiling of the Holy Quran and use of derogatory remarks in respect of the Prophet Muhammad, his wives, family, companions and the first four Caliphs of Islam. The last two clauses (298-B and 298-C) categorically prohibit Ahmadis—who self-identify as Muslims—from calling themselves Muslims, using Muslim names and titles, using any the Islamic practices and propagating their faith. The earlier passages inherited from the British legislation had a consideration for *intent* to hurt religious feelings as a crucial component to them. The later clauses added by Zia-ul-Haq do not consider intent in punishing acts or words that may be deemed hurtful and insulting to Muslims. The amended legislation also prescribes much harsher punishments, including the death penalty, for the offences described (see the Appendix for the full text of the clauses).

The original legislation was written in English, as is the current Pakistan Penal Code (PPC) because English remains one of the official languages of the state. The English words used in the legislation for the offence being discussed include injuring, defiling, insulting, desecrating, damaging, misusing, posing (as Muslims), outraging and using derogatory remarks. Some of these words—for example, desecrating—do indeed overlap with the meanings of blasphemy according to the *Oxford English Dictionary*.[1] Nonetheless, it appears that the phenomenon being talked about is not merely sacrilegious, it is also connected to people's feelings and perceptions. Hurting people's feelings or undermining their perceptions is as significant an offence, if not more so, as hurting the Prophet or other Holy personages. The language of Pakistani law, however, remains vague and does not clearly define *what* is deemed hurtful and insulting (Siddique and Hayat 2008: 359). To better understand the nature and definition of the offence under consideration, it is therefore pertinent to investigate the meanings people associate with it.

The offence in public consciousness

The Urdu terms associated with the offences referred to as 'blasphemy' offer some insights into the public understanding of these offences. I studied a range of sources—religious publications, sermons, political banners and pamphlets, the statements of accusers and witnesses in the courts—to trace the words and phrases most commonly used to refer to the offences concerning religion and other related fields. The most recurrent words and phrases people use are: *gustaakhi, bey-hurmati, tauheen-e-risaalat, namoos-e-risaalat, shaan-e-rasool, hurmat-e-rasool, ghayoor, ghairatmand* and other derivatives of these terms (see Table 1 for a summary of literal meanings).[2]

---

[1] 'Blasphemy', in the *Oxford English Dictionary*, is defined as: 'The action or offence of speaking sacrilegiously about God or sacred things; profane talk'.
[2] Translations of all foreign words in this book are my own unless otherwise specified. Translations of Urdu words and phrases used by others I quote in this book are also mine (presented inside square brackets within the quotes).

Table 1. Frequently used Urdu terms in relation to the offence of blasphemy and their meanings

Urdu term	Meaning
Gustaakhi	Irreverence
Bey-hurmati	Sacrilege
Tauheen-e-risaalat	Insult to the Prophet
Namoos-e-risaalat	Honour of the Prophet
Shaan-e-rasool	Grace/pride of the Prophet
Hurmat-e-rasool	Sanctity of the Prophet
Ghayoor/ghairatmand	Honourable

Notes: Words in green define the offence; words in blue refer to what is at stake when the offence of *tauheen-e-risaalat* is committed; words in yellow refer to the honour of faithful Muslims who punish offenders.

These terms can be grouped into three broad categories. The first category (shaded green) contains words defining the offence: *gustaakhi*, *bey-hurmati* and *tauheen-e-risaalat*. These are the terms in the local language closest to what I have been referring to as 'blasphemy'. These three words are used in slightly different contexts: *gustaakhi* is often committed against holy personalities, *bey-hurmati* is usually committed against physical objects and places considered holy[3] and *tauheen-e-risaalat* is specifically an insult to the Prophet. Insults to God or to abstract ideas, such as sacred norms related to religion, do not form specific categories (unlike the Western concept of blasphemy in which the immediate connotation is insult to God). This does not mean that the insult to God or to abstract ideas is not offensive; rather, it is most often seen in terms of an insult to either certain personalities (most importantly, the Prophet) or sacred objects or places. There is a hierarchy of insults/offences in the first category, the highest offence being an insult to the Prophet. Insults to other holy personalities and physical objects and places can, however, be described as being in effect an insult to the Prophet and this increases the intensity and seriousness of the offence. The second category of words (shaded blue) refers to what is at stake when the offence of *tauheen-e-risaalat* is committed: the honour and sanctity of the Prophet. Again, other offences can very easily be framed as an attack on the honour of the Prophet—for example, sacrilege of the Quran can be described as an offence against the honour of the Prophet because the Quran was revealed to the Prophet.

---

3   The reverence of holy objects and places is more a South Asian phenomenon, expressed by South Asian Muslims and other religious communities in South Asia.

The third category of words (shaded yellow) refers to the honour of those faithful Muslims who safeguard holy personalities, the holy objects and the holy Prophet by punishing offenders. Let us now consider some of the specific connotations of each of these terms to understand the sociocultural context of the offence.

Gustaakhi, *bey-hurmati* and *tauheen-e-risaalat* are the words most frequently used to refer to acts and words of disrespect or insult towards Islam and its holy personalities. However, they all have very specific connotations. The word *gustaakhi* usually means irreverence, impudence or insolence. It is most commonly used in the context of hierarchical relations. For example, a father is considered higher than his son and should be approached with certain reverence by his son. Any act or expression not conforming to the expected behaviour of a son towards a father will be termed *gustaakhi*. Given the context of hierarchical relations, *gustaakhi* is more a form of transgression than an insult. The one who commits *gustaakhi* is called *gustaakh*. Nevertheless, *gustaakh-e-rasool* is a common term used to refer to those accused of 'insulting' the Prophet, *rasool* being the Urdu word for Prophet.

The term *bey-hurmati* is derived from the word *hurmat*, which means honour and dignity in common usage. The prefix *bey* is similar to the English prefix 'dis'; the term *bey-hurmati* thus means dishonour or disrespect. *Hurmat* is derived from the Arabic root *h-r-m*, which is considered one of the most ambiguous terms in that language (Marmon 1995: 6). Derivatives of this root have various meanings, including 'sacred', 'inviolable', 'forbidden' and 'taboo' (Marmon 1995: 6). Words derived from *h-r-m* may also have rather disparate connotations—for example, they may refer to 'unlawfulness' as per Islamic law, on the one hand, and 'veneration' of sacred objects on the other (Schick 2010: 69). Thus, the root *h-r-m* refers to sacredness, honour and respect, on the one hand, and to forbidden and illegitimate acts according to Islamic moral principles on the other.[4] The term *hurmat*, derived from this root, has connotations most commonly associated with sacredness, honour and respect. *Bey-hurmati* thus means sacrilege, dishonour or disrespect.

---

4   The word *haram* derived from the root *h-r-m*, for example, is used for a man's wives and other women of the household whose honour and respect must be protected (Schick 2010: 70), as well as for illicit and prohibited acts and foods, such as alcohol, pork and extramarital sex (Adamec 2009). It is used to refer both to women who a man is sexually allowed (his wives, slave girls) and to women with whom sexual relations are prohibited (mother, sister). It is used for sacred sites, such as the house of Allah, Kaaba, in Mecca and for acts that are forbidden inside those sacred sites, such as shedding blood.

Interestingly, *bey-hurmati* of a sacred or honoured entity (space or object) is often caused by approaching it without taking proper ritualistic procedures into account—for example, entering the house of God without ablution—or by crossing certain boundaries prescribed by various religious interpretations. Again, the underlying offence is a transgression of perceived boundaries.

Tauheen means 'insult' and *risaalat* means 'prophethood' (of the Prophet Muhammad in this context). Thus, *tauheen-e-risaalat* means insult to the Prophet Muhammad. Compared with *gustaakhi* and *bey-hurmati*, *tauheen* has a more direct connotation of insult. It is also the most commonly used of the three terms; however, it is used specifically in relation to the Prophet Muhammad. The term *tauheen-e-risaalat* evokes the strongest of emotions and hence is used to intensify an offence in public discourse even if the original offence is not an insult to the Prophet. The public political discourse concerning the issue of 'blasphemy' is centred on the personality of the Prophet Muhammad. The Prophet is thus central to the conception of what people refer to as 'blasphemy' in Pakistan, even though most of the offences are not directly against the Prophet. Together, these three terms—*gustaakhi*, *bey-hurmati* and *tauheen*—suggest that the offence being discussed is the insult, disrespect or dishonour of a revered personality, object or order, as well as a transgression of perceived boundaries and hierarchies.

Namoos-e-risaalat, *shaan-e-rasool* and *hurmat-e-rasool* are frequently used to refer to the honour, dignity and respect of the Prophet Muhammad. I have already mentioned the meanings of *risaalat* (the prophethood of Muhammad) and *rasool* (the Prophet). *Namoos* means honour; *shaan* means dignity, grace and pride; and *hurmat* also means honour and respect, as already discussed. While the actual cases of religious offences range from presumed disrespect of printed Arabic words on pamphlets and banners to misspelling the name of Muhammad, the public discourse is centred on the honour of the Prophet. This is because various forms of perceived insults and transgressions can be understood and portrayed, in effect, as insults to the Prophet. For example, an insult to the beard of a Muslim man can be described as an insult to the Prophet since the beard is a symbol associated with the Prophet. Thus, the actual accusations can be quite arbitrary but have the potential to be framed as an insult to the Prophet. Once the offence is framed as an insult to the Prophet, its severity and intensity are increased significantly, and the discourse is built around the honour of the Prophet. Therefore, it is important to highlight the centrality of the honour of the Prophet as far as the popular meaning and discourse of blasphemy in the local language are concerned.

Honour is an extremely important value in the South Asian culture in general, and even more so in the Punjabi culture where I conducted my research. Honour needs to be maintained, protected and actively reemphasised to establish a man's worth as honourable. A man's honour is usually associated with the standing of the women of the house, and transgressions against one's women are punished through several means, including honour killings of the transgressors. The underlying assumption is that an honourable man is supposed to protect his honour (which is associated with women's sexuality in this case), and as a part of his duty to protect he must punish the transgressors. There are similar reasoning and value systems behind protecting the honour of the Prophet and punishing the transgressors and offenders of the Prophet. It can be argued that the honour of the Prophet is in effect the honour of Muslim men—associated with the Prophet as it is associated with women's sexuality—which needs to be protected.

Ghayoor and *ghairatmand* are two other terms frequently used in the context of religious offences. The word *ghayoor* refers to a person (usually a man) who has due concern for honour, who knows how to protect that honour and is capable of doing so. Hence, a *ghayoor* or *ghairatmand* (synonymous) man will go to any length to defend and emphasise his honour, which in this case is associated with the honour of the Prophet: *namoos-e-risaalat, shaan-e-rasool, hurmat-e-rasool*. The words *ghayoor* and *ghairatmand* are frequently used to mobilise people to punish the alleged transgressors and to refer to those who have successfully done so. The usage of these words further indicates that it is the honour of the defenders that is under threat rather than the honour of the Prophet. Those who believe in punishing the ones who insult the Prophet do indeed proclaim that the Prophet does not need protection or defending, but being his faithful and *ghayoor* followers, it is the test of *their* faith whether or not they punish the transgressors. They believe that the Prophet is above the attacks and criticisms of people, but as believers, *their* loyalty to the Prophet requires affirmation by punishing offenders.

The public discourse on blasphemy thus highlights two important principles that constitute the meaning and social reality of the phenomenon within the context of the local language: honour and transgression. Why, then, do I use the word 'blasphemy' in this book?

If there was one particular word or term in the local language to describe the offence, I would have defined it first and then used it throughout the rest of my writing. Instead, there are multiple words and terms, each with their specific connotations, none of which captures the whole essence of the offence on its own. Therefore, for the sake of simplicity, I choose to use the term blasphemy in this book, as it is a word conveniently understood in the English-speaking world. Nevertheless, it should be understood within the context of local meanings I have discussed here. The word blasphemy in this book therefore means disrespect, dishonour and transgression, particularly in relation to sacred persons and objects. While these meanings overlap with and are reflected in the legislation, they cannot be reduced to the same. They incorporate a wider public understanding of morality, which is centred on honour, symbolic social-physical boundaries and hierarchies.

Consideration of the public discourse further highlights that the public meanings associated with the offence are also vague and open to interpretation and manipulation—just like the legal definitions of the offence according to the state. Both aspects (legislative and public meanings) remain imprecise as to *what* constitutes insult, disrespect or transgression. The very vagueness of the relevant legislation as well as of public meanings of blasphemy forms the basis for ongoing contestation between the state and the public—and between various sections of the public—as to what can or cannot be deemed blasphemous. The open-endedness of the meanings of the offence also means that practically anything—from sexual transgressions to mere existence as a member of a minority community—can be framed as a religious offence, as this book demonstrates.

Who are the public?

To whom am I referring with the word 'public' when I talk about the public consciousness or the public meanings of an offence? It would be wrong to assume that all Pakistanis agree with the public meanings of blasphemy discussed here. It would also be wrong to assume that all Pakistanis support violent punishment of blasphemers. Who, then, is offended and who believes in punishing the offenders? This question is hard to answer statistically, specifically for those who *do not* support the punishment of blasphemers, because their lack of support can itself be construed as support for blasphemy, therefore inducing silence on their behalf. We can get some clues about the number of those who *do* support the idea of the offence and the punishment of blasphemers and are politically active in their support. The most recent figures are from the 2018 general elections in Pakistan in which a political party specifically rallying for the cause of violently punishing blasphemers, Tehreek-e-Labbaik Pakistan (TLP), emerged as the fifth-most popular party nationwide and third-most popular in Punjab (ECP 2018). The party bagged more than 2.2 million of the roughly 50 million votes cast in the general election (FAFEN 2018).

The winning party of the 2018 elections, Pakistan Tehreek-e-Insaf (PTI), had also previously supported the punishment of blasphemers within Pakistan and protested against blasphemy in an international context within the first few weeks of its election (Barker 2018; Crisp and Farmer 2018). The former ruling party, the Pakistan Muslim League (PMLN), which was the runner-up in the 2018 elections, has also supported punishment of blasphemy on various occasions (Zaidi 2017). This does not imply that all supporters of these political parties unanimously support the punishment of blasphemy. However, it does indicate the central importance of the issue of blasphemy in the popular consciousness of Pakistani people such that all major political parties *must* cater to this concern at some point—in one way or another. It is safe to say that there is significant public support for the punishment of blasphemers in Pakistan and that this support is not limited to what some studies describe as radical, extremist or militant religious groups (Forte 1994: 35; Hayee 2012: 51; Saiya 2016). Instead, supporters of anti-blasphemy violence are present in almost all sections of society, and include those who are seen as moderate or progressive Muslims.

Different sections of society support different means of punishment of blasphemers. There are those who support only state punishment of the accused; others support state *and* nonstate punishment. There are also those whose opinions vary on a case-by-case basis. Hence, there are varying levels of concern about blasphemy and multiple positions among the supporters of punishment for blasphemers. Regardless, my research shows that most Pakistanis are offended with respect to their religious and moral beliefs at some point, although varying in their perception of what constitutes the threshold of offence, and most support retribution in one form or another when that threshold is reached. This book is mostly concerned with those who support violent punishment of blasphemers, whether by the state or by nonstate actors.

It must also be noted that there is a growing number of people who sympathise with the accused and the victims of violence. Those who disagree with the violent punishment of the accused are certainly not as organised as the supporters of violent punishment but there are a significant number of such voices. Like the supporters of violent punishment, those who sympathise with the victims of blasphemy-related violence are also present in all sections of society. I have had discussions with people from diverse backgrounds such as those with no formal education, housewives, taxi-drivers, lawyers and university professors who condemn violence against those accused of blasphemy. There are also local activists and organisations that are actively campaigning against blasphemy-related violence in Pakistan. However, those who oppose violent action against the accused have never been able to mobilise in numbers comparable with those who have publicly demonstrated their support for violent punishment of alleged blasphemers.

Who are the accused?

As mentioned earlier, more than 1,500 cases of blasphemy accusations and 75 incidents of nonstate killings following such accusations were reported between 1987 and 2017. To put these numbers in context, it is pertinent to point out that there were only 10 cases reported between 1927 and 1986 under the British-era legislation (Dawn News 2010). The number of accusations has risen sharply since the amendments made to the law by General Zia-ul-Haq (Rumi 2018: 327). However, it should also be noted that these figures do not represent the actual number of incidents, as there are many cases that are never reported or taken to a court of law. Incidents of nonstate violence against those accused of blasphemy have also risen since the amendments to the law (Rumi 2018: 327). In fact, all the killings following blasphemy accusations in Pakistan so far have been carried out by nonstate actors. While the state prescribes the death penalty for various offences related to religion and the courts have sentenced several people to death, none has so far been executed by the state.

In terms of geographical distribution, 74 per cent of all reported cases have been in Punjab, the most populous province of Pakistan, which is home to 55 per cent of the country's total population (Jacob 2018). However, notwithstanding its large population, Punjab stands out as the most likely locus of blasphemy-related incidents. This is not surprising as Punjab is also the hub of most active religious organisations, particularly the Barelwis, who are at the forefront of anti-blasphemy campaigns in Pakistan. Barelwis are the largest subsect of the majority Sunni Muslims in Pakistan, followed by Deobandis, Ahl-e-Hadith and various other Sunni subsects (Suleman 2018: 6). Of the 95 per cent Muslim population of Pakistan, Sunnis make up somewhere between 75 and 80 per cent of all Muslims according to unofficial estimates; the remainder are mostly Shia Muslims (Suleman 2018: 6). Rivalries between sects and various groups within each sect are common and are often the basis of blasphemy accusations.

According to data collected by the Centre for Social Justice in Lahore, 46.48 per cent of the 1,549 cases of blasphemy reported between 1987 and 2017 were against Muslims (Ahmed 2018). The data do not differentiate between different Muslim sects, but my survey of individual cases suggests that minority sects, such as Shias, are more likely than others to be accused of blasphemy. Even rivalries between subsects, such as between Barelwis and Deobandis, often lead to blasphemy accusations. More than 50 per cent of all the cases are, however, against non-Muslims, who form less than 5 per cent of Pakistan's total population. Christians, who represent 1.50 to 1.59 per cent of the total population of Pakistan, were accused in 15.4 per cent of the total cases. The most striking figures, however, are for the Ahmadis, who form roughly 0.25 per cent of Pakistan's population but are accused in 33.31 per cent of all the blasphemy cases in Pakistan (see Table 2).

The data for nonstate killings of the accused tell a slightly different story. While Muslims are still the largest group, forming 52 per cent of all the accused killed so far, Christians and Ahmadis make up 31 per cent and 12 per cent, respectively, of the total number of reported killings (see Table 2). These numbers imply that, while Ahmadis are most likely to be accused, Christians are more likely to be killed after an accusation of blasphemy. One potential explanation for this discrepancy may be that Ahmadis generally belong to higher socioeconomic sections of society than Christians in Pakistan, which means they have more resources available to escape vigilante action compared with Christians. Nevertheless, the figures presented so far indicate that religious minorities are disproportionately affected by blasphemy accusations and subsequent violence in Pakistan.

Table 2. Distribution of persons accused and killed by religious identity in Pakistan, 1987–2017

Religion	Total no. accused	Percentage of total accused (1,549)	Total no. killed	Percentage of total killed (75)	Percentage of total population
Muslim	720	46.48	39	52.00	95–98
Ahmadi	516	33.31	9	12.00	0.25
Christian	238	15.36	23	30.67	1.5–1.59
Hindu	31	2.00	2	2.67	1.6
Other	44	2.84	2	2.67	n.a.

n.a. not available

Existing studies and gaps in research

The issue of blasphemy in Pakistan has received significant academic attention in recent years. In this section, I aim to trace major trends in the existing literature and lay out my own theoretical framework for the rest of this book. I will start with literature specific to the issue of blasphemy in Pakistan and move to bodies of more general literature that are relevant to the topic.

Instrumental use of blasphemy laws

As the numbers in the previous section indicate, certain minority groups are disproportionately affected by blasphemy accusations and subsequent violence. The discriminate use of blasphemy laws against religious minorities in Pakistan has been demonstrated—and argued against—by several existing studies of the issue. Many of these studies highlight flaws in the design of, and procedural inadequacies associated with, the Pakistani legislation, rendering both the form and the function of anti-blasphemy laws problematic (see, for example, Forte 1994; Gregory 2012; Jahangir and Jilani 2003; Julius 2016; Rumi 2018; Siddique and Hayat 2008). This body of literature shows that the design of the legislation concerning blasphemy is inherently flawed as it does not take into account the intent of the accused. Moreover, due to a lack of adequate safeguards, the laws lend themselves to abuse against the vulnerable in society. The emphasis of this critique has been on the discriminatory nature of the laws, as well as their instrumentalisation to target certain sections of society, particularly religious minorities. The use of the blasphemy laws against vulnerable people is a valid issue; however, these studies largely fail to explain *why* certain groups are targeted by blasphemy accusations and *why* accusations of blasphemy—and not of any other offence, for instance, adultery—are instrumentalised to settle personal scores.

There are some exceptions. For example, Rumi (2018: 334) points to the identity of Pakistan as 'an Islamic fortress pitted against the outsider-infidel' and draws attention to national narratives that glorify past acts of violence against alleged blasphemers as enabling the present violence in the name of blasphemy. I expand this argument to propose that certain religious minorities and groups are targeted by blasphemy accusations because they represent the face of the *other* and are perceived as a threat to the imagining of the self, the community and the state for Pakistani Muslims. There is a significant lack of literature that looks into microlevel interpersonal dimensions of the issue to understand what leads people to accuse someone of blasphemy and engage in violent action. One noteworthy exception is Asad Ali Ahmed's (2009) ethnographic work in contemporary Pakistan in which he demonstrates how everyday conflicts between different sects—two subsects of Sunnis, in his case study—find expression in the form of blasphemy accusations. I take this project further by presenting more ethnographic examples of how various conflicts in people's everyday lives—which may not be religious in nature—lead to blasphemy accusations and subsequent violence. I propose that blasphemy accusations are chosen as *the method* by the individuals involved in making accusations due to the symbolic power of blasphemy embedded in the prevalent religious-national narratives, as Rumi (2018) pointed out.

Freedom of speech and moral injury

Another body of existing studies looks at the (il)legitimacy of Pakistan's anti-blasphemy laws in the context of international law, which is binding on Pakistan (see, for example, Bohlander 2012; Dobras 2009; Hayee 2012; Khan 2015; Uddin 2011). The authors of these studies see freedom of expression as an inalienable right of every individual and assess the credibility of the limitations imposed on individuals in the name of religion. They argue that Pakistan's blasphemy laws violate the principle of universal human rights by allowing and promoting religious violence. Asma T. Uddin (2011), for example, argues that instead of justifying the use of blasphemy laws to silence dissent in maintaining public order, the Government of Pakistan should take responsibility to confront and curtail violent elements. She asserts that religion, like all other political and/or cultural ideologies, is open to criticism and thus critical views of religion should not be treated as blasphemous. Similarly, Dobras (2009: 360) opposes the Pakistani Government's stance that 'Islamic law supersedes international human rights' and that 'freedom of speech and expression never justify offending religious feelings' (p. 359). While arguing that it is the believer who merits the right to protection, not the religion or belief itself, she relies heavily on the element of 'intent' in any expression. Hence, she contends that 'punishing speech that involves no hateful intent violates freedom of expression' (Dobras 2009: 356). Along similar lines and making a case for freedom of speech and human rights, Bohlander (2012) argues that blasphemy cases and trials in Pakistan constitute crimes against humanity.

The idea of freedom of speech as the basis for understanding blasphemy has been criticised, most strongly by Saba Mahmood and Talal Asad in their work on secularism in Western societies. Asad (2009) argued that the concept of freedom of speech is not neutral; rather, it is a product of the specific historical developments in Western political thought. He also suggested that those in power decide what is allowed under the concept of 'freedom of speech' (Asad 2009: 54). Mahmood (2009: 70), in her essay on Muslims' reactions to Danish cartoons published in 2005, argued that the notion of freedom of speech dismisses the 'moral injury' experienced by Muslims. She described this moral injury as emanating from 'the perception that one's being grounded as it is in a relationship of dependency with the Prophet, has been shaken' (Mahmood 2009: 78). The perceived offence, she argued, was not against a religious commandment but 'against a structure of affect, a habitus, that feels wounded' (Mahmood 2009: 78). I agree with Mahmood and Asad that the concept of freedom of speech is too reductive and Western-centric to comprehend the issue of blasphemy. In fact, the notion of freedom of speech is even more problematic in the case of Pakistan because it assumes that those who are accused of blasphemy are punished for exercising their freedom of speech to criticise the religion of Islam, which is not true in most cases. As already mentioned, blasphemy accusations in Pakistan can be triggered by perceived transgressions that are not at all religious in nature and even by the mere existence of some people as different. Furthermore, as Mahmood (2009) demonstrated, the idea of freedom of speech does not consider moral and affective dimensions that are crucial to understanding how blasphemy is perceived and the reactions it provokes.

Nonetheless, Mahmood's and Asad's critiques also have their limitations when it comes to understanding the issue of blasphemy within the specific context of Pakistan. Mahmood (2009: 89) herself noted that her argument concerned majority–minority power relations in the European context. According to her, Muslims as a minority in European countries are understood through the normative lens specific to Western religious and political thought. In the case of Pakistan, however, Muslims are a majority and their sentiments are recognised and protected by the dominant political and legal structures. Therefore, the moral injury of the *minority* Muslim community in Europe cannot be equated with the moral injury of the *majority* Muslim community in Pakistan, whose religious sentiments are protected by law. There is a different set of power relations in Pakistan in which moral injury to Muslims is not a marginalised phenomenon; rather, it is the dominant mode of social control against those who are deemed to be different or transgressive. Moreover, in most instances of blasphemy accusations in Pakistan, it is not the same essentialised religious ethos of the Muslims, as described by Mahmood, that is at stake. While the mobilisation for violent action against those accused of blasphemy indeed revolves around the personality of the Prophet Muhammad and invokes the specific ways of relating to the Prophet that Mahmood discussed, the initial accusations are triggered by a much wider and more culturally specific moral framework.

This book demonstrates how norms related to sexual behaviour, social hierarchy and purity are subsumed within this wider moral framework. Thus, while the ideas of moral injury and the affective dimensions of this injury are extremely important to understanding blasphemy accusations and subsequent violence in Pakistan, the moral system is not as bounded (connected to the Prophet) and universal (shared with Muslims across the globe) as Mahmood's work depicted. In fact, the moral framework of Pakistani Muslims within which the blasphemy accusations take place may be closer to the sociocultural ethos of non-Muslim communities within South Asia than to Muslim communities around the world. Interestingly, as the discussion in Chapter 2 will demonstrate, the proponents of anti-blasphemy violence in Pakistan themselves demand their sentiments be recognised as belonging to a unique religious ethos, as argued by Mahmood. Hence, I find that, while Mahmood's argument aligns with the vocalised arguments of those who support anti-blasphemy violence in Pakistan, it is not supported by the ethnographic details of individual incidents of such accusations. My research shows that blasphemy accusations in Pakistan are based on moral injury that corresponds to specific sociocultural moral frameworks rather than a universal religious morality.

A more useful conception of 'moral threat' was offered by Hassner (2011: 24) in his description of the hurt felt by Muslims in response to the Danish cartoons. While Mahmood (2009) had located the moral injury experienced by Muslims in the distinct subjectivities enshrined in their Islamic ethos, Hassner (2011: 29) described the same in more general terms of symbolic boundaries such as purity/danger and sacred/profane that are present in all societies and the transgression of which may be perceived as moral injury. The notion of symbolic boundaries encompasses social, cultural, religious and political ideas on which a group draws to distinguish itself from its *others*. From this point of view, any threat to the preconceived notions of the group's identity (and its purity) can lead to moral injury of the group in question. Hassner used this theoretical framework to study Muslims' reactions to blasphemous cartoons at a macro level, focusing on several Muslim countries. I also find the framework of symbolic boundaries useful in understanding blasphemy accusations in response to microtransgressions within interpersonal relationships in Pakistan. I demonstrate in this book how the cultural notions of purity/impurity, sacred/profane and the social hierarchies/boundaries based on such symbolic structures enable the blasphemy accusations and subsequent violence to take place.

There are a few other issues in the literature discussed so far that I would like to address. First, there is an exclusive focus on state law in the literature concerning the instrumental use of 'blasphemy laws' as well as the studies looking at Pakistan's legislation within the context of international law. As already mentioned, many blasphemy accusations are not even taken to court, and, so far, all of the blasphemy-related killings in Pakistan have been carried out by nonstate actors. Therefore, any study of blasphemy in Pakistan must go beyond the legislation and its failures. Second, there seems to be a rift between instrumental use and moral/affective responses as explanations of anti-blasphemy violence. The literature that focuses on the instrumental use of blasphemy laws largely ignores the aspects of moral outrage and affective dimensions of the conflict, and the studies focusing on moral injury or moral threat seem to exclude the possibility of the instrumental use of blasphemy accusations. The instrumental use argument seems to be privileging *reason*, whereas the moral injury argument locates the issue within the realm of *emotion*. Admittedly, these are two different bodies of literature dealing with two distinct contexts: the literature on the cases of blasphemy *within* Pakistan mostly looks at the instrumental use and the literature on the issue of blasphemy in a global or European context focuses on the moral injury of Muslims. Nevertheless, I believe that both reason and emotion—instrumental use and moral threat—are crucial to understanding accusations of blasphemy and related violence within Pakistan.

Beyond state law

The case of Mashal Khan, discussed at the beginning of this Introduction, shows that blasphemy accusations and subsequent violent punishment have legitimacy beyond the law in Pakistan. Pakistan's legal system is not the only, or even the superior, source of authority that legitimises punishment of those accused of blasphemy. There are a few studies that have looked at the wider sociopolitical dimensions of the issue—beyond the laws of the state. For example, Hoffman (2014) analyses the role of social pressure and vigilantism in influencing the outcome of blasphemy cases in Pakistan. He sees the prevalence of violence and vigilantism as the 'extra-legal system of blasphemy law enforcement' (Hoffman 2014: 371). While he acknowledges and emphasises the role of vigilantism and 'extralegal' action, he still sees these phenomena with reference to the blasphemy laws. In seeing vigilante action as a mechanism of blasphemy law enforcement, he assumes that state law is the foremost and ultimate source of authority and legitimacy for violence. Such analyses are based on a law-centric approach that takes the laws of the modern nation-state (a Western category) as the reference point to understand conflict in a society. This approach does not help us understand the wider legitimacy of the punishment of alleged blasphemers delivered outside and beyond the law of the state.

Moving beyond the law-centric approaches, this book investigates the broader understandings of legitimacy, justice and authority among the accusers, killers, their supporters and wider society in Pakistan through the lens of *legal pluralism*. Legal pluralism is a theoretical paradigm based on the premise that any society has a multiplicity of forms of law present within it (Rouland and Planel 1994: 51). Theorists of legal pluralism have argued that Western legal systems and those imposed or inspired by the West are not the only moral systems through which people govern and order their lives (Fitzpatrick 1983; Griffiths 1986). Legal anthropologists have also argued against law-centric approaches to understanding and engaging with the diverse social-moral systems of people even if they belong to the same 'class of phenomena' as modern law (Pirie 2013: 7–9). Hence, the nation-state's legal system is not the *only* system of authority, morality and legitimacy in a society. There are usually multiple sources of morality and legitimacy within a society, which may overlap, contradict or overtly clash with the state's legal system at any point (Tamanaha 2001). From this perspective, accusations of blasphemy and subsequent violence against the accused in Pakistan must be seen as situated in a broader public domain of justice, morality and legitimacy rather than simply the domain of state law. I argue that, while state laws reflect and extend public morality concerning the issue of blasphemy, the latter cannot be reduced to state law and legality.

Legal anthropologists have also criticised the exclusive use of the terms 'law' and 'legal' for the state's systems of moral regulation as state-centric. For example, Hoebel (1954) argued for inclusion of nonstate systems of moral regulation in the definition of law. According to him, a:

> social norm is legal if its neglect or infraction is regularly met, in threat or in fact, by the application of physical force by an individual or group possessing the socially recognised privilege of so acting. (Hoebel 1954: 28)

Other scholars, such as Woodman (1998: 45), understand law as 'a continuum which runs from the clearest forms of state law to the vaguest form of informal social control'. According to these definitions, the punishment of alleged blasphemers by nonstate actors would be considered a legal and legitimate form of social control in the minds of the proponents of such punishment. While I agree that we should not limit our understanding of law and legality to that of the state, I also find all-encompassing definitions of law more obscuring than explanatory in understanding different positions, conflicts and contestations of moral systems in a society. In this book, I deal with contestations, overlaps and cooptations of multiple ideas of justice, legality and legitimacy. Therefore, instead of describing all of these competing ideals as 'law', I will differentiate between different forms of legality as either *state* or *nonstate*.

While legal pluralism is a helpful theoretical tool with which to understand nonstate violence against those accused of blasphemy in Pakistan, it is mainly a descriptive theory. That is, while it helps us understand the causes of and motivations behind nonstate violence without restricting our analysis to state law, it does not suggest any resolution of the conflict between state and nonstate ideals of justice. There has been a tendency in legal anthropology to idealise nonstate justice systems to some extent—a position that assumes an inherent agreement among all local people about what customary law is (Benda-Beckmann 2009: 50). However, as Harris (1996: 6) argued, 'it would be romantic to idealise local, customary morality and demonise state law' because custom is ambiguous:

> [O]n the one hand it represents the possibility of acts of violence against women, against ethnic minorities, against those whose actions have offended the local powerholders; on the other hand it invokes local values against an alien and imposing state.

Similarly, as Benda-Beckmann (2009: 50) highlighted, customary or 'folk' law is often 'the law of local elites and/or the senior male population'. In the case of blasphemy accusations in Pakistan, the sanction of public morality applies to those who offend local powerholders or religious elites. In such situations, 'state law is the only defence of subordinate groups or individuals who transgress local moral norms and values' and 'the "rule of law" becomes a defence against tyranny' (Harris 1996: 6). Hence, I use the theory of legal pluralism as a descriptive, but *not* normative, framework. It is not to say that the nonstate justice system is somehow worse—more violent—than the state legal system; rather, the point is to emphasise that it is simply *another* manifestation of violence that is already enshrined in Pakistan's legal system. The state legal system reflects public morality insofar as it prescribes violent punishment for those accused of blasphemy, but it does not hold a monopoly on identifying blasphemy and delivering punishment. Therefore, while it is helpful to look at the state and nonstate sources of legitimacy and authority, I do not intend to endorse or idealise the existing situation of *legal pluralism* with respect to the punishment of blasphemy in Pakistan.

Beyond the reason–emotion dichotomy

As mentioned earlier, most studies locate the causes of blasphemy-related violence in either reason or emotion. It is either rational actors strategically choosing to instrumentalise blasphemy accusations to settle their personal scores or emotive actors driven by moral outrage rooted in their exceptional religious ethos. My research in Pakistan shows that, in most cases of blasphemy accusations and subsequent violence, the actors are driven by rational and emotive elements at the same time. There are some studies that incorporate both cognitive and emotive aspects in their analyses. For example, Blom (2008) interviewed protestors from an anti–Danish cartoon rally in Lahore in 2006 and wrote about the affective dimensions of their motivations. She suggested that we should look beyond the 'emblematic figure of an outraged protestor'—what she called the stigmatised Muslim 'rage boy'—to gain deeper understanding of individual subjectivities (Blom 2008: 1). She argued that participation in anti-blasphemy protests is driven by affect and emotion, cognitive understanding of the situation and public performance of emotions (Blom 2008: 2). She has published similar work on 'outraged communities' in the broader context of South Asia that describes 'outrage' as a 'juncture between the moral and the emotional realm' and argues that 'instigating, staging, and managing this "righteous anger" is a crucial dimension' in mobilisation around cultural symbols in South Asia (Blom and Jaoul 2008: 7–8). According to these arguments, affect (bodily or visceral responses), emotion (bodily responses imbued with meaning), cognition (thought processes used to make sense of the world) and morality (shared world views) are all interdependent. Dispelling the reason–emotion dichotomy, Blom and Jaoul write:

> Some false dualisms certainly need to be clarified. The first dualism is the debatable opposition between emotions and reason, as if only one or the other could shape behaviour at any one time. This disjunction, inherited from the rational actor perspective, proves to be fragile, because ostensibly any rational calculus also implies a range of affects. (Blom and Jaoul 2008: 13)

In the same vein, studies of collective violence in South Asia and beyond have argued that participants' motivations lie simultaneously in the realms of emotion and reason. For example, Veena Das (1990: 25) contended that communal violence is both highly organised and emotionally charged. Similarly, Tambiah (1996: 284) and Sidel (2006: 13) have demonstrated in their studies of ethnic and religious violence that the aggressors are usually motivated by both strategic or instrumental goals and emotional attachments to cultural symbols. While these studies focus mostly on collective action, which is an important aspect of blasphemy-related violence in Pakistan, they do not deal with the intersubjective experiences leading to blasphemy accusations and driving individuals to carry out punishment of alleged blasphemers. I find the notion that emotion and cognition are mutually constitutive helpful in understanding not only the collective violence, but also the motivations of individual accusers and aggressors in cases of blasphemy in Pakistan. This book demonstrates that elements of strategic or instrumental use and moral outrage can be found in most instances of blasphemy accusations and subsequent violence.

Subjective and structural forms of violence

So far, I have focused on individual subjectivities in the formation of violence. However, individual subjectivity—'the felt interior experience of the person that includes his or her positions in a field of relational power' (Das and Kleinman 2000: 1)—is also embedded in wider political and economic processes. My arguments in this book are built on the crucial premise that violence is meaningful action within a sociopolitical domain. As Schröder and Schmidt (2001: 19) argued, violence is 'performed as well as imagined by reflexive, socially positioned human beings under specific historical conditions for concrete reasons'. The performance of violence is necessitated, conditioned and legitimised within given structural constraints. Žižek (2008: 9–15) argued that we are so engrossed in the immediacy of the 'subjective violence' (violence carried out by visible subjects) that we effectively ignore the violence inherent in the system, the violence that is not visible because it is *designed* to escape our eyes, the violence he calls 'objective violence'. Žižek thus described systemic or objective violence as one of the three types of violence he identified— the other two being subjective and symbolic. Schinkel (2013) also gave a similar classification of 'regimes of violence', which he called '*trias violentiae*'—namely, private, state and structural violence. Both Žižek and Schinkel are concerned with violence inherent in the foundations of the state, in the all-encompassing systems such as capitalism and neoliberalism, and its manifestations within private or visible spheres.

The violence inherent in the ideology and foundation of the state of Pakistan, as well as within the existing structures of power at national and global levels, is of crucial significance to understanding violence related to blasphemy in the everyday lives of common people. Scheper-Hughes and Bourgois (2004) argued that the violence of the everyday/ordinary is not entirely separate from the violence of the extraordinary; there is, rather, a continuum between its structural and its everyday forms. Following this argument, I demonstrate in this book how the structural and the everyday forms of violence not only manifest in each other, but also constantly construct each other in the case of blasphemy accusations and related violence in Pakistan. I focus on multiple locales of power and authority: the state, religious leaders and local and regional powerholders in intersubjective relationships.

To sum up, in this book, I take the premise that blasphemy-related violence is meaningful at both subjective and structural levels. At the subjective level, the immediate perpetrators of violence are driven by both emotion and reason. The subjective violence is embedded in culturally specific idioms and also reflects interpersonal power relations. The legitimacy of the subjective meanings of violence is not confined to the state legal system; rather, it is based on wider understandings of morality and justice. At the structural level, the violence is a manifestation of the state's claims to represent public morality and shared religious ideals. It reflects the systemic construction of certain cultural, religious and political identities as central to the project of the nation-state. It is also a consequence of larger forces of modernity, globalisation and the neoliberal world order. This book demonstrates how subjective and structural forms of violence enable and reinforce each other.

I borrow from the fields of anthropology of law, anthropology of emotions and affect, anthropology of violence and critical theory to construct my arguments. However, to limit myself to any of these disciplinary categories would be to reduce a complex phenomenon to only a few of its many dimensions. This book looks at collective action and motivational processes, escalation, resolution of conflict in society, statecraft and discursive production of religious-political ideology, processes of self-making and community-building, as well as the wider dynamics of global politics. This is indeed a massive task, as Skoggard and Waterston (2015: 117) put it:

> We anthropologists have probably set ourselves up for the impossible: to capture lived experience, emotionality, and perception; small and large-scale interactivity; intimacy; and sociality, power, politics, and ever-changing material conditions of social life without reducing one to the other.

However, this contextualisation and attention to the interconnectedness of various aspects of a phenomenon are what make the anthropological perspective valuable. Keeping that in mind, I aim to study the symbolic power of blasphemy accusations and subsequent violence in Pakistan and offer an anthropological perspective to the existing scholarship on the issue. This book by no means covers the entire breadth and complexity of the problem, but I hope to contribute to the ongoing discussions and provide more ethnographic material on which to build future research.

This book is divided into three parts. Part I, comprising Chapters 1 and 2, describes the broad religious-nationalistic landscape of Pakistan within which blasphemy accusations and subsequent violence take place. Chapter 1 establishes the historical context necessary to understand the problem of blasphemy in contemporary Pakistan. I highlight the processes of self-making, community-making and state-making—from precolonial times to the present day—that have led to the widespread uncertainties and moral anxieties among Pakistani Muslims. The discussion deals with the concepts of modernity, nationalism and globalisation, and their impact on shaping the popular consciousness in Pakistani society. The aim of this chapter is to demonstrate that the current issue of blasphemy-related violence in Pakistan is a product of specific historical and political contingencies. Chapter 2 highlights the prevalent religious discourse and politics that shape public morality around the issue of blasphemy in Pakistan. Through a study of religious publications, sermons and my interviews with religious scholars, I demonstrate how political competition over legitimacy and moral authority affects the positions of religious scholars and politicians on the punishment of blasphemy, and how these positions shape public religious thought amid widespread uncertainty and moral anxiety. The aim of this chapter is to unpack the religious aspect of the issue of blasphemy, as it is the prime justification given by the proponents of violence against the accused.

Part II, comprising Chapters 3 and 4, focuses on the everyday, the subjective and the lived aspects of blasphemy accusations and subsequent violence. Chapter 3 focuses on microlevel interactions between people to demonstrate how everyday conflicts (religious or otherwise) lead to blasphemy accusations. Based on my ethnographic research, this chapter shows that most of the accusations—and subsequent violence—take place among people who are already known to each other. I describe how familiarity and interpersonal power relations are crucial to understanding individual accusations. The aim of this chapter is to understand people's motivations—beyond personal rivalries—in accusing known others of blasphemy and examine the symbolic value of these accusations to those involved. Chapter 4 explains how the accusations, once made, are transformed from interpersonal to communal conflict and how various actors contribute to the making of the violence. The aim of this chapter is to show that accusations do not automatically—and inevitably—lead to violence and that various actors in addition to the accuser determine the outcome of the conflict once it has escalated.

Part III, comprising Chapters 5 and 6, focuses on the issues of legality and the legitimacy of different forms of punishment for those accused of blasphemy. Chapter 5 demonstrates how the state's claim to a monopoly over legitimate violence is contested by narratives of popular justice when it comes to the punishment of alleged blasphemers. The aim of this chapter is to contest the popular understandings of legitimacy—associated with the state legal system—and demonstrate that wider understandings of morality, justice and authority determine the accepted ways of punishing those accused of blasphemy. Chapter 6 analyses the discourse of two groups that exist at the nexus of the state and the society: lawyers and judges. I present my ethnographic study of a specific group of lawyers who support both state and nonstate punishments of blasphemers. I discuss the sources of legitimacy on which these lawyers draw to construct coherent narratives in which state and nonstate punishments are not dissonant but exist on a continuum of legitimacy. I also discuss the discourse of judges to highlight how they construct the legitimacy of state punishment of blasphemy while also endorsing narratives that glorify nonstate punishment. This chapter shows that state and nonstate systems of justice are not entirely contradictory; rather, they are extensions of each other. The aim of this chapter is to show how state and public morality shape each other and operate in a system of shared sovereignty in Pakistan.

Part I

1
Historical roots of anti-blasphemy violence in Pakistan: Formation of self, community and the state

In the old city of Lahore, at the Miani Sahib graveyard—one of the oldest in the region—lies a shrine adorned in white marble and dressed in embroidered sheets and flower petals. Every year, thousands of devotees visit the shrine to pay their respects to the person buried there. The archway leading to the shrine reads: 'The passionate lover of the Prophet, Ghazi Ilmuddin Shaheed'. It is the final resting place of the highly revered Ghazi Ilmuddin Shaheed, successful warrior and martyr. Ilmuddin was a 19-year-old Muslim man who was executed by the British government in 1929 for killing a Hindu publisher, Mahashe Rajpal, who had published an allegedly derogatory book about the Prophet Muhammad (Khan 2011: 60). The book, titled *Rangila Rasul* (*Colourful Prophet*), was published in 1924, leading to widespread protests by Muslims for its portrayal of the Prophet Muhammad's 'sexual dalliance' (Stephens 2014: 45). In 1927, after Rajpal had been tried for hate speech—after complaints by Muslims—and acquitted by the British courts, as many as 70,000 Muslims gathered in Delhi to protest the acquittal (Nair 2013: 323), raising slogans of 'death for defamation of the Prophet', which eventually led to the killing of Rajpal by Ilmuddin. After his trial and then execution by the British courts, Ilmuddin was turned into a Muslim hero, 'who had the courage to avenge the disrespect for [the] Prophet Muhammad' by meting out 'the punishment which the British colonial government could not award' (Rumi 2018: 323). His act of defending the honour of the Prophet by killing Rajpal was lauded by prominent religious leaders of the time and the founding fathers of Pakistan (Rumi 2018). In present-day Pakistan, Ilmuddin is revered as a saint and a national hero; the anniversary of his death attracts enormous crowds of devotees, is celebrated in textbooks and popular cinema, and there are government buildings named after him (Rumi 2018: 322–23).

In an apparent act of history repeating itself, Mumtaz Qadri—the young man who killed the Governor of Punjab, Salman Taseer, on allegations of blasphemy in 2011—was hailed as the 'Ilmuddin of our time' by his supporters. Much like Ilmuddin, Qadri also earned a shrine and hordes of devotees after his execution by the state for murder in 2016. His funeral was also attended by masses and his life and personality have since been similarly valorised in a multitude of ways. Farhat Haq, in her recent (2019) book on blasphemy politics in Pakistan, calls the entanglement of Ilmuddin's and Qadri's stories 'a tale of two saints'. The similarity between the two tales of veneration suggests that anti-blasphemy violence in present-day Pakistan has deeper historical roots than the introduction of the current anti-blasphemy legislation by General Zia-ul-Haq—the event from which most scholars trace the origins of anti-blasphemy violence (see, for example, Dobras 2009; Hayee 2012; Hoffman 2014; Saiya 2016; Siddique and Hayat 2008). However, as Haq (2019: 17) rightfully reminds us, there are some significant contextual differences between the acts of the two assassin-saints: Ilmuddin killed a Hindu publisher who had deliberately mocked the Prophet Muhammad amid the rising insecurities of Muslim-minority colonial India; Qadri killed a Muslim politician who had publicly proclaimed his faith and his love for the Prophet while criticising the procedural inadequacies of the anti-blasphemy laws in Muslim-majority Pakistan.[1] These differences suggest that, while the symbolic significance of love for the Prophet and the act of protecting his honour remain central to both stories, the perception of what constitutes an attack on the Prophet and Islam has evolved. This chapter traces the continuities and discontinuities in the individual and collective consciousness underlying the veneration of the two saints,

---

1   Farhat Haq, in her remarkable work on the political history of Pakistan's blasphemy problem, provides a detailed account of political rivalries, parliamentary debates and historical developments that got us to this point, where 'the so-called blasphemy laws' have become sacralised to an extent that 'criticising them could make one a target for murder' (2019: 17). I leave most of these details out and instead focus on the development of individual and collective consciousness concerning identity. I encourage readers to consult Haq's book for further historical and political context of the current anti-blasphemy legislation in Pakistan.

Ilmuddin and Qadri, almost a century apart. I demonstrate how anti-blasphemy attitudes and violence in contemporary Pakistan—aggravated and intensified since Ilmuddin's case—have evolved over time.

Anti-blasphemy sentiments in contemporary Pakistan must be understood within the context of the wider religious and political sensibilities of Pakistani Muslims—specifically, their anxieties concerning individual, communal and national identities. These anxieties have taken shape through the wider processes of modernisation, colonisation, nationalism and neocolonialism over the past two centuries. I focus on four key historical developments that I believe are crucial to understanding anti-blasphemy attitudes in contemporary Pakistan: 1) the development of a morally anxious modern Muslim self under the influence of colonial-era reform movements on the Subcontinent; 2) apprehensions related to the self-contradictory religious and national identity harboured by the Pakistan Movement; 3) anxieties about difference and dissent inculcated by state policies to achieve a uniform and homogeneous national identity after the creation of Pakistan; and 4) widespread concerns about Pakistan's and Islam's place and reputation in the neocolonial world order, particularly in the context of 9/11 and the subsequent rise of Islamophobia. While Ilmuddin's case was influenced by the first point—the politicisation of modern individual and collective Muslim identity under colonial rule—the subsequent developments are crucial to understanding the making of Qadri a century later. The following discussion will demonstrate how these interlinked processes bear on the contemporary lives of Pakistani Muslims at individual, communal and national levels and shape the deep-rooted understandings of blasphemy and its punishment.

Modernity, reform movements and transformation of the self

Modernity—an era commonly understood to have started in seventeenth-century Europe—is seen by anthropologists, sociologists and critical theorists as comprising specific social processes, attitudes, discourses and economic conditions. Some of the widely recognised markers of modernity include industrialisation, the rise of capitalism and the market economy and the development of nation-states (Berman 2010: 16–30; Giddens 1991: 6). The underlying features of modern institutions include standardisation, centralisation and all-encompassing control of human life, on the one hand, and individualism, liberation, emphasis on free will and loss of certainty on the other (see, for example, Bauman 1990, 2000; Giddens 1991). Similarly, modernity has been characterised by both emancipation from religion and religious revival (Hervieu-Léger 1990; Lambert 1999). While these characteristics of modernity are considered to be universal, as is the transition to modernity itself, the specificity of modernity to different local contexts—multiple modernities—has also been acknowledged (Delanty 2007; Eisenstadt 2000).

British colonisation of the Subcontinent in the eighteenth century is largely seen as the trigger for the onset of modernity in South Asia. However, some of the changes in the Subcontinent's political sphere *prior* to the arrival of the British were also headed in the general direction of modernity—for example, consolidation of the Mughal Empire under the rule of the last Mughal emperor, Aurangzeb (r. 1658–1707), whose policies tended towards standardisation of laws and governance (Malik 2008: 189–95). There were also general reformist tendencies influenced by Muslim scholars such as Sirhindi, who aimed to revive Islamic practices in society (Malik 2008: 179–80).

Nevertheless, despite the unifying efforts of the Mughal emperors and the reformist tendencies of some Muslim scholars, the internal diversity of Muslim society prevented centralisation from being fully implemented (Malik 2008: 209). Under Mughal rule, Indian Muslims socially identified themselves according to their lineage and regional ties rather than their 'Muslim' identity. In the Mughal courts, the Muslim elite identified themselves as Persians or Turks; among the general populace, family history (kinship ties), language, locality and ethnicity were sources of identification and even divisions (Robinson 1998: 271–72). In most instances, the lower castes of Hindus and Muslims identified more closely with each other due to shared exigencies of their everyday lives (Malik 2008: 172).[2] While religion had its role in the empire and in the lives of the elite Muslim scholars, it was not the primary basis of categorisation in society. In fact, religion as such did not exist as a category separate from other spheres of life.

---

2   The presence of caste among South Asian Muslims was documented from as early as the thirteenth century (Malik 2008: 157). I will discuss caste in the context of purity, hierarchy, transgressions and blasphemy accusations in Chapter 3.

The colonisation of the Subcontinent by the British completely transformed the sociopolitical institutions and life-worlds of the Indian population. Several historians have attributed the reification of Muslim identity—as well as the religious identities of other South Asian communities—to circumstances created by British colonial policies aimed at modernising and secularising the Subcontinent (see, for example, Metcalf 1982; Zaman 2002). The British brought Western conceptions of modernity with categorisations such as religious/secular and private/public at the heart of their policies. Thus, the forced categorisation of political, legal, religious and cultural as distinct from each other was essentially a modern phenomenon with an imperialist aim to govern and control colonial subjects (Zaman 1999: 297). On the one hand, the colonial rulers made religion the prime identifier of their subjects, differentiating between Hindus, Muslims and other religious communities at the official level. On the other hand, they aimed to push the religious aspects of people's lives out of the public sphere (van der Veer 2002: 179). These apparently contradictory moves were driven by the political project of secularisation—a normative concept rooted in British religious history.[3] The consequence was the simultaneous reification of religious identity and forced elimination of religion from public life. It was only a matter of time before the reified religious identities would return to the public sphere with a renewed and intensified political spirit.

British policies of educational and legal reform are of particular relevance to my argument. Under Mughal rule, the *madrasahs* (educational institutes) were spaces of comprehensive learning where religious education was integrated with training in law, mathematics, philosophy and many other subjects. These *madrasahs* produced elite religious scholars, *muftis*, who were incorporated into the courts of the empire as official interpreters of Islamic law. Colonial policies altered this arrangement significantly; while the educational reforms eliminated religious

---

3   It must be noted that the political project of 'secularisation', as Talal Asad (2003) has argued in his book *Formations of the Secular*, is a historically specific development. Asad problematised the simplistic understanding of secularism as separation of religion and politics and assumptions about its neutrality or opposition to religion. He also questioned the uniformity and singularity of the notion of secularism. He instead demonstrated that *secularisms* as practised in modern Western states today are products of specific historical developments within Christianity and Western philosophy. The secularism that the British were trying to implement was also a particular political system with its roots in British religious history. It was not based on the separation of the church and the state; rather, the two were intricately linked. In fact, the Church of England established several dioceses in India during colonial rule. Peter van der Veer's (2001, 2002) work also shows how the specific religious agenda of the British was pushed in the guise of secularity and neutrality towards religion.

education from school curriculums,[4] the legal reforms removed *muftis* from the courts (Zaman 1999, 2002). Colonial governance effectively reduced the role and influence of traditional Muslim scholars to private religious education and Muslim personal law—matters of marriage, divorce, children and inheritance.[5] The British policies thus challenged the authority of Muslim scholars and left them feeling alienated from the political and administrative spheres.

The Muslim scholars, feeling disenfranchised and threatened, then took it on themselves to preserve Muslim culture and religion, partly to carve out a new space for themselves in the changing society. They emerged as the custodians of a newly developed concept of a private *religious sphere* and its role in public life. After losing their place in the religious and administrative setup, the religious scholars left the big cities and moved to smaller towns and villages, where they started their efforts for the revival of Islam (Metcalf 1982: 85). They attributed the decline of Muslim political power to Muslims' failure to adhere to *true Islam*. Their campaigns aimed to:

> restore the perceived pristine glory of Islam, both politically and religiously, by way of cleansing its prevalent modes of practices and sets of beliefs from what were felt to be later-day accretions [*bid'at*]. (Qasmi 2011: 32)

The past glory of Islam—the golden era—was imagined as a 'political and social utopia' that the reformists aspired to re-create (Malik 2008: 200).

Reform movements are nothing new in the history of Muslim societies as, 'from the beginning of the Islamic era, Muslim societies have experienced periods of renewal' (Robinson 2008: 259). In fact, as already noted, there were reform movements during the Mughal era as well. However, the conditions created by British colonisation—imposed modernisation and secularisation—of the Indian Subcontinent in the eighteenth and nineteenth centuries were unique and gave rise to a host of reform movements not only among Muslims, but also among Hindus and

---

4   Despite claims of secularisation of the education system, much of the British education system was 'in the hands of Christian missionaries', whose explicit aim was to convert the local population to Christianity rather than provide religiously neutral education (van der Veer 2001: 98).

5   In modernising the law, the British introduced distinctly secular and personal laws. The latter were community-specific laws—based on religious affiliations—that would regulate personal matters such as marriage, divorce, children and inheritance.

other religious communities (van der Veer 2001: 110).⁶ It was within this context that the reform movements that arose among South Asian Muslims under colonial rule were often defined by their 'opposition to Western cultural and political hegemony' (Robinson 2008: 261). The aims of these movements can therefore be described as both religious revival *and* anticolonial resistance.

Despite their anticolonial spirit, these movements employed uniquely modern ways of thinking and incorporated Western knowledge and technologies where appropriate (Robinson 2008). Their use of print media, for example, helped religious scholars reach the masses. They even published in vernacular languages and used simplified writing styles to address ordinary people as opposed to their specialised religious writings for traditional audiences within the scholarly community. Previously, 'the referential works of the scholars of the past, Quranic commentaries and Hadith collection could not be mass-produced and widely disseminated' (Qasmi 2011: 31). The print medium and the use of simplified language made the message of religious scholars accessible to a much wider audience.

There were various reform movements that began at different points in the modern history of the Subcontinent, each with slightly different goals and motivations. They all used—deliberately or otherwise—modern technologies and tools of thinking to varying degrees. Historians have described the Islamic reform movements variously—as *Islamic modernism*, adapting Islam according to modern times; *Islamic fundamentalism*, rejecting modern/Western knowledge and technologies and returning to the perceived fundamental elements of Islam; and many variations in between (see, for example, Qasmi 2011: 240; Robinson 2008: 260). These variations are best seen as a spectrum, with different configurations of modernity and what was thought to be tradition at their heart. Regardless of which configuration was adopted, all of these movements were essentially modern in their nature since they took religion as a distinct, reified category and aimed to rationalise it in the modern world. Some of the common characteristics that pervade these reform movements include: rejection of past authority, the rise of independent reasoning, an emphasis on human will and individual responsibility, and rationalisation

---

6   The strengthening of Hindu identity and the Muslim reform movements went hand in hand and were both the cause and the effect of each other (in a dialectic relationship).

of religious knowledge (Metcalf 1982: 12; Robinson 2008: 261). Francis Robinson (2008: 279–80) describes these processes in South Asian Islamic reform movements:

> Islamic reform destroyed much of the authority of the past, making possible a more creative engagement with the present. It emphasised human will, preparing the way for the modern understanding of undiluted human instrumentality in the world. It set off transformations of the self that we associate with modernity, the emergence of an internal landscape and the affirmation of the ordinary things of life. It helped set off a rationalisation and reification of Islam, which, amongst other things, prepared Muslims to engage with a broad-based political identity and conceive of their faith as an entity, even a system. And finally, it set going processes that offered both a disenchanted world and one in which paradoxically the transcendent was reasserted, indeed, the world itself was re-enchanted.

The changes of the self, which Robinson calls *transformations of the self*, are of crucial significance to my argument in this book. There was a notable shift towards personal and individual moral reform as the religious scholars turned to the masses to regain their influence in society. Since they had the private religious sphere—separate from the secular public sphere—available to them, the religious scholars directed their focus to reforming the private moral lives of individuals. They aimed to inculcate a renewed sense of piety and virtue among individuals through various methods of proselytising. They preached to ordinary people on the higher standards of faith and morality based on the reformed religious ideals. The individual moral life was thus subjected to much greater scrutiny and regulation. Even the *fatwas* (religious verdicts) of that time demonstrated a move away from matters of governance to matters of individual morality and piety (Qasmi 2011: 38).

Through their preaching and publications, the religious scholars disseminated ideals of *authentic* Islam widely among ordinary Muslims. This led to an enhanced burden of responsibility falling on the shoulders of individuals as:

> it was the individual human conscience, working with this knowledge, which now had sole responsibility to ensure rightly guided behaviour. Thus, reformed Islam was a willed faith, a 'protestant' faith, a faith of conscience and conviction. (Robinson 2008: 269)

Preoccupied with 'the individual and its subjectivity', the reformist tendencies are thus:

> a process of self-making, which may include the reinterpretation of religious traditions, and in which the self seeks its completion in particular social and political acts that express its authenticity. (Verkaaik 2004: 45)

The modern Muslim self was, therefore, defined by an increased focus on individuality and authenticity (Roy 1994). The enhanced focus on human will and individual responsibility, along with the increased expectations of adherence to Islam to be a proper Muslim, gave rise to newer technologies of the self in which the self was constructed primarily as a sinner in need of purification. This transformation also led to a greater emphasis on the bodily practices involved in the purification of the self. Technologies of the self, as defined by Foucault (1988: 18),[7] are techniques:

> which permit individuals to effect by their own means or with the help of others a certain number of operations on their own bodies and souls, thoughts, conduct, and way of being, so as to transform themselves in order to attain a certain state of happiness, purity, wisdom, perfection, or immortality.

The modern reformist movements' emphasis on individual piety and moral goodness prompted an inward turn and a reflective approach to being a Muslim, such that 'Muslims had to ask themselves regularly if they had done all in their power to submit to God and to carry out His will in the world' (Robinson 2008: 272). They had to constantly measure themselves against the perfection and purity they were supposed to achieve. This inward turn was nothing new as there have been ascetic and reflective tendencies within Muslim societies throughout history. What was new, however, was the essentialising of the self as lacking and in need of correction. Hence:

---

7   Foucault explained his concept of technologies of the self in a 1982 lecture in which he compared the hermeneutics of self in the Greco-Roman philosophy of the early Roman Empire (the first two centuries CE) with the Christianity of the late Roman Empire (fourth and fifth centuries). He noted that the technologies of the self in the classical period consisted primarily of the 'care of the self' by subjecting the soul to questions of truth and morality. By the late Roman Empire, the technologies of the self had transformed to an emphasis on bodily discipline—renunciation—and a disclosure of the sinful self. At the end of the lecture, Foucault briefly referred to a further break in the technologies of the self in the modern era whereby the self is constituted positively—without renunciation—through scientific knowledge. It can be argued that the technologies of the self emerging in modern colonial India were a combination of the sinful self in need of purification and the modern self subjected to positivist, scientific/rational modes of knowledge.

while in the past, the reflective believer, the mystic, might have meditated on the signs of God, the new type of reflective believer reflected on the self and the shortcomings of the self. (Robinson 2008: 273)

The newer self was thus constructed through constant purification and expulsion of impurities.

At the heart of this development was the tension between the lived life and one's ideals. As Gilmartin (2014: xxxvii) indicates, such a tension had always existed, emanating from 'the interactions between the particular and the universal within Islamic civilisation'. The universal ideals of Islam and its strong ties to the land of its origin, Arabia, were never completely synchronised with the local lives of South Asian Muslims, who constructed a composite culture. However, these tensions were exacerbated by the colonial interventions and modern categorisation of religion as a distinct system—which was then perceived to be at odds with local life. The newly created 'tensions between ideals and worldly realities' were 'layered onto the older tensions between core Islamic civilizational ideals and lived realities' (Gilmartin 2014: xxxii). The underlying tension between the *universal* and the *particular*, the *ideal* and the *lived* persisted and aggravated the moral anxieties of ordinary Muslims. Muslims were increasingly conscious not only of the shortcomings of their selves with respect to the ideal Muslim self, but also of the deviations of society from the idealised essence of Islam.[8] Thus, the inner or reflexive turn was also inherently political—eventually culminating in movements for wider social change.

Driven by similar anxieties and with similar aims at their heart, the reform movements developed in various—often conflicting—directions. Three of the most important reformist groups—still relevant to Pakistan—that emerged among the Sunni Muslims of South Asia were Deobandis, Ahl-e-Hadith and Barelwis. Each emphasises returning and adhering to the original sources of Islam—the Quran and the *Sunnah* (the prophetic traditions). However, they also have their own specific trajectories of development and ideas of reform. For example, Ahl-e-Hadith do not deem it necessary to follow any school of law or *fiqh* (Islamic jurisprudence), while Deobandis and Barelwis continue to follow the established schools of jurisprudence

---

8   Joel Robbins's (2004) book, *Becoming Sinners*, presents a similar account of 'moral torment' among the Urapmin of Papua New Guinea in the face of tension between local tradition and changes brought about by the ideals of Christianity.

within Sunni Islam[9]—the Hanafi school being the most popular among them (Behuria 2008: 59). Deobandis and Ahl-e-Hadith, however, do not accept 'local cultural and custom-based practices' and other shrine-related rituals (Qasmi 2011: 34–35). Barelwis, on the other hand:

> accept customary practices of mediation closely associated with the *pirs* [spiritual guides] of the shrines and the evocation of the supernatural powers and blessings of other revered figures from the Muslim past. (Qasmi 2011: 34–35)

Thus, as argued by Osella and Osella (2008), there is no uniform reformism, but a period of renewal was experienced by almost all sections of Muslim society despite their internal differences.

One of the major points of contestation between different reformist groups was the nature and place of the Prophet Muhammad in *true Islam*. The increased emphasis on the personality of the Prophet and his significance to Muslims' faith have also been described as a new development within the colonial context. Muslims became increasingly conscious of the image of the Prophet due to encounters with Christian missionaries and other politicised reformist religious groups within South Asia, such as certain factions of Hindus (Qasmi 2011: 39). In an increasingly hostile environment and in the wake of interaction with Western powers who challenged the status of the Prophet Muhammad, this became the pivotal point of contestation between different reformist groups. They ardently debated the minutest of details related to the life and personality of the Prophet, as they aimed to come up with a model personality for Muslims to follow. They argued over issues such as the bodily appearance of the Prophet (clothing, length of facial hair, and so on), his method of praying (the positions and postures) and the details of his everyday life. Such an emphasis on the person of the Prophet has also been linked to modernity's emphasis on the individual self, as Qasmi argues:

> This growing emphasis on the person of the Prophet as the exemplar of human perfection and presentation … can also be attributed to an enhanced focus on the individual self—a colonial/ capital by-product. The Prophet's 'new' image, thus constructed, emphasised a wide array of his human virtues and projected him as beloved, charitable, frugal, a lover of children, steadfast, successful

---

9   There are four widely recognised schools of jurisprudence in Sunni Islam: Hanafi, Maliki, Shafi'i and Hanbali (Coulson 1964: 86). These schools were consolidated in the ninth and tenth centuries and have been sources of guidance, debate and authority for Muslims since then (Melchert 1997: 1).

and so on. This can be taken as an expression of the growing sense of the self amid a newly emerging middle-class Muslim world forced to fall back upon, and coming to terms with, its inner resources. (Qasmi 2011: 39)

Malik (2008: 202) describes this shift in the modes of attachment to the Prophet as a transformation from 'mystical piety' into 'prophetic' or 'action piety', in line with the newer technologies of self, discussed earlier. Within the context of these developments, the scholars of Islam engaged in renewed studies of the prophetic tradition (*hadith*)—the transmitted knowledge of the Prophet. These new studies shortened the chain of narrators, making a quick and effective attachment with the Prophet possible. This form of attachment focused on imitating the everyday life of the Prophet—what Malik (2008) calls 'imitatio muhammadi'. Thus, the Prophet's *sunna*—his way of being in this world—became the pivotal point of social and political reform, resulting in the 'Sunnatisation' of Muslims' life-worlds (Malik 2008).

The Barelwis—followers of Ahmed Raza Khan Barelwi (1856–1921)—are often seen as the least radical of the reformers as they did not call for complete eradication of local customs. Instead, their movement was deeply embedded in the South Asian culture of shrines and reverence for holy personalities and objects. Nevertheless, they were the ones who were most vocal in denouncing others as disrespectful and inappropriate Muslims when it came to the issue of the personality of Muhammad and the appropriate means of attachment to him. The Barelwis leader issued *fatwas* against other religious leaders deemed disrespectful of the Prophet (Qasmi 2011: 40). These *fatwas* focused on improper ways of speaking about the Prophet, inappropriate understanding of the 'true nature' of the Prophet and inadequate modes of attachment to the Prophet.

Debates on the nature and place of the Prophet in Muslim society led to polemics concerning respecting him as early as the nineteenth century. These concerns were manifested not only in the personal, but also in the political, domain as they later developed into several emotionally charged mass movements to protect Islam's holy symbols—the Quran, mosques, the Prophet—in early twentieth-century colonial India.[10] Gilmartin

---

10 This development, however, was not exclusive to Muslims, as other religious communities in South Asia, such as Sikhs and Hindus, also displayed passionate attachment to their religious symbols—for example, through the cow protection movement in the late nineteenth and early twentieth centuries (Brass 1991: 77–80). The central place of emotion in South Asian public life has been recognised and described as the 'moral outrage' that has characterised popular mobilisations on the Subcontinent for a long time (Blom and Jaoul 2008: 1–2).

(1991), in his essay on colonial Muslim politics, wrote about the rise of Muslim emotionalism in the political sphere in twentieth-century pre-Partition India. He argued that the emergence of Muslim publics and community identity in colonial India was rooted in rational self-control of the individual as well as the autonomous realm of the individual heart and emotion (Gilmartin 1991: 131).[11] Autonomous individuals driven by emotions and engaged in self-making came to form the new Muslim community. It was manifested in the symbolic action in the movements in the 1920s and 1930s for the protection of *Khilafat* (the Ottoman caliphate),[12] the Prophet and mosques. In these movements, the discourse of personal and emotional identification with Islamic symbols was translated from the press into public action (Gilmartin 1991: 133).

The *Rangila Rasul* publication controversy of the 1920s—discussed at the beginning of this chapter—was turned into 'a symbolic test of "love" of the Prophet' (Gilmartin 1991: 134). It was:

> the *public* display of the heart in the active protection of the honour of the Prophet that defined the real existence of a Muslim community during the Rangila Rasul crisis. (Gilmartin 1991: 134; italics in original)

The glorification of Ilmuddin's killing of Rajpal established 'action in the name of the heart as the most telling validator of Muslim identity' (Gilmartin 1991: 135). By 1935, one of the most powerful movements for the defence of holy symbols had emerged in Lahore, Punjab, to protect the Shahidgunj mosque from demolition by Sikhs. Gilmartin (2014: xxxiii) argues that this movement 'drew on the mosque as a symbol of a transcendent, universalising morality', which was enabled by 'new forms of direct individual attachment to the ineffable core of civilisation'. Thus, it was the modern Muslim self, conscious of their individual responsibility and with the urge to achieve personal and societal purification, who

---

[11] The shift of emotion into the public sphere was also facilitated through Urdu poetry. Poets such as Maulana Zafar Ali Khan and Muhammad Iqbal brought the long-established literary idioms of inner emotions and desires into the realm of public debate through political poetry and publishing. The emotions in Urdu poetry were sometimes seen as 'irrational', and sometimes as intuitive, giving access to inner Sufi knowledge. However, with the politicisation of poetry, emotion was also politicised, leading up to the 'movement of the inner world directly onto the political stage' (Gilmartin 1991: 132).

[12] The Khilafat Movement (1919–24) was led by South Asian Muslims against the sanctions placed on the Ottoman caliphate after World War I. The aim of the movement was to restore the caliph of the Ottoman Empire, who was considered a leader of the Muslim world and an upholder of the Islamic system of governance in the modern world.

participated in the emotional politics. The centrality of emotions and passionate attachments to the public life of Muslims in twentieth-century South Asia should not be seen in opposition to reason and rationality, as it was through the modern techniques and language of reason that the emotional attachments were articulated in the public sphere. Muslims were not only driven by their modern sensibilities but also engaged with the language of rights and 'the logic of secular regimes of law' to express their emotional grievances on the political stage (Stephens 2014: 46–47). While they glorified an act of nonstate killing, they also demanded the state change its legal structure to acknowledge the killing of Rajpal as legitimate—the introduction of clause 295-A in the penal code being a response to this demand (Stephens 2014). Reason and passion, therefore, were components of the same popular consciousness.

The development of the religious sensibilities of Muslims concerning certain holy symbols should therefore be seen within the context of modernity, reformation and transformation of the self, giving rise to a newer consciousness of religious identity not only at the individual but also at the collective level. The development of the new religious identity was also a direct result of colonisation and forced secularisation. The increased consciousness of religious identity, however, does not automatically and necessarily lead to nationalism, and even less so to a specific separatist nationalist movement—the Pakistan Movement, in this case. In the next section, I explain how the heightened sense of religious identity led to the specific outcome of a separate nation-state for Muslims: Pakistan.

Nationalism, religious identity and the Pakistan Movement

Nationalism, like modernity, has been described as a global phenomenon. There is a small group of scholars—usually referred to as 'primordialists'— who see nationalism as an inherent tendency of human beings, who have formed social groupings and attachments since the beginning of time (Coakley 2018: 327–29). However, most theorists of nationalism—such as Ernest Gellner, Benedict Anderson, Paul Brass and Eric J. Hobsbawm— see it as a distinctly modern development dating back to the French Revolution, and qualitatively different from all previous forms of social groupings. Ernest Gellner (1983: 1) defined nationalism as 'primarily a political principle that holds that the political and the national unit should be congruent'. Gellner's theory of nationalism postulates that:

> nations as a natural, God-given way of classifying men, as an inherent though long-delayed political destiny, are a myth; nationalism, which sometimes takes pre-existing cultures and turns them into nations, sometimes invents them, and often obliterates pre-existing cultures: *that* is a reality, and in general an inescapable one. (Gellner 1983: 48–49)

The modern world, therefore, has been characterised by the emergence of nation-states—political entities claiming sovereignty based on ideas of shared culture.

Following a modern global trend of nationalism, the Indian Subcontinent also saw the rise of numerous nationalist movements in the twentieth century. These movements drew on many of the universally identified characteristics of nationalism such as imagined communities, linguistic standardisation and cultural homogeneity. Modern nations are described as 'imagined communities' because the members of these nations do not personally know all other members, and will never meet them, but have a shared notion of their communion (Anderson 1991: 5–7). Many of the Muslim nationalist movements that arose on the Subcontinent also imagined a community of all Muslims of South Asia and beyond. The imagined community was brought together by cultural elites through standardisation of Urdu as the language of Muslims through the print medium and a supposed sameness of the community. Other features of modern nation-states, such as the 'invention of tradition' (Hobsbawm 1983) and manipulation of 'cultural symbols' (Brass 1991), which I discuss in more detail later, were also present in the nationalist movements of the Subcontinent.

While espousing some of the general characteristics, the nationalist movements of the Subcontinent were at the same time culturally and regionally specific. Partha Chatterjee (1993) discussed the emergence of postcolonial nations and how their nationalisms are both specific to their local contexts and products of the universal move towards nationalism. He objects to Anderson's argument that the colonial world copied Euro-American models of nationalism. Chatterjee instead contends that the colonised people had their own imagined communities and their nationalisms emerged out of their specific imaginations

(1993: 5). He argues, in the context of India, that the colonial subjects resisted and developed their own sense of nationalism by developing an 'inner' spiritual domain, which they held as sovereign, and refused interventions by colonial powers in this inner domain. While colonialism transformed the outer (material) world of administration, laws, policies, statecraft, science, economics and infrastructure—which led to apparent imitation of Western nationalism—the local nationalist movements developed a distinct spiritual sphere that was specific to their imagined community. According to Chatterjee (1993: 6), the spiritual is the 'inner' domain bearing 'essential' marks of cultural identity. Within this spiritual domain, 'nationalism launches its most powerful, creative, and historically significant project: to fashion a "modern" national culture that is nevertheless not Western' (Chatterjee 1993: 7). Muslim nationalist movements on the Subcontinent were also rooted in this 'inner' domain.

In the previous section, I demonstrated the construction of a peculiarly modern inner sphere for Muslims that was then politicised and brought into the public sphere. It was this *inner* sphere that was crucial to the establishment of certain cultural symbols as central to Indian Muslims' nationalist imaginations. While nationalist movements everywhere relied on some central symbols defined by the cultural elite for their collective imaginings, the particularly spiritual and religious nature of symbolism in India is of significance. Thus, as Paul Brass (1991: 76) argues:

> Muslim separatism was not pre-ordained, but resulted from the conscious manipulation of selected symbols of Muslim identity by Muslim elite groups in economic and political competition with each other and with elite groups among Hindus.

Of course, manipulation of certain symbols by elite groups is possible because people have certain meanings attached to those symbols in the first place. However, those meanings are not fixed in time and are also a product of historical circumstances. As we have already seen, the centrality of the Prophet Muhammad's personality and the attachment to certain symbols such as mosques were outcomes of specific developments within the individual as well as the collective lives of Muslims in India. The politicisation of religious symbols through appeal to popular meanings of those symbols is what gave rise to Muslim nationalism.

Muslim separatism—culminating in the creation of Pakistan—is seen as one of the most powerful nationalist movements to emerge in British India. In a recent book, Qasmi and Robb (2017) trace the trajectory of Muslim nationalism on the pre-Partition Indian Subcontinent. They argue that the sharpening of Muslim identity did not automatically lead to the idea of a separate nation-state (Qasmi and Robb 2017: 9). The Muslims of South Asia were transformed first into a community, then a minority and then a nation. Their heightened consciousness of religious identity led them to see themselves as a community who then demanded their rights as a minority community within the undivided India. It was much later that the idea of attaining sovereignty based on their collective identity as Muslims became popular. Even so, this trajectory did not lead to a single, uniform Muslim nation. Instead, there were several, often conflicting, theories of Muslim nationalism prevalent in pre-Partition colonial India. The idea of Pakistan, peddled by the political elite of the All India Muslim League (AIML), was a specific, albeit triumphant, outcome of *one among many* notions of Muslim nationalism prevalent in twentieth-century India (Qasmi and Robb 2017).

The major trends in the imagining of a nation by Muslims on the Subcontinent ranged from a pan-Islamic community of Muslims (*ummah*) to regional communities held together by language and culture rather than religion. Tanweer Fazal (2015), in his detailed account of the subject, recounts a range of competing ideas of Muslim nationalism. Pan-Islamism—the concept that Muslims from around the world form a spiritual community regardless of their regional, territorial, ethnic and other affiliations—was supported by several prominent religious leaders and reformers (such as Abul A'la Maududi) as well as the ideological founder of Pakistan, philosopher and poet Muhammad Iqbal. These ideologues saw the Western concept of territorial nationalism as materially based, compared with their notion of spiritual Islamic universalism (Fazal 2015: 64–65). Another noteworthy trend was that of 'composite nationhood', championed by the likes of Maulana Abul Kalam Azad, a congressional leader, and Islamic scholar Husayn Ahmad Madani, who was the head of a Deoband seminary and president of Jamiat Ulama-i-Hind, a prime collective of Indian *ulema* (religious scholars). They advocated for a common nationality for Hindus and Muslims based on their shared cultural and historical ties. Like the pan-Islamists, the composite nationalists also referenced the Quran and other religious sources to prove that their theory was in line with the Islamic concept of nationalism (Fazal

2015: 66–68).[13] The third-most important, and eventually triumphant, take on Muslim nationalism was based on the Western concept of a territorial nation-state, which was championed by the Western-educated elite leadership of the AIML when they proposed a separate nation-state for the Muslims of India in 1940. However, they modified this idea to suit their own purposes. They argued for the shared history, geography and language of Muslims as the basis for their nationality but at the same time suggested that religious identity should supersede all other affiliations. The idea of a separate state for Muslims thus proposed was not entirely Western but a compromise attempt between a territorial nation-state and a universal Islamic community. Muhammad Ali Jinnah, the principal leader of AIML and the founder of Pakistan, based his argument for such a state on French philosopher Ernest Renan's conceptualisation of subjective nation formation based on a collective 'moral consciousness' and 'will of the aggregate' (Fazal 2015: 73).

Many religious leaders (Deobandis, Jamaat-e-Islami, Jamiat Ulama-i-Hind) were suspicious of the Westernised leadership of the AIML and opposed the demand for Pakistan. Despite the antagonism, the AIML succeeded in materialising the idea of Pakistan within just seven years. This was made possible by several factors, including the lack of other feasible options, manipulation of religious symbolism and formation of strategic alliances. On a practical level, as Qasmi and Robb (2017: 4) argue, it was the sheer lack of viable alternatives offered by their opponents that worked in favour of the AIML during the political negotiations. On a more strategic level, the leadership of the AIML manipulated the symbols of Muslim identity to gain political influence over the masses. For example, as Fazal (2015: 75) notes, many 'prominent Leaguers took to praying in public to establish their commitment to their faith'. They also appealed to the heart and emotions of the 'autonomous individual Muslim voter' by using 'deeply rooted language of religious commitment' (Qasmi and Robb 2017: 26). Another strategic move was AIML's courting of Barelwis, particularly the landowning *pirs* (spiritual leaders) who had significant influence over their local populations. Barelwis had a longstanding rivalry with the Deobandis and they supported the idea of Pakistan to counter

---

13   Contestations of the ideas of *ummah*, *qoum* and *millat* (three different words referring to community) were at the heart of these formulations. For example, while *ummah* referred to the spiritual community of all Muslims, *qoum* meant a regional community for some but a political religious community for others. These three words have varying meanings that have also overlapped and shifted.

the position of the Deobandis on Muslim nationalism. They formed a significant population in the provinces Jinnah was demanding for Pakistan but supported the AIML only on the condition of making the new state an Islamic one (Qasmi and Robb 2017: 73–75).

Furthermore, while campaigning for Pakistan, its proponents employed a 'two-nation theory', which held that Muslims were qualitatively different from Hindus (Cohen 2004: 28). The theory postulated that Muslims and Hindus had different cultures, different religious traditions, different customs and norms, and hence could not live together. Some validation and political currency were provided to this theory by competitive mobilisation by Hindu nationalists, who used Hindu symbols to lay exclusive claims to Indian territory (Fazal 2015: 72–73). Prominent historians of Pakistan such as Ayesha Jalal and Barbara Metcalf argued that the Pakistan Movement was concerned with the power-sharing arrangements between the Muslims and the Hindus of India due to the minority status of the Muslims. Metcalf (2004: 1) wrote:

> The Pakistan movement should not be considered 'Islamic': it was a movement for a secular, liberal democracy, although once the country was established there certainly were voices that sought to create an Islamically ordered state.

According to Jalal (2014: 40):

> Religion is often thought to have been the main impetus behind the creation of Pakistan. The historical evidence militates against such certitude. The demand for Pakistan was intended to get an equitable, if not equal, share of power for Indian Muslims in an independent India.

However, the two-nation theory, in constructing a distinct Muslim identity, went far beyond the discourse of the economic and political rights of Muslims as a minority in a united India. As already mentioned, the use of religious symbolism and the politicisation of religious identity were crucial to the success of the Pakistan Movement. Jalal and Metcalf also agree that 'Muslim identity' was the rallying point for the movement. The leaders of the movement constructed the Muslims of India as 'a homogenous category' while disregarding their regional, ethnic, linguistic and class differences (Jalal 2014: 8).

The two-nation theory as the basis for a separate nation-state was inherently contradictory, as it was anti-territorial (in creating a pan-Indian Muslim identity) and territorial (demanding a separate geographical territory) at the same time. The relationship between the proposed unifying Muslim identity and the demand for territorial sovereignty remained uncertain even for the chief architect of Pakistan, Jinnah. While propagating the idea that the Muslims of India were one nation, the leaders of the Pakistan Movement did not demonstrate any concerns about the Muslims living in Hindu-majority areas of India when they demanded the chunk of India with Muslim-majority areas be designated as a separate nation-state for Muslims (Jalal 2014: 51). Hence, Jalal (2014: 10) contends, 'reconciling the imperatives of citizenship in a territorial nation-state with the supra-territorial claims of Islamic universalism based on affinity to a worldwide Muslim community was a challenging proposition'. The inherent contradictions in the idea of Pakistan imply a conflation of religious, territorial and national identities.

Faisal Devji's (2013) noteworthy work on the concept of Pakistan as 'a political idea' combines the modern, religious and nationalist elements at play in the creation of Pakistan without reducing the motives behind its creation to either religious or secular. He compares Muslim nationalism in South Asia to Zionism in Europe and draws parallels between 'the political ideas' of Pakistan and those of Israel (Devji 2013: 3). What this political idea essentially means is a territorial nation-state claimed on the basis of a universal (anti-geographical) idea of a nation, bringing together all Muslims of India and severing their regional, ethnic and linguistic ties. Devji describes both Pakistan and Israel as exceptions to the norm of nation-states around the world due to their juxtaposition of territorial and universal claims. The underlying contradictions of the political idea of Pakistan become clearer when he notes:

> As early as 1948, in a speech made at a mammoth meeting in Dacca, the Governor-General of a recently created Pakistan made it clear that his new nation would have to repudiate not simply its colonial and more generally Indian past, but even the regional identities of its own Muslim majority, which fearfully compared to nations in waiting. It was as if Jinnah's own 'two-nation theory' had returned to haunt Pakistan with the spectre of more partitions to come, leading him to recommend a politics of unity that was, in appearance, at least, difficult to differentiate from that which characterised his rivals in the Indian National Congress. What

distinguished Pakistan's unity from that of its giant neighbour's, however, was the elimination of everything that its people had inherited from their past. (Devji 2013: 10)

The exceptional 'politics of unity' thus formed the foundation of the state of Pakistan from the very beginning. Islam was not only the most important rallying cry for the Pakistan Movement, but also the only unifying and binding factor for the nascent state of Pakistan (Qasmi 2011: 239). Religious identity was imagined and promoted as the sole basis of unity among the residents of Pakistan, while historical and geographical ties were actively downplayed. Official history was written to inculcate a strong religious and nationalist ideology among the people. Despite all these efforts, the fears of Jinnah of which Devji speaks in the excerpt quoted above materialised only two decades later in 1971 when East Pakistan (now Bangladesh) separated from West Pakistan (now Pakistan) due to ethnic and linguistic differences, despite a common Muslim identity. Hence, the viability and adequacy of religion as the sole basis of national unity were not only questioned but also strongly refuted by the separation of Bangladesh.

Regardless of whether the leadership of the AIML had wanted a secular or a theocratic state, it is important to understand *how* the idea of Pakistan was sold to ordinary Muslims—already living with moral anxieties under colonial rule—and what it meant for their imaginations, aspirations and expectations. The self-contradictory idea of the territorial nation-state of Pakistan based on religious identity rather than cultural, historical and geographical ties left Pakistanis with a deep sense of *identity crisis*. This crisis was worsened by the separation of Bangladesh, which questioned the very basis of the idea of Pakistan. I argue that the moral anxieties of Muslims triggered by modernity, colonisation and forced secularisation were compounded by the anxieties related to their national identity after the creation of Pakistan. The underlying tensions of the ideal versus the lived, the imagined versus the real and the universal versus the local persisted and continued to haunt the post-Partition lives of Pakistanis as individuals as well as a community. In the next section, I will discuss how the state of Pakistan has tried to deal with these anxieties by creating a religious and national ideology that aims to suppress differences to achieve uniformity and homogeneity.

Construction of homogeneous national subjects and the passion for exclusivity

The people of the newly created state of Pakistan included those who had supported the idea of Pakistan and those who were against it. Even among those who supported the idea, there were variations in their understanding of what it entailed and their expectations of it (Jalal 2000: 538). There were many who were indifferent, if not hostile, to the idea. Nevertheless, in the process of Partition, supporters and non-supporters alike suffered great losses. Millions migrated across the newly drawn borders to be part of the new state of Pakistan (Brass 2003a: 75), but not all migration was voluntary as many were forced to leave India due to intercommunal violence that accompanied Partition. A major section of the population of Pakistan suffered immense losses—of homes, property, loved ones and livelihoods—in the process (Pandey 2003: 14). Having to rebuild their lives from scratch, they needed a strong sense of purpose to justify their losses. Since religious identity had been sold as the fundamental basis for the creation of Pakistan, and due to a lack of common historical and geographical ties to define the newly formed nation, Islam became the refuge, the motivation and the purpose for a majority of Pakistanis. Discourses of sacrifice were invoked, glorifying the losses incurred during Partition, to achieve communal solidarity (Pandey 2003: 176). The idea that Muslims sacrificed everything for an Islamic state in which to practise their religion in peace became a common public narrative. However, there was no consensus as to what that Islamic state meant. If anything, the Muslims of Pakistan aspired to a diversity and multiplicity of Islamic practices.

Moreover, Pakistan was formed out of regions that were ethnically and linguistically diverse. These regions had their own organisational structures, customs and even local religious practices. The religiously and ethnically diverse population of the new country was unsure what the nature of the new state would be. The inherent contradictions of the idea of Pakistan were a source of fear and anxiety concerning religious and national identity. These fears were exacerbated by doubts about Pakistan's ability to survive. There were both real and imagined threats to the security of Pakistan. India's belief that the idea of Pakistan was bound to fail instilled further fear and anxiety among the populace (Jalal 2014: 51–52). The state of Pakistan did not have enough resources to run the country and there were massive material and political challenges to the survival of the state (Jalal 2014). These challenges, in addition to the contradictions and uncertainties inherent in the idea of Pakistan, left people with deep anxiety concerning their national identity.

There was therefore a need for a coherent and unifying policy to control and appease the population in the process of state-making. Interestingly, many prominent protagonists of the reform movements—such as Mawdudi of Jamaat-e-Islami—who had previously opposed the Pakistan Movement, formed their own pressure groups and political parties to mould the policies of the new state according to their own religious ideals (Jalal 2014: 56–57). Meanwhile, the leadership of the Pakistan Movement—those who formed the first Government of Pakistan—wanted 'Islamic modernism' as the principle of the state's formation. An 'Islamic state', for them, meant a democratic state that ensured equality and justice for its populace (Jalal 2014: 56; Qasmi 2011: 239–40). The religious ideologues—often contradicting each other—had their own ideals for the state. The clash of ideals thus began soon after the creation of Pakistan. It was no longer just a matter of individuals trying to live up to the ideals of *good Muslims*; it was now also a matter of whose ideal would define the *ideal Islamic state* that had just been created. Hence, the question for the political leaders of Pakistan at its creation was not whether or not Islam would have a role in the state, but 'the *kind* of Islam' that would form the basis of the state's policies (Qasmi 2011: 239; emphasis added). This led to vehement 'politics of Islam' becoming a critical force in state-making.

Given that Pakistan was founded on a unifying nationalist ideology based on religious identity, with a homogeneous conception of Islam and Muslims at its heart, religious exclusivity was inherent to the idea. This unifying narrative was built on the absolute dismissal of Hindus as inferior *others* by ignoring their shared cultural, social, linguistic and historical similarities. Such an emphasis on *exclusivity* and *unity* at the same time came to define the state-making of Pakistan. The diverse groups of Muslim and non-Muslim citizens of Pakistan were supposed to be unified under the banner of Islam while ignoring their differences. Instead of acknowledging the differences, the state aimed to suppress them through construction of one nation, one language[14] and one religion. Unity, singularity and homogeneity became the emphases of the nationalist

---

14   The imposition of Urdu as the national language on linguistically diverse populations was one of the major reasons for the rise of the separatist movement in East Pakistan, culminating in the creation of Bangladesh.

project whereas internal differences came to be regarded as 'undesirable', 'unacceptable' and 'un-Islamic' (Nelson 2009: 604). Homogenised social identities of citizen subjects became crucial to the making of the state in Pakistan (Ali 2008: 8).

National television, textbooks, public history books and all other possible media were used for the propagation of the principles of exclusivity and unity (Jalal 2014: 51–52). The writing of history thus employed what Hobsbawm (1983: 14) called the 'invention of tradition'—a technique modern nations use to construct national history. The invented tradition can be:

> a set of practices, normally governed by overtly or tacitly accepted rules and of a ritual or symbolic nature, which seek to inculcate certain values and norms of behaviour by repetition, which automatically implies continuity with the past. (Hobsbawm 1983: 1)

Pakistan's national history thus fashioned was replete with ideas of continuity, unity, oneness and homogeneity. Nosheen Ali, in her study of textbook representations of religious differences in Gilgit, described the state of Pakistan as an assemblage of contested discourses and micropractices of discipline and power. As she succinctly puts it, 'such discursive practices embody "politically organised subjection" and "moral regulation" through which the social identities of citizen-subjects are cultivated, and state rule accomplished' (Ali 2008: 2). These discursive practices of subjection and control of differences are a common feature of modern nation-states and have been extensively theorised—for example, Bourdieu (1973) called them mechanisms of cultural reproduction and Althusser (1971) called them ideological state apparatuses. Contemporary nation-states have been known to exercise 'taxonomical control over difference' by domesticating it, curbing it and exploiting it for their interests (Appadurai 1990: 304).

The attempt to domesticate differences also led to the creation of newer forms of selfhood. As Bauman (2000: 106) argued:

> [T]he more effective the drive to homogeneity and the efforts to eliminate the difference, the more difficult it is to feel at home in the face of strangers, the more threatening the difference appears and the deeper and more intense is the anxiety it breeds.

In the case of Pakistan, the new anxious self of Pakistani Muslims was constructed around the elimination of religious differences, as noted by Iqtidar (2012: 1023):

> The majority that is being created out of the diverse classes, ethnicities and other divisions within Pakistan remains elusive. But the possibility of that uniform, homogenous majority animates a specific kind of selfhood—one that is impatient with the idea of doctrinal difference even as it is increasingly confronted with the practice of it, of more choices given the proliferation of religious groups in contemporary Pakistan.

State-making in Pakistan, however, was not a one-way project involving imposition of exclusivist policies and indoctrination from top to bottom. It went hand in hand with the modernist self-making processes that had been initiated much earlier, as I have argued. Imposing a unifying narrative was in the interests of the state, but it was also at times a response to public demands. This was because the exclusivist tendencies had already been popularised through various movements of Muslim nationalism in the pre-Partition era. Thus, having separated themselves from the Hindu *others*, Pakistani Muslims turned to look for *lesser others* among themselves to continue their exclusivist project. Soon after the creation of Pakistan in 1947, the question of 'Who is a Muslim?' was raised as authorities deliberated about the state-sanctioned definition of 'Islam' and 'Muslims', which was also in line with what many people wanted. In 1953, there were widespread protests by religious groups and citizens demanding the official declaration of Ahmadis, who claim to be Muslims, as 'non-Muslims' (The Punjab Disturbances Court of Inquiry 1954). Three years later, in 1956, Pakistan was declared an Islamic republic, reaffirming its Islamic identity and leaving open in popular consciousness the questions of legitimacy and authority as to what is Islamic and who is a Muslim.

The following decades saw the religious and nationalist passion for exclusivity metastasise into fully fledged sectarian conflicts, with widespread communal violence between different sects of Muslims. In addition to the government, the religious groups and the common people, another player—probably the strongest—was the Pakistan Army, which contributed to the country's exclusivist tendencies. The decades of the 1970s and 1980s were particularly significant in the aggravation of sectarian tensions, further enabling the spread of violence against religious minorities. Three major political events during these years have been described as the cause of worsening sectarian tensions: Zia-ul-Haq's military rule (1977–88), the Iranian revolution of 1979 and the Afghan war (1979–92). Zia-ul-Haq came to power in a military coup in 1977 and used popular Islamic symbols to legitimise his rule (Ahmad 1998: 14). Zia-ul-Haq's Islamisation was seen as a form of Sunni Islamism in response to Iran's Shia Islamism that culminated in the Iranian revolution (Nasr 2000a: 175). Zia-ul-Haq's Islamisation project was supported by the mainstream Sunni political parties, such as Jamaat-e-Islami, for various reasons, including Zia-ul-Haq's appeal as a good Muslim and as an 'embodiment of their concept of a true Islamic ruler' (Ahmad 1998: 13). He was also supported by Saudi Arabia to promote Salafi/Deobandi—a reformist sect of Sunnis—ideology in Pakistan (through heavy funding of *madrasahs*), mainly because they wanted to erect a 'Sunni wall' around Iran (Nasr 2000a: 178) to protect their political and ideological interests in the region.

These developments coincided with the Afghan war during which the Pakistan military provided training and resources to Deobandi seminary students (Taliban) and other Sunni militant organisations such as Sipah-e-Sahaba Pakistan (SSP) and Harkat-ul-Ansar (Nasr 2000a: 178). These Sunni militants—supported, trained and indoctrinated through the collaboration of the United States, Saudi Arabia and Pakistan—fought as *mujaheddin* (wagers of holy war) against the Soviet Union (Nasr 2000a: 179). The collaboration of the US Central Intelligence Agency (CIA) and Pakistan's Inter-Services Intelligence (ISI) to create militant Islamists to counter the growing Soviet influence in Afghanistan, along with heavy funding for the ideological training of *mujaheddin* from the Gulf region, worsened sectarian tensions (Toor 2011: 153–54). The inflow of weapons and funds during the Afghan war militarised sectarian outfits and contributed to the violence against Shias in the years to come (Ahmad 1998: 28). In addition to the sectarian violence, the military was also involved in the ethnic conflicts across the country. The biggest tragedy in terms of ethnic conflict was Bangladesh's independence war in which the Pakistan military played a huge role. There have been other ethnic conflicts—such as in Baluchistan—where no *war* was declared but the military has been involved in curbing what they call separatist movements. Moreover, as Ali (2008: 12–13) shows in her study of violence against Shias in Gilgit, there have been occasions when political dissent has been portrayed as sectarian conflict to depoliticise it and suppress dissident voices.

Thus, the process of state-making in Pakistan has been a constant struggle between civil governments, military leaders, religious groups and ordinary citizens. Some groups with leftist, progressive, civil and human rights agendas have existed throughout the history of Pakistan, but they have been on the fringe and have often been persecuted in the religious and political spheres. Some political parties—for example, the Pakistan Peoples Party—claim to have left-leaning manifestos but have used religious symbolism and alliances with religious groups whenever it served their political interests.

Appadurai's (1990) formulation of 'the nation and the state' as 'another's projects' is a useful concept to understand the processes of state-making in Pakistan. He writes: '[N]ations (or more properly groups with ideas about nationhood) seek to capture or co-opt states and state power, states simultaneously seek to capture and monopolise ideas about nationhood' (Appadurai 1990: 303). He describes it as a 'disjunctive relationship between the nation and the state', which argues is a characteristic of most states in the era of a global political economy (Appadurai 1990: 304). In Pakistan's case, both the nation and the state are incomplete, and are constantly being made. However, I argue that, through a convergence of the focus of all the major players in this process on religious exclusivity and national unity, the possibility of differences has come to be a threat at individual, communal and national levels. The consequence is that various groups and individuals with their own ideas of Islam and of Pakistan seek to eliminate the differences to legitimise and consolidate their religious and national identity.

Neocolonialism, globalisation and the state of present-day Pakistani Muslims

The processes of self-making, community-making and state-making discussed so far have led to the present condition of Pakistani Muslims: experiencing deeply embedded anxieties related to their religious and national identities, and constantly striving to become *good Muslims* by purging impurities within themselves and their imagined collective identity. Naveeda Khan (2012) highlighted 'scepticism' (of the self and the other) and 'aspiration' (to become a good Muslim) as central features of the everyday lives of Pakistani Muslims in her groundbreaking ethnography. Other scholars have noted similar trends—for example,

Jalal (2014: 5–6) contends that Pakistan is 'a visibly perturbed' nation, 'pondering the reasons for their country's perilous condition and seeking a reprieve from violence and uncertainty'. I also found religious and nationalistic anxieties prevalent among most of the Pakistani Muslims I met during my time in Pakistan—both as a researcher and as a part of the community. In addition to their concerns about the different and the deviant within their imagined national and religious communities, they harbour deep-seated apprehensions about 'the West': the powerful, anti-Islam and anti-Pakistan nations of the world threatening the existence of Islam and Pakistan.

'The West' has been associated with godlessness and moral corruption in South Asian consciousness for a long time—and particularly since the colonial era. Colonialism was also seen as a direct attack on Islam and Muslim identity, as discussed earlier. Present-day Pakistani Muslims' apprehensions and concerns, however, are rooted more specifically in neocolonialism, globalisation and the rise of Islamophobia in the post-9/11 world. Despite the end of direct colonial rule on the Subcontinent in 1947, Western nations have continued their involvement in Pakistan through direct or indirect political intervention, development and humanitarian aid and other economic impositions. This involvement is often imperialist in nature and has left Pakistanis feeling threatened and powerless in the face of a new hegemonic global order. The political and economic hegemony of the West is augmented by cultural imperialism through various media—a softer but much more effective instrument of alienation. This neocolonial subjugation is further exacerbated by the rise of Islamophobic tendencies across the globe since the 9/11 attacks. Pakistani Muslims, even if they have never travelled abroad, are acutely aware of these tendencies and see them as a threat to their already fragile religious and nationalistic identities. Globalisation, particularly through new forms of media, has positioned Pakistani Muslims on an international stage where they must constantly defend their religious-national image from broad-stroke associations with terrorism. Therefore, a majority of Pakistani Muslims feel under attack and threatened by the West and its influence on local ways of life, and are on the lookout for the enemy within.

The threat from the West in the wake of neocolonialism, Islamophobia and globalisation is layered on top of the threats already felt from Pakistan's rivalry with India—and from ethnic and religious differences within Pakistan. There are multiple identities that Pakistani Muslims navigate in their everyday lives: the pan-Islamic identity, the national identity and sectarian and ethnic identities. Some of these identities conflict with others—for example, a Sunni Muslim likely feels strongly Sunni in relation to Shias or other minority sects, but feels strongly Muslim in relation to the rest of the world in the context of the global image of Islam. The shifting identities of Pakistani Muslims, however, are a cause of the uncertainty and anxiety that characterise their individual and collective lives.

The religious and nationalistic moral anxieties of modern Pakistani Muslims directly contribute to accusations of blasphemy and subsequent violence. I will demonstrate this with a particular example. Altaf is a Sunni Barelwi Muslim man from Lahore aged in his mid-thirties. He accused a Muslim woman from his neighbourhood, who used to teach his children, of having insulted the Prophet Muhammad. The woman allegedly told his children that 'the prophetic traditions are not as reliable as the Quran itself'. I met Altaf in the Lahore Sessions Court, where his case was being heard. I attended several court hearings with him and talked to him before and after those hearings. One morning, as we were having tea while waiting for the hearing, he said to me:

> Pakistan—despite being created for the rightful practice of Islam—is inundated by a flood of sins these days. The horrendous number of blasphemy cases in today's Pakistan is evidence of that. Our society has been corrupted—corrupted by the filth of blasphemous thoughts and practices all around us. What else is to be expected with the rise of Western influence in [the] media, in our schools and colleges, and everywhere else? It is up to each one of us to fight this filth, and to purify our society, to achieve the ideal Islamic land for which our ancestors sacrificed their lives.

Altaf, like many other accusers to whom I spoke about blasphemy cases, referred to the moral decline of society, the influence of the West seeping into society and the unfulfilled ideals of an imagined collective national identity. While most blasphemy accusations are made within hierarchical interpersonal relationships and are triggered by a range of dynamics within those relationships (as will be shown in later chapters), they occur in the context of widespread moral anxieties among Pakistani Muslims. Even if these moral anxieties are not the immediate triggers of such accusations in most cases, they provide legitimation and justification to accusers and enable violent exclusion of the accused from society.

Conclusion

Blasphemy accusations and related violence in present-day Pakistan must be understood within the context of the uncertainty and anxiety that pervade the individual, communal and national lives of Pakistanis. These anxieties are not entirely unique to Pakistanis, as issues of sameness and difference, the particular and the universal, the lived and the ideal are common to all societies. Especially in the modern globalised world, 'the triumphantly universal and the resiliently particular' pose a pertinent challenge for all societies, and the struggle between sameness and difference is 'the central feature of global culture today' (Appadurai 1990: 308). What makes the state of present-day Pakistani Muslims peculiar is the historically specific amalgamation of various anxieties concerning their individual and collective identities. The reformist emphasis on the purification of the self under the influence of modernity, and in response to British colonisation, gave rise to moral anxieties that were exacerbated by the inherent contradictions of the idea of Pakistan and its national identity. Neocolonialism, globalisation and the rise of Islamophobia in the post-9/11 world have further contributed to these anxieties. Such religious and nationalistic moral anxieties are inherently related to the gap between reality and the ideal, the lived and the imagined and aspiration and achievement. It is the sense of lack and inadequacy that defines Pakistanis' struggles for religious and national identities. Sidel (2006: 137) aptly captures this sense in the context of his study of 'religious violence' in Indonesia:

> At the core of any 'identity' is always a constitutive sense of lack, of inadequacy, or of a 'theft' that can be imputed to an Other who deprives 'us' of the full enjoyment of those material, discursive, and social practices, which, we imagine, [would] allow 'us' to be fully 'ourselves'.

The 'politics of Islam' as exercised by various players involved in the state-making of Pakistan created the conditions for violent expression of these anxieties by promoting an exclusivist national ideology. It is not certainty about that identity but doubt, not uniformity of religious and national ideals but a multiplicity of them, that enable the violent exclusion of others.

Blasphemy accusations and subsequent violence form but one manifestation of the uncertainties and anxieties about religious and national identities in present-day Pakistan.

2
Religious discourse concerning blasphemy: Politics of uncertainty and legitimacy

Batla do gustaakh-e-nabi ko, ghairat-e-Sunni zindaa hai
Deen pe mar mitnay ka jazba, kal bhi tha aur aaj bhi hai!
[Tell the blasphemer of the Prophet, the honour of Sunnis is alive
We always had the passion to die for our religion, and still have it!]

Jaag uthay hain ahl-e-sunnat, goonj utha ye naara hai
Door hatto aye dushman-e-millat, Pakistan humara hai!
[Ahl-e-Sunnat (Sunnis) have awakened, and their slogan is echoing:
Get out of the way, O enemy of the nation! Pakistan belongs to us.]

Sunnio, apnay aap ko ghair syasi kehna chor do,
Ab baat namoos-e-risaalat ki hai
[O Sunnis, stop calling yourselves apolitical,
It is about the Prophet's honour now!]

These are some of the slogans that have been popular among various Sunni groups, particularly the Barelwis, over the past decade or so. Arising as a reformist movement in colonial India, the Barelwis—the largest section of Sunni Muslims in Pakistan—have always played a political role in Pakistan's history through street protests, lobbying and political coalitions (Khan 2011: 61; Philippon 2014). However, they have become increasingly politicised since the 2000s, actively defending 'their religious identity and heritage' (Epping 2013: 1). Barelwis have been popular targets for sectarian violence—such as bombing of their shrines and religious celebrations—at the hands of Deobandis, another Sunni reformist group (Khan 2011: 64). Barelwis' increased political activism is therefore often understood as a response to Deobandi militancy against them (Epping 2013; Khan 2011). It has also been argued that the rise of Barelwi activism is a direct result of the post-9/11 institutionalisation of Barelwi Islam by Pakistan's government in an attempt to combat Deobandi terrorist outfits, whom the government and the military had previously sponsored (Suleman 2018). Nevertheless, today, Barelwis are at the frontline of campaigns to defend the honour of the Prophet and punish all blasphemers.

While scholars of almost all sects, schools of thought and religious groups in contemporary Pakistan[1] support the mandatory death sentence for a blasphemer, the Sunni Barelwi groups have, in particular, established the issue of blasphemy as the pivotal point of their political claims in the recent past (Basit 2020). They have positively aligned the ideology of Pakistan with the aim of defending the honour of the Prophet, as indicated by the following slogan:

> *Pakistan ka matlab kya? La illaha illallah*
> *Dastoor-e-reyasat kya hoga? Muhammad ur Rasool Allah*
> [What does Pakistan mean? There is no God but Allah.
> What shall the principle of our state be? Muhammad is the Prophet of Allah.]

The first line is popularly known as the political slogan of the Pakistan Movement in the pre-Partition campaign for a separate homeland for Muslims (Butt 2016: 11).[2] The second line is an extension recently added by the Sunni Barelwi groups engaged in anti-blasphemy campaigns. It is a claim as to what 'the idea of Pakistan' means and how it should be implemented by the state. As discussed in the previous chapter, the process of state formation in Pakistan has always been characterised by competing ideas of nationhood. In this chapter, I will demonstrate how certain groups are (re)imagining and campaigning to promote *their* ideas of the state in Pakistan, participating in the ongoing 'battle of imagination'

---

1   There have been some attempts to challenge the dominant interpretations about the punishment of blasphemy from within the religious traditions, but they remain minority voices without much support. One religious scholar, Javed Ahmed Ghamidi, questioned the existing law and argued that it was not in accordance with the Quran, but he had to flee Pakistan in fear of his life. Currently, Arafat Mazhar, a young scholar, is involved in challenging the religious scholars and inviting them to debate the theological basis of the punishment of a blasphemer (Alvi 2015; Mazhar 2018).
2   However, researchers have shown that this slogan was not supported by the leadership of the Pakistan Movement, and that it was under Zia-ul-Haq's regime that this slogan was written into history as *the* slogan of the Pakistan movement (Paracha 2013; Wasti 2009: 4–5).

(Appadurai 1990: 303–4). Love of the Prophet Muhammad and defence of his honour have come to be central to contemporary ideas about nationhood among the dominant religious groups.

I argue that mainstream religious leaders and scholars have popularised an absolutist discourse about blasphemy and its punishment to gain political legitimacy and religious authority for themselves, in the process granting certain symbolic meaning and significance to the issue of blasphemy. This symbolic meaning is then harnessed by more individuals and groups to gain influence, legitimacy and power in the religious and political domains. The symbolic power of blasphemy works by generating certain affective responses from believers, through their bodily and sensory experiences as well as their devotion to the cause. Thus, I contend that the popular religious discourse around blasphemy should be understood within the context of a power struggle between religious scholars, the meaning it holds for believers and the affective responses it generates.

Affect, meaning and power: An integrative approach

> There is only one punishment for the blasphemer of the Prophet
> Beheading, beheading!
> O blasphemer of Muhammad! You are not safe anymore
> We will lay down our hearts and our bodies for the sake of the honour of the Prophet
> [We] Muslims will behead all the blasphemers!

This is the chorus from a *na'at* ('song') praising the Prophet often played at anti-blasphemy gatherings and protests. The first two lines are also used as a slogan, chanted, printed and sung by anti-blasphemy campaigners—particularly Sunni Barelwis. The original video for the song, sung by Aftab Qadri, shows a young bearded man in embroidered attire and a glittery turban standing in front of trees lit by fairy lights, singing the above lines to a very catchy tune.[3] The singer begins with an extremely passionate recitation to warn blasphemers of the power of Muslims' faith and love for the Prophet. The vocals and the music invoke certain visceral responses by creating a sense of urgency and instilling a sense of empowerment. While listening to this *na'at*, I experienced an increased heart rate and felt

---

3   The video can be found on YouTube: www.youtube.com/watch?v=jyPmYFVefr8.

a surge of energy course through my body. After listening to it a few times, I was also subconsciously humming the chorus. No wonder it is a popular slogan and is used in religious gatherings to generate affective responses from the crowd.

Affective responses are understood by psychologist Silvan Tomkins (2009: 163) as the 'primary innate biological motivating mechanism'. Affects are thus understood as non-linguistic and non-ideological aspects of human behaviour related to the senses and bodily processes that are not entirely located in consciousness. My heart rate increasing while listening to this *na'at* was thus an affect—my body's natural reaction to the aural experience—even though the words being uttered had no meaning for me. Brian Massumi (2002: 30–35), a leading affect theorist, distinguished between affects and emotions, arguing that affects are purely subconscious and autonomous whereas emotions are imbued with meaning. He argues that affects have an intensity of their own that can produce certain effects and motivations in individuals and groups of people (Massumi 2002).

Such an understanding of affect has been criticised as anti-intentionalist, giving an autonomous and pre-personal existence to 'affect' as a 'natural' element of the human body, rather than constructed within social conditions (Leys 2011: 470). Leys argues that affect theory discerns affects as 'inhuman', 'pre-subjective', 'visceral' forces and 'intensities that influence our thinking and judgments but are separate from these' (2011: 437). In her view, affect theorists put an almost excessive emphasis on bodily and corporeal processes stripped of meaning and social conditions, to counter post-structuralist theory's obsession with meaning, ideology and discourse (Leys 2011: 440–41). The resulting theory then sees:

> the subject's affects and its cognition or appraisal of the affective situation or object, such that cognition or thinking comes 'too late' for reasons, beliefs, intentions, and meanings to play the role in action and behaviour usually accorded to them. The result is that action and behaviour are held to be determined by affective dispositions that are independent of consciousness and the mind's control. (Leys 2011: 444)

The disconnect between ideology and affect thus underplays the role of ideas and beliefs in people's behaviour and motivations (Leys 2011: 451). Even though the *na'at* about beheading blasphemers evoked a physical response in me, it did not produce any *motivation* because I do not subscribe to the ideas being presented. Therefore, I agree with Leys's criticism of affects as the 'primary innate biological motivating mechanism' devoid of meaning. Physical responses certainly have a role to play in individual and collective life; for example, participants at anti-blasphemy protests respond with a certain fervour to Arabic and Persian recitations—languages most of them do not understand but associate with religious value. The sensory experience of hearing recitations, music and poetry at religious gatherings does indeed produce certain affective responses. However, the biological responses alone cannot produce motivations and judgements.

The symbolic meaning associated with Arabic and Persian recitations is what turns the biological responses into devotion. While I can be drawn into subconsciously humming the chorus of a song, I do not automatically feel motivated to act on it. Nor does the sound of the chorus autonomously produce any devotion in me. For the people participating in anti-blasphemy protests, on the other hand, the same chorus not only produces devotion and motivation, but may also lead them to act and kill alleged blasphemers. They are already committed to an ideology or set of ideas—seen as secondary by affect theorists—that generate passionate reactions. Thus, I see affect as crucial to understanding the dominant discourse on blasphemy, but only in conjunction with the meaning transmitted through this discourse. Affect, in my understanding, *adds intensity to meaning* instead of meaning adding purpose to intensity. That is, the affect—or intensity—is not prior to the meaning. The intensity generated by the affect, however, turns ideas into passions and meaning into embodied devotion.

Geertz (1993: 90) emphasised the significance of symbolic meaning in producing religious 'moods and motivations'. He understood religion as a system of interconnected symbols that give meaning to religious experience. He defined religion as:

> (1) a system of symbols which acts to (2) establish powerful, pervasive, and long-lasting moods and motivations in men by (3) formulating conceptions of a general order of existence and (4) clothing these conceptions with such an aura of factuality that (5) the moods and motivations seem uniquely realistic. (Geertz 1993: 90)

I follow the Geertzian concept of symbolic meaning to understand how religious discourse creates certain moods and motivations in the supporters of anti-blasphemy violence. Thus, I analyse the popular religious discourse concerning blasphemy with attention to the affect *and* the meaning it engenders among believers.

While Geertz (1993: 125) acknowledged that religion as a system of symbols is also related to 'socio-structural and psychological processes' and is culturally specific (p. 123), Asad (1983) criticised him for ignoring the role of power in determining historically specific understandings and experiences of religion. Emphasising the role of historical power relations and processes, Asad argues that we should pay attention to:

> the conditions (discursive and non-discursive) which help to explain how symbols come to be constructed, and how some of them are established as natural or authoritative as opposed to others. (Asad 1983: 240)

I agree with Asad's emphasis on the role of power in the construction of meaning. I focus on the discursive construction of the symbolic meaning of blasphemy—following a long tradition of Foucauldian discourse analysis. For Foucault (1971: 8), discourse means whatever determines the way in which at a given point in history one can think, speak or write about a social object or practice. Discourse is historically specific and grounded in the sociopolitical context, which implies that, in a given context, reality or truth is the function of what can be thought, written or said at a given point in time (Foucault 1971: 15). The historical circumstances are the conditions of possibility that constrain discursive formations. Therefore, social imagination is determined by a particular set of material conditions and their representations at any given point in history (Foucault 2002: 145). Following this conception, I understand the symbolic meaning of blasphemy as being constructed discursively within the context of power relations.

However, I also argue that the symbols thus constructed may attain power of their own and can empower more people in their course. Therefore, as Geertz pointed out in an interview in response to Asad's critique, the religious symbols cannot be *reduced* to power relations (Micheelsen 2002: 8–9). While power relations determine which symbols become important and what meaning they hold, the symbols also provide meaning for those concerned and at the same time generate for them certain affects. While the religious discourse concerning blasphemy in present-day Pakistan has obvious political undertones and is a product of specific historical and political circumstances, it also provides *affective meaning* to those involved in the discourse, whether they are religious scholars or ordinary people. Thus, I contend, power relations and (affective) meaning cannot be entirely separated from each other; rather, they share a dialectic relationship in which power creates (affective) meaning and meaning can grant power in turn.

The discussion of the dominant religious discourse in the first section of this chapter is mostly concerned with the *affective meaning* this discourse holds for believers. In the second section, through a discussion of the role of religious authority and political motivations that determine the religious discourse about blasphemy, I will demonstrate, in line with Asad's argument, that historically specific power relations determine religious symbols, as well as the moods and motivations they produce in people.

The dominant religious discourse concerning blasphemy

Despite a general consensus among religious groups on the punishment for an alleged blasphemer, there is a proliferation of literature and speeches on the issue of blasphemy. I studied more than 50 book-length publications from Islamic scholars of all major sects and religious groups on the topic of blasphemy. These included (semi-)fictional stories as well as nonfiction interpretational texts. The (semi-)fictional stories—such as the novelette *Shaatam* (*Blasphemer*) by Mukhtar Alam—revolve around stories of blasphemers. These stories almost always start from their birth as 'illegitimate' children. The storylines lead up to the offence of blasphemy, or *tauheen-e-risaalat* ('insult of the Prophet'), committed by them and their *ibrat-naak anjaam* ('horrifying destiny') at the hands of the 'heroes', or *aashiqan-e-rasool* ('lovers of the Prophet'), who kill them. These stories are imbued with passion and are a source of affective meaning for their devoted readers.

A pattern can also be drawn out of the interpretational texts in terms of the structure and content of these publications. Most publications include some form of the following components: the centrality of love for the Prophet Muhammad to Muslims' faith; examples of love for the Prophet from his companions and later Muslims; the absolute authority of the

Prophet; Quranic and prophetic traditions regarding punishment for those who insult or question the Prophet; what actions, words, gestures and attitudes constitute insult to the Prophet; examples of 'blasphemers' who met their destined 'horrific' deaths at the hands of Muslims; characteristics of blasphemers; and blasphemy as a conspiracy of the West, non-Muslims, Jews or anti-Islam forces to undermine Islam. These texts are written in passionate language and are sources of emotional as well as ideological meaning for readers.

In addition to the Quranic references and prophetic traditions, many of these publications include verses from the modernist South Asian philosopher-poet Allama Muhammad Iqbal, who is commonly known as a passionate lover of the Prophet and the visionary of Pakistan. Specifically, his verses dealing with love of the Prophet and the call for Muslims to be active against the enemy—the colonial forces at the time he was writing—are often cited. Not surprisingly, the same topics and references were popular in religious sermons and speeches made at protests and were highlighted by religious scholars during my interviews with them. Based on such religious publications, sermons, speeches and my interviews with religious scholars, I will discuss some of the key themes mentioned above that make up the prevailing discourse on blasphemy and its punishment in Pakistan. I will begin with the discourse of contemporary scholars from three religious groups and then discuss the religious sources or Islamic juristic literature to which they refer.

The religious scholars to whom I refer are also active politicians. In fact, most of the religious groups and organisations actively engaged in the anti-blasphemy campaigns in Pakistan are also political parties. Some of them have been in existence since the conception of Pakistan and have played an active role in achieving Pakistan's anti-blasphemy laws as they exist today; others have entered the political scene much more recently, specifically rallying around the issue of blasphemy. I will focus on three religious political parties—formed at different stages in the history of Pakistan—that are currently engaged in the anti-blasphemy discourse around the country. Jamaat-e-Islami (JI) Pakistan was formed in 1941, Pakistan Awami Tehreek (PAT) was formed in 1989 and Tehreek-e-Labbaik Pakistan (TLP) was formed in 2015. All three of these parties belong to the Sunni sect, with PAT and TLP representing the Barelwi subsect of Sunni Islam.

Love for the Prophet Muhammad

Ki Muhammad se wafa'a tu ne tou hum teray hain
Ye jahan cheez hai kya, Loh-o-qalam teray hain
[Be loyal to Muhammad, and you will have me on your side;
The world is nothing, you will command My Pen of Destiny.]
— Allama Muhammad Iqbal, 1913

The above verse appears in Iqbal's poem 'Jawab-e-Shikwa' ('God's Answer to Muslims' Complaint'), which was a sequel to his poem 'Shikwa' ('The Complaint'). Together, these poems are in the format of a dialogue with God. In the first poem, Iqbal complains about the miserable situation of Muslims on the Subcontinent and beyond despite them being the followers of the rightful religion. In the second part, God responds to highlight the shortcomings of Muslims that are responsible for their abject condition in the world and offers ways to rectify that. The verse quoted above is the closing couplet of the second poem. Thus, loyalty to Muhammad is argued to be the answer to all of Muslims' problems in the contemporary world. This couplet is one of the most popular references to Iqbal's poetry made by the anti-blasphemy campaigners in present-day Pakistan. The couplet engenders intense passion among believers and is quoted in books, recited in sermons and has also been sung as a *na'at* in praise of the Prophet. The verses are employed to argue that love of the Prophet and faithfulness to him are the most powerful tools in the hands of Muslims. Love of the Prophet is what distinguishes Muslims from the rest of the world and is the only way to achieve success and power.

The figure of Muhammad has been a popular subject of devotional literature in most Muslims societies (see, for example, Asani et al. 1995). However, while the centrality of the Prophet to Muslims' faith is common to most sects and subsects in Pakistan, the Barelwis have been known for their exceptional devotion and passionate attachment to the personality of Muhammad. For Barelwis, 'a true Muslim is an "Ashiq-e-Rasool", or a "Lover of the Prophet"', who is 'obligated to protect the sanctity of the Prophet' (Khan 2011: 60). The Prophet is the spiritual axis of faith as well as the perfect role model for living in this world. Even mentioning the name of the Prophet invokes affective and emotional responses—such as a lowering of the gaze—because of the meaning attached to his personality. However, this is precisely the concern for which different Barelwi groups compete among each other—and against other Sunni subsects—in the shared religious-political sphere. The following discussion deals specifically with the popular ideas of love of the Prophet among Sunni Barelwi groups in Pakistan.

One of the senior lecturers at Minhaj-ul-Quran, a Sunni Barelwi religious institute affiliated with PAT, who teaches postgraduate students and prided himself on having supervised many theses, told me that the starting point of my PhD thesis should be the different conception of the Prophet in Islam compared with that in 'the West'. He emphasised the 'relative concept of prophethood' and the 'different concepts of insult in Islam as compared with other religions' as crucial to understanding the issue of blasphemy in Pakistan. He said:

> Our conception of the Prophet is very different from that of the West for whom their prophets[4] are just like other human beings. For us, Prophet Muhammad is not merely a human being. He is a transcendental spiritual being, with the highest status even amongst the spiritual beings. An insult against human beings cannot be compared to insult against the highest spiritual being— our Prophet Muhammad.

According to him, insult of the Prophet is not merely hate speech (a Western concept that he mentioned); rather, it is the most serious of sins. When I asked him to elaborate, he responded:

> Because our faith is based upon unconditional love for the Prophet Muhammad. It is what sets us apart from other religions. This love is the condition of our faith; one cannot be a Muslim if one does not hold the Prophet Muhammad in the highest reverence and dearer than his own life, wealth, family and children. The unconditional love demands that we do not tolerate even a little doubt on the personality of Muhammad and the religion he brought to us.

Interestingly, similar arguments about the different conceptions of the Prophet in Islam compared with those in the West, and the different understandings of insults to the Prophet in contrast with the Western notion of hate speech, have also been made by anthropologist Saba Mahmood (2009) in her work on Muslims' reactions to the Danish cartoons. She argued that there is a different 'modality of attachment' between a devout Muslim and the Prophet Muhammad, embedded in a different 'economy of signification' (Mahmood 2009: 76). In this economy of signification,

---

4 Referring mainly to Christianity and Judaism.

the Prophet Muhammad is 'a figure of immanence in his constant exemplariness, and is therefore not a referential sign that stands apart from an essence that it denotes' (Mahmood 2009: 76). The moral injury thus experienced by insult to the Prophet:

> emanates not from the judgment that 'the law' has been transgressed but from the perception that one's being, grounded as it is in a relationship of dependency with the Prophet, has been shaken. (Mahmood 2009: 78)

Hence, she argued that the moral outrage of Muslims in response to the insult of the Prophet is embedded in their unique religious ethos, which is qualitatively different from that of Western societies.

However, the supposedly unique ways of attaching to the Prophet—the distinctly Muslim ethos—is very hard to define. In fact, it is one of the major points of difference between various groups and sects within Islam. Barelwis and Deobandis, for example, passionately disagree on the nature of the Prophet's existence and appropriate modes of attachment to him. The former believe the Prophet is not only a physical existence; rather, he is a part of the *noor* ('light') of God that existed before anything else was created and will last beyond everything in the universe; and, by virtue of this spiritual existence, the Prophet's physical death does not mark his disappearance from the world; he is all-present and always existing (Khan 2011: 59). Deobandis, on the other hand, believe that while Muhammad was a prophet of Allah, he was a human being like all other human beings, who died a physical death after fulfilling the role he was assigned to play (Khan 2011). They believe that the conception of Muhammad as anything more than a human being elevates his status to divinity and this corrupts the monotheistic spirit of Islam (Khan 2011).

While all sects agree on the authority of Muhammad and respect for him, different conceptions of the nature of the Prophet also entail distinct ways of attaching to and displaying love for him. One group's way of respecting the Prophet may be seen as an insult by the other group. Therefore, Sunni Barelwis and Deobandis, Wahabbis, Salafis and Ahl-e-Hadith accuse one another of blasphemy. Even among Barelwis, there are different conceptions of how to love the Prophet. Love for the Prophet, therefore, becomes the domain in which they actively compete against each other, to establish themselves as more authentic lovers of the Prophet than others. Thus, while they all agree on the centrality of the Prophet Muhammad to Muslims' faith, they contest what the appropriate reverence accorded to the Prophet must look like and, by corollary, the understandings of what is blasphemous and what is not. Here I will only discuss in detail some of the examples of 'how to love the Prophet' as promulgated by the two Barelwi groups, PAT and TLP.

Despite their beliefs concerning the *spiritual* aspects of Muhammad's existence, Sunni Barelwis put an almost obsessive emphasis on reverence of the *physical* being of Muhammad. Love of the Prophet in the present world, for them, is marked by imitating his physical features (for example, facial hair), eating what he ate, drinking what he drank and living life as closely as possible to his. There are numerous traditions of the Prophet's everyday life referred to in the everyday lives of Pakistani Muslims. The standards of love for the Prophet were set by his companions who lived in his time, according to the prevalent religious discourse among Sunni Barelwis. They quote acts of reverence accorded to the Prophet by his companions to set forth a model for believers, who are supposed to love the Prophet more than they love their own lives, families and wealth. One such example of his companions' reverence for the Prophet, narrated by Muhammad Tahir-ul-Qadri, the founder of PAT, is as follows:

> The companions of the Prophet highly revered anything associated with the Prophet and everything that came in contact with his Holy body. Urwa bin Mas'ood, who converted to Islam, narrated: 'By God, he [the Prophet Muhammad] would spit and his companions would collect it on the palms of their hands and rub it on their faces.' Whenever any discharge from Prophet Muhammad's mouth or nose dripped, his companions would rush towards him to collect it on their hands and rub it on their faces and bodies. Now, we must pay attention to who was indulged in these acts: it was [the three caliphs] Hazrat Abu-Bakr Siddique, Hazrat Umar Farooq, Hazrat Ali and fifteen hundred other companions of the Prophet ... The Prophet did not stop them, neither did any revelation from Allah. How could it be stopped? This intense passionate relationship with the Prophet is the very spirit of the faith—the truth of the faith—that was well acknowledged by the companions of the Prophet. (Tahir-ul-Qadri 2013: 49)

Other similar examples narrate how his companions would not allow the water used during the Prophet's ablution to go to waste, how they kept the Prophet's hair from falling to the ground, how their eyes looked down and their voices stayed low in the presence of the Prophet, and so on. Reverence of the Prophet is often talked about in terms of *ghulaami* (lit.: 'slavery') to the Prophet as the ideal to be achieved and a source of pride for his followers. Tahir-ul-Qadri (2013: 52) writes:

> Destroying one's self in the Prophet's slavery is the only complete faith and crossing all limits in his respect and veneration is the true devotion to the Prophet, and devotion is the pinnacle of faith.

Thus, there is an emphasis on complete devotion to the Prophet—not only in thoughts, but also through the body. A lover of the Prophet submits to him cognitively, physically and affectively—all at the same time.

The late Allama Khadim Hussain Rizvi, leader of TLP, while addressing a crowd on the anniversary of the death of Amir Cheema—a young engineering student who died in 2006 in a German prison after attempting to assassinate Roger Köppel, editor of the German daily *Die Welt*, which published cartoons of Muhammad—gave an example of crossing the limits. He narrated the story of a woman who drank the Prophet Muhammad's urine and then went on to describe its 'delightful' taste and smell as priceless. He called it 'blind love for the Prophet Muhammad' and aroused the crowd by rhetorically asking them what *they* had done to show their love for the Prophet? The crowd was impassioned and chanted slogans of praise and reverence for the act of drinking the Prophet's urine. In his speech, Rizvi asserted that, in the present day, giving one's life to protect the honour of the Prophet Muhammad is the ultimate act of love, as shown by Amir Cheema, Mumtaz Qadri and many others who died while guarding the honour of the Prophet. Those present in the crowd raised their hands and registered their physical presence to reaffirm that they were willing to lay down their bodies in love for the Prophet.

The emphasis on love for the holy Prophet as a bodily practice appears to be the underlying theme of notions of love for him, especially among Sunni Barelwis.[5] This understanding of love is connected to biological processes, from identifying with the body of the beloved in certain ways and revering their bodily fluids, to sacrificing one's own body for the sake of the beloved. Similar examples of embodied devotion have been cited in the wider literature on Sufi practices in South Asia (for example, Werbner and Basu 1998: 10). Parallels can be drawn with the emphasis on bodily practices with respect to the holy in South Asian religious communities

---

5   Similar notions are found in Shia conceptions of love for holy persons in Pakistan, as well as in some other sects.

in general. In particular, in Hinduism, the notion of holiness is overtly manifested in the physical world. From using cow's dung to consecrate physical spaces to drinking cow's urine for purification purposes, the relationship between the ordinary (profane) and the holy (sacred) is conceived in terms of physiological and bodily processes (Korom 2000: 193–95). The centrality of notions of purity to such a conception of love for the holy is also significant.[6] It is the holy that can not only transcend the normally perceived boundaries of the pure and impure, but also purify the impure. If the impure crosses the boundary, it is a transgression. However, what is normally perceived as impure—such as urine—is not only pure but also purifying when it comes from a holy body.

Muslims in Pakistan widely condemn Hindu practices such as drinking the urine of a cow, but at the same time, at least some groups glorify the act of drinking the Prophet Muhammad's urine. It can be argued that such a conception of love for the Prophet has developed within South Asian culture and draws on the same ideas of physicality, sacredness and purity as do Hindus. Barelwi Muslims, while claiming to oppose Hindu rituals, themselves subscribe to notions of purity and holiness as embedded in bodily processes. There is another significance of relating to the Prophet—or any holy symbol—through bodily practice: it is visible to others and is therefore an act of *public* performance. It is within the public sphere that it becomes a marker of identity, embedded in the body—or the death of the body. The ways of loving the Prophet are thus embodied techniques of the self, as they enable individuals to discover *meaning* for their own selves and establish their purity in contrast to *others*. The emphasis on the body adds intensity to meaning and inculcates embodied devotion. It is through the body that love for the Prophet must be expressed, and an offence against the Prophet must also be avenged such that the body of the offender bears the punishment. It is visible to the world and a clear sign—engraved on the bodies of the avenger (the lover of the Prophet) as well as the offender (the blasphemer)—of the pious *self* as distinct from the *other*.

---

6 While Dumont's (1980) thesis on purity and impurity as the primary basis of India's caste system has been challenged (see, for example, Marglin 1977; Olivelle 1998), the significance of the ideas of purity and impurity to the South Asian cultures is generally acknowledged.

'Religious sources' concerning the punishment of blasphemy in popular discourse

As mentioned earlier, religious scholars from all schools of thought in present-day Pakistan agree that whoever insults the Prophet Muhammad must be killed. Most accusations that include the act of insulting anything related to the religion of Islam, its dominant understanding and practices and even the authority of religious scholars can be framed as *tauheen-e-risaalat* ('insult to the Prophet'). According to the Pakistan Penal Code (PPC), religious offences other than insult to the Prophet Muhammad are punishable by life imprisonment and fines rather than death. However, in the popular discourse, such distinctions are rarely made, and the death penalty is promoted for a wide range of offences. For example, in justifying the murder of Salman Taseer, who did not directly insult the Prophet Muhammad but questioned the misuse of anti-blasphemy laws against religious minorities, religious scholars described his crime as insulting the 'law of God'. They argued that it was in effect an insult to the Prophet. Consequently, the popular term used to rally against Taseer for his offence was *tauheen-e-risaalat*. Similarly, religious scholars have described acts as various as insulting men's beards, criticising the Pakistan Army and supporting religious minorities as *tauheen-e-risaalat*. Thus, almost anything can be subsumed as an insult to the Prophet, deserving death as punishment.

Religious scholars refer to various sources in the Quran and *hadith* literature to support their belief that anyone who insults the Prophet must be killed. Such references add authenticity to *meaning* for people. Tahir-ul-Qadri, in his book *Tahhafuz-e-namoos-e-risaalat* (*Defending the Honour of the Prophet*) refers to Quranic verse Al-Ahzab 33:61:

مَلْعُونِينَ ۖ أَيْنَمَا ثُقِفُوا أُخِذُوا وَقُتِّلُوا تَقْتِيلًا

[They shall be cursed from all around and they shall be ruthlessly killed wherever they are seized.][7]

---

[7] There are multiple translations and interpretations of the verses of the Quran, which I am not concerned with here. My aim is not to confirm or contest the authenticity of the interpretations but to highlight the prevalent discourse.

In his interpretation of this verse, Tahir-ul-Qadri (2013: 21–22) writes:

> Thus, the Almighty is saying, 'O man! Don't show any empathy or leniency towards those who insult the sacred personality of my beloved [Prophet Muhammad]. Don't allow them any sort of consideration because they have gone miles away from my mercy; rather [they] have become totally devoid of it. So, where and whenever you find them, destroy their irreverent existence. Because even my merciful nature cannot tolerate their obscenities against my beloved. I cannot bear fearless existence of their filthy bodies on my pure and sacred land.'

He further comments on the choice of words by 'the Almighty' in the abovementioned Quranic verse. He asserts that the final two words (ٱلۡثِیتَقَت اوۡلَتَنُقَو) are a repetition of the Arabic word for *killing*, which implies that not only should blasphemers be killed, but also 'they should be killed as is the right to be killed'—that is, 'as brutally as possible' (Tahir-ul-Qadri 2013). Once again, through an emphasis on the physical act of killing, the meaning of punishment is intensified. Tahir-ul-Qadri (2013: 22) goes on to argue that this Quranic verse forms the basis of the 'eternal, indispensable law of God' concerning the punishment of a blasphemer and no human can make even a slight change to it. He argues that this is a *hadd* ('mandatorily enforced law') rather than a *tazeer* ('discretionary law'). He defines *hadd* as a punishment 'prescribed by Allah, that cannot be amended or altered by anyone except Allah' (Tahir-ul-Qadri 2013: 25). Hence, he argues, there is no room for forgiveness of a blasphemer. One of the senior scholars at JI headquarters described a similar position to me:

> It is not possible to forgive the blasphemer. The biggest example is the conquest of Mecca when the Prophet forgave everyone except those who had committed blasphemy. Even if one is himself sinful, it is mandatory to punish the blasphemer. One's sins can be forgiven by Allah; not practising Islam properly is a personal matter between him and Allah. However, not believing and insulting the religion of Islam is an unpardonable sin.

A similar distinction between lesser sins (related to the practice of faith) and the ultimate sin (insulting the religion and the Prophet) is drawn by Tahir-ul-Qadri. He argues, if one practices every component of Islam faithfully but does not appropriately revere the Prophet, he remains an infidel. On the other hand, one who does not practise Islam properly, but whose heart is filled with love for the Prophet, is still a Muslim and has hope for salvation from their sins. The former is *kharij-al-imaan* ('outside the circle of Islam') while the latter is *na'qas-al-i'maan* ('incomplete in faith') (Tahir-ul-Qadri 2013: 35). He also suggests that blasphemy is equal to infidelity and apostasy. In effect, this means that the private practice of faith is treated differently to insult or denunciation of the religion, which is carried out in the public sphere. Insulting the religion or the Prophet is treated as a *public offence* that is subject to regulation and punishment by the community. Hurting *the religious feelings of others* is therefore the ultimate offence.

However, in his commentary on 295-A, the clause of the PPC according to which anyone can be punished for insulting any other person's religion or religious feelings, Tahir-ul-Qadri also argues that the punishment for hurting the *religious feelings of non-Muslims* is *tazeer* but hurting *Muslims' religious feelings* is a *hadd*. This is because:

> when it comes to the insult of Prophet Muhammad, it no more remains an issue of hurting Muslims' feelings; it becomes an issue of destabilising Islam ... and only Islam is the religion of truth in the present world whereas all other religions are either false, adulterated, or obsolete. (Tahir-ul-Qadri 2013: 29)

An insult to Islam and the Prophet of Islam is therefore a threat to the *public order* as perceived by Muslims. Similar arguments are made by other religious scholars. A senior scholar of JI with a doctorate in Islamic studies said in an interview with me:

> There are several such cases within the lifetime of the Prophet that demonstrate that neither the Prophet nor Allah tolerated anyone who insulted the Prophet or questioned his authority. Even in the Quran, Allah says, whoever hurt my beloved Prophet will be damned in the world as well as in the hereafter. In another place in the Quran, Allah says, kill the blasphemers wherever you find them. The Prophet did not punish those who took it upon themselves to kill the blasphemers. It doesn't matter if those killers [lovers of the Prophet] practise the religion properly or not or offer their prayers or not.

There are plenty of references to other prophetic traditions with a similar message. Below are (summarised versions of) some of the most quoted prophetic traditions, across the three religious organisations on which I am focusing, which are used to support the killing of blasphemers:

- There was a blind man, who killed his slave girl. He came to the Prophet and confessed that he had killed his son's mother. He said he killed her because she used to constantly say derogatory words about the Prophet Muhammad. He stopped her a couple of times, but she did not stop insulting the Prophet. On hearing this, the Prophet did not denounce his act. Rather, he praised it and said this murder was void—that is, there would be no repercussions for the killer.

- On the occasion of victory over Mecca, the Prophet graciously announced public forgiveness for everyone in the city. However, he did not forgive the blasphemers. He issued a list of five or six people who used to say blasphemous things about the Prophet. The Prophet ordered that they should be killed even if they were found sticking to the walls of Kaaba, the house of Allah, where it is normally forbidden to shed blood. One of the blasphemers identified by the Prophet was ibn-e-Khutl. He used to write derogatory poems about the Prophet and publicised them through women singers. He was killed as per the order of the Prophet.

- In another instance, there was a doubting and hypocritical Muslim man. He had a fight with a Jewish man. They took it to the Prophet Muhammad, who decided in favour of the Jew because he was right. The Muslim man was suspicious and took the matter to Hazrat Umar (one of the companions of the Prophet who later became caliph). He asked Umar to do justice because he felt that Muhammad had not been just in his decision. Umar asked him to confirm whether the decision was made by the Prophet Muhammad? He said, 'Yes.' Umar went inside his house, came back with a sword and beheaded the Muslim man. Umar said, 'This sword will decide the fate of whoever does not accept the judgement of Muhammad'. The Muslim man's family went to the Prophet to complain but the Prophet said that Umar did the right thing because the man insulted the Prophet by not accepting his decision.

- There was another man, named Utab bin Ashraf, who was very rich and used to write insulting verses about the Prophet. The Prophet one day asked all his companions, 'Who will save me from the evil of this man?' There was a companion called Muhammad bin Muslima, who stepped forward and killed that man.

Hence, there are certain Quranic verses and prophetic traditions that appear in almost all religious publications, sermons, pamphlets, social media posts and so on. Not surprisingly, then, these are the same 'sources' that are quoted by almost every supporter of blasphemy-related violence to whom I talked. I did not explicitly ask any of them to share their religious knowledge with me; they themselves felt the need to refer to 'sources' to authenticate their beliefs and passion concerning blasphemy and its punishment. These people ranged from working-class Muslim men to government-employed, middle-class men, and from religious clerics to lawyers. Such religious discourse is thus not limited to religious scholars; it is widely distributed and is reflected in the everyday conversations of ordinary Muslims. It includes even those rural sections of society who would normally be dismissed as illiterate masses. During my research, I came across many such people who had not received any formal education, could not read or write, but who quoted Quranic verses and prophetic traditions to me. They had learnt these 'sources' and their interpretations from their local imams in Friday sermons and from other preachers on television.[8]

Moreover, ordinary people—even those belonging to lower socioeconomic classes and from rural backgrounds—have access to social media these days and are not only consuming but also participating in the dominant religious discourse online. This discourse provides them with meaning and inculcates passion. Hence, many religious scholars as well as common people passionately argue that anyone who commits blasphemy must be killed and does not deserve forgiveness, according to 'religious sources' and Islamic law. Their motivations are thus simultaneously embedded in cognition/reason and affect/passion. Since all refer to the 'sources' of Islamic law, it is pertinent to provide a brief overview of the traditional sources of Islamic law and their positions on the issue of blasphemy and its punishment.

Blasphemy in Islamic juristic literature

While the Quran and *sunnah* ('prophetic traditions') are accepted by most major sects in Pakistan as the basis of Islamic law, they mostly rely on the interpretations of major scholars from established schools of thought

---

8   Academic scholars have debated the authenticity and authority of the religious sources used in the current dominant religious discourse around blasphemy in Pakistan and have argued that they are not a true representation of Sharia—that is, Islamic—law (see, for example, Haq 2019). I am not concerned with the question of whether or not the dominant religious discourse is 'truly Islamic'—a question many scholars find central to studying blasphemy in Muslim societies. For me, the dominant religious discourse is significant with respect to the value and meaning it holds for people engaged in the discourse as religious scholars or their followers.

and *ijma'a* ('consensus among scholars'). There are four major schools of thought within Sunni Islam (Hanafi, Shafi'i, Maliki and Hanbali) and one major school of thought in Shia Islam (Jaafari) that are practised in Pakistan. The juristic discourse between different schools of thought is mostly theological and uses legal reasoning to derive conclusions. However, there are instances of impassioned debate between Islamic jurists when it comes to the issue of protecting the honour of the Prophet and Islam. The most significant value of the juristic sources, nevertheless, lies in the authenticity and authority they grant to contemporary religious discourse.

The English word 'blasphemy'—referring to the conceptual category of sacrilege—does not correspond to a distinct respective category in Islamic jurisprudence. In Islamic literature, the words most commonly used for the concept of sacrilege include *sabb* ('insult'), *shatam* ('abuse', 'vilification'), *takdhib* or *tajdif* ('denial'), *iftira* ('concoction'), *la'n* or *la'ana* ('curse') and *ta'n* ('accuse', 'defame') (Wielderhold 1997: 40–45). Moreover, the concept of sacrilege often overlaps with those of *kufr* ('unbelief'), *fisq* ('depravity') and *ridda* ('apostasy') (Khan 2014: 65). Kamali (1997: 208) argued that there is a tendency in the traditional practice of *fiqh* ('jurisprudence') to treat blasphemy, apostasy and infidelity as 'substantially concurrent and interchangeable'. However, the concept of blasphemy is subsumed under apostasy with reference to Muslims only; a non-Muslim cannot commit the Islamic offence of apostasy. Blasphemy can, on the other hand, be committed by Muslims and non-Muslims alike (Kamali 1997: 210). Accordingly, the punishment for blasphemy has traditionally been thought of in two separate categories—that for non-Muslims committing blasphemy and for Muslims committing blasphemy.

In the case of non-Muslims, most of the Islamic juristic literature deals with those non-Muslims who live in the land of Muslims, either through invasion or through the spread of Islam such that it took hold of domestic political power (Arzt 2002: 21). Thus, the literature concerning punishment of non-Muslim blasphemers is relevant mostly in situations when the majority in society are Muslims and/or the political power belongs to Muslims. In either case, non-Muslims are given the status of *dhimmis*: a minority bound to pay *jizya* ('a form of tax', 'minority tax') to the government in return for protection of their lives (Emon 2012: 37). Under this pledge of security, the Muslim government is responsible for the lives and safety of non-Muslims living in their lands (Emon 2012).

There are varying opinions on the punishment of a member of the *dhimmi* non-Muslim community who commits blasphemy (insults Islam, the Prophet or Muslim authority).[9] The Hanafi school of thought—the most widely practised in Pakistan—maintains that the offence of disbelief or infidelity is the most serious crime for which non-Muslims cannot be punished if they pay *jizya*; thus, they cannot be killed even if they insult Islam. The punishment of a non-Muslim blasphemer is, then, discretionary (*tazeer*), based on what the ruler of the time deems appropriate. It can be death if the blasphemer is also a combatant, or else arrest, caning and so on. All other schools of thought (Shafi'i, Maliki, Hanbali and Jaafari) believe that *dhimmis* break their social contract by committing blasphemy and hence lose the protection of their lives accorded to them in return for their taxes, and therefore must be killed. The Shafi'i, Maliki and Jaafari schools have some provisions for forgiveness if the non-Muslim blasphemer converts to Islam and becomes devout.

The punishment prescribed for Muslims committing blasphemy is often harsher. They are treated as apostates because, by insulting the Prophet or the religion of Islam, they also demonstrate their unfaithfulness, disbelief and denial of Islam (O'Sullivan 2001: 82). In fact, in most cases, they are also punished for treason under the pretence of blasphemy. The punishment for apostasy, blasphemy and treason committed by a Muslim is disputed among various scholars and schools of thought. The Islamic juristic literature portrays apostasy as an unforgiveable sin that must be punished by death unless the person in question repents and returns to Islam (Saeed 2011: 32). In some cases, even repentance is not an option, and anyone suspected of apostasy is considered liable to be killed. As noted by Friedmann (2003: 123–24), 'killing the unrepentant apostate is mandatory, while an "original" unbeliever is killed only if he is a combatant'. Thus, a brief survey of the legal opinions of jurists from different schools of thought on the matter of the prescribed punishment for an apostate indicates that an adult Muslim male must be put to death unless he is not in full possession of his faculties; this is agreed on by all major schools of thought.

---

9   The opinions presented here are summarised from the online archive of Islamic juristic texts compiled by Engage Pakistan. Available at: engagepakistan.com/engage/digital-library-of-classical-fiqh-texts/.

Shafi'i, Maliki and Hanbali jurists agree that an apostate should be given a chance to repent. The Hanafi school of law considers the option of repentance a desirable but not mandatory course of action. Jaafari jurists concur that an apostate should be given a chance to repent, but they limit the availability of this option only to *murtadd milli* ('a Muslim convert who later rejects Islam'). The exact duration allowed for the incumbent to repent is debated among the different schools, and sometimes within one school of thought as well. However, the most common view is that an apostate should be allowed three days to repent. The ruling is somewhat different regarding female apostates in some of the schools of law. According to Hanafi and Jaafari jurists, female apostates should not be killed; rather, they are to be imprisoned, or tortured by their masters if they are slaves, until they accept Islam again. According to the Hanbali, Maliki and Shafi'i schools of thought, however, women are also put to death (Jordan 2003: 62).

As we have seen, while there is debate as to whether an apostate should be imprisoned first or executed without delay, the duration of repentance allowed to an apostate and the punishment of an apostate depending on gender, there is wide consensus among Muslim jurists on the death penalty for an apostate. Most of these jurists based their verdicts on the Quran and *sunnah*—the two basic sources of Islamic law. While some of the scholars mentioned above have referred to Quranic verses in their writings to support their arguments or judgements, many rely mainly on the *hadith* literature to justify the imposition of the death penalty on apostates.

What we learn from the discussion of the traditional Islamic juristic literature is that the punishment of blasphemers and apostates has always been a matter of debate among Islamic scholars and jurists. In the traditional Islamic juristic literature, as well as in the views of the major Islamic scholars of the Subcontinent (including the founders of major subsects such as Barelwis and Deobandis) in the pre-Partition era, there have always been certain qualifications of the argument concerning the punishment of blasphemers (Mazhar 2015). Comparing this with the current positions adopted by scholars, we see that the nuances of debate concerning the frequency and intent of the offence, the possibility of repentance and different punishments prescribed for Muslims, non-Muslims, slaves, free people, men and women have largely been lost.

Competing claims to religious authority and the rise of absolutist claims

The present consensus among religious scholars on the killing of blasphemers, as demonstrated by the dominant religious discourse, reflects a shift towards absolutist claims regarding the punishment of blasphemy and all other offences it subsumes. I argue that the current absolutist claims regarding the punishment of alleged blasphemers are an outcome of the dual nature of modernity: its desire for order and neat categorisation, on the one hand, and the anxiety caused by a growing multiplicity of opinions on the other. The modern condition is characterised by simultaneous homogenisation and heterogenisation, as described by Appadurai (1990: 295). Following Appadurai's theory, I argue that there are two distinct characteristics that define the prevalent religious discourse concerning blasphemy in contemporary Pakistan:

1. The homogenisation of the concept of the offence of blasphemy and the understanding of its punishment in absolutist terms.
2. The heterogenisation of religious authority, marking a shift from traditional structures to an unregulated multiplication of opinions and scholars.

First, we see that the various qualifications of the argument concerning the punishment of a blasphemer are removed, leading to absolutist understandings of the offence and its punishment. Representatives of most major sects and subsects in present-day Pakistan seem to have a homogeneous conception of the punishment for a blasphemer. The punishment of death for anyone who commits blasphemy against the Prophet Muhammad is arguably a unique point of consensus between all sects. Moreover, as noted earlier, various categories and concepts of offences are now subsumed under the popular imposed/appropriated Western term 'blasphemy' or the Urdu term *tauheen-e-risaalat*. Various offences, including that of apostasy, are labelled under these terms in the popular religious discourse. Even though there is no punishment for apostasy in the PPC, the offence of apostasy—particularly with reference to Ahmadis—is understood as blasphemy and, more particularly, as an insult to the Prophet. Thus, we see modernity's emphasis on neat categorisations and the desire for order and homogenisation reflected in the contemporary absolutist religious discourse.

Second, compared with traditional religious authority, religious authority in contemporary Pakistan is a lot more fluid and dispersed. While Islam never had a consolidated central orthodoxy like Christianity, there were established schools of thought that were accepted as legal and juristic authorities after the initial formative period. In his work on continuity and change in Islamic legal authority, Wael Hallaq (2004: 123) highlighted that a multiplicity of doctrinal narratives was a norm even during the era of consolidation of the major schools of thought in Islam. He argued that discursive and hermeneutic practices were always a part of Islamic juristic traditions (Hallaq 2004: 127). However, the discursive changes in traditional schools of thought, as Hallaq (2004: 166) argued, took place within the established structures of authority. The new and emerging scholars were first trained in established schools of thought, and their interpretations were then produced and defended, rejected or recognised within the existing structures. The structure of religious authority and the relevant discursive practices are quite different in present-day Pakistan. The new scholars do not have to be trained in any formal system of religious education. Their authority is mostly self-proclaimed, and legitimacy is drawn from their charisma and popularity rather than juristic training.

Robinson (2008: 265–68) argued that the modernist reformist movements among South Asian Muslims qualitatively changed the nature of religious authority. As noted in the previous chapter, some of the reformist groups completely broke away from the established schools of jurisprudence, while others, such as Deobandis and Barelwis, continued to follow the established schools of thought within Sunni Islam. Nevertheless, all the reformist groups, including the Deobandis and Barelwis, questioned the authority of the past and established newer ways of relating to the traditional schools of thought through a renewed focus on *ijtihad* ('independent reasoning') (Robinson 2008: 262). According to Robinson (2008: 268):

> [T]he breaking of the continuous link with the past has enabled new forms of religious authority to emerge, an authority that could be made and remade in each generation and make use of the new resources of the times—a very modern kind of authority.

The newer modes of religious authority, therefore, did not require formal affiliation with an established institution of learning and could be claimed by anyone who could read the religious texts that became widely available in local languages due to the print revolution in the nineteenth century.

The dispersal of religious authority was further enabled in Pakistan by government interventions in the institutes of religious learning. As Vali Nasr (2000b: 146–47) noted in his study of religious scholars and the rise of sectarian violence in Pakistan, the *ulema* ('religious scholars') are no longer trained in traditional intellectual tools and forms of knowledge associated with Islamic theological and juristic education. On the contrary, since the government's sponsorship of *madrasahs* during the Soviet war, the emphasis of religious education has been highly political. He writes:

> So notable was the impact of the government initiative that Islamist and self-styled Islamic groups—whose members were predominantly lay and had received modern education—began to establish madrasahs of their own. (Nasr 2000b: 147)

There has been not only a proliferation of self-proclaimed religious scholars with no formal religious education, but also a striking overlap of political parties and centres of religious learning. As already pointed out, most of the religious scholars dominating the discourse around blasphemy are also politicians. The number of politicians-cum-religious scholars has been expanding exponentially due to lack of formal requirements, such as recognition by traditional authority. There is a shift towards more organic, charismatic forms of religious authority. It is possible for anyone who can speak on matters of religion with a certain conviction and passion to establish himself as a legitimate scholar.

Hence, we see the dual forces of modernity—that is, simultaneous homogenisation and heterogenisation at play in determining the popular religious discourse and the construction of religious authority in Pakistan. The inherently contradictory nature of modernity has been pointed out by several theorists. For example, Bauman (2000: 106), a prominent theorist of modernity, argued that ambivalence and duality were inherent characteristics of modernity. On the one hand, the emphasis on categorisation, rationalisation and predictability was supposed to achieve order, homogeneity and domestication of chaos. On the other hand, the drive for homogeneity breeds uncertainty, differences and anxiety about those differences (Bauman 2000). The heterogenisation of religious opinions and the constant flow of information expose common people—as well as religious scholars—to different and conflicting views, leading to the prevalence of uncertainty. The lack of one established truth when the modern nation-state emphasises the need for a metanarrative leaves people anxious and desiring certainty. The desire for certainty is then expressed in terms of absolutist claims, describing everything in terms of black and white, pure and impure, to reassert boundaries. The absolutist claims, however, concern the punishment of blasphemy and do not define what it is to blaspheme in any certain terms. The lack of definition as to what can be deemed blasphemous is in fact an added source of uncertainty. In this context, the competition of various groups and individuals for religious authority is what describes the current religious discourse concerning blasphemy in Pakistan. It is the competition for authority and legitimacy that constructs the *affective meaning* that the religious discourse holds for people. I will now discuss the politics of the three religious parties—JI, PAT and TLP—to demonstrate how they compete against each other to achieve legitimacy and authority in the face of the uncertainty arising from the multiplication of claims to religious authority.

Politics of uncertainty and legitimacy

JI was conceived in 1941 by Abul A'la Maududi, a reformist Sunni Muslim scholar, as a modern, pan-Islamist, anticolonial movement on the Indian Subcontinent. Initially opposed to the idea of Pakistan, JI has been a significant political party since the state's creation. While it has never won a significant number of seats in elections, it has periodically liaised with ruling and opposition parties to influence political decision-making, particularly in favour of Islamist policies. JI has always emphasised its text-based, urban, reformist Islam. Its headquarters in Mansoora, Lahore, has extensive libraries with a plethora of publications on the issue of blasphemy.

The other two organisations, PAT and TLP, represent Sunni Barelwis—followers of the reformist-Sufi movement headed by Ahmed Raza Khan Barelwi in the early twentieth century. PAT was formed in 1989 by Tahir-ul-Qadri, a Pakistani Canadian Barelwi scholar. Tahir-ul-Qadri had been running the Minhaj-ul-Quran institute since 1980 and was also intensely involved in religious textual discourse. This organisation is registered as a university and has libraries, bookshops and publication houses associated with it. Tahir-ul-Qadri has written hundreds of books of religious interpretations, many of which concern the issue of blasphemy exclusively. He is also famous for his sermons aired through Minhaj-ul-Quran's own TV channel, as well as other media. While Tahir-ul-Qadri spends most of his time in Canada, he occasionally visits Pakistan and has arranged events like Namoos-e-Risaalat Convention ('Honour of the Prophet Convention') in the past.

TLP is the most recently formed political organisation, registered in 2015. It emerged out of the religious organisation Labbaik ya Rasool Allah, formed by supporters of Mumtaz Qadri exclusively with the aim of protecting the honour of the Prophet (Basit 2020). This organisation was headed until his death in November 2020 by Allama Khadim Hussain Rizvi, a disabled man in a wheelchair who travelled across the country to address his followers. Rizvi connected with his supporters in the Punjabi vernacular popular among the working classes. TLP's discourse is disseminated largely through religious sermons given in mosques and in the street, their recordings and live screenings posted on social media, pamphlets, street protests, banners and so on.

Together, these three organisations are actively involved in producing the dominant discourse about the punishment of blasphemy in Pakistan. Despite the proliferation of religious scholars claiming religious authority and political power, their political claims greatly overlap. All three of the political parties under discussion have mandates concerning widespread social and political reforms based on Islamic ideology. JI's constitution (Article 4) defines their mission as 'the establishment of the *Deen* ['Divine Order' or the Islamic way of life] and in essence the achievement of Allah's pleasure and success in the Hereafter'. They further explain the scope of the establishment of 'Divine Order':

> Establishment of *Deen* does not mean establishing some part of it, rather establishing it in its entirety, in individual and collective life, and whether it pertains to prayers or fasting, Haj or Zakat, or political issues of life. No part of Islam is irrelevant, but the whole Islam is necessary.

In the recent past, JI has been very active in anticorruption campaigns against the government, using the slogan 'Corruption-free Pakistan'. In March 2016, it led a 'train march' against corruption across the country—from Peshawar to Karachi (The News International 2016). Its members have also raised their voices against terrorism and the government's weak efforts to curb it. In a recent 'Resolution on the economic conditions in the country', they declared that, 'contrary to the government claims, the economy of the country was on the decline'.

After quoting figures showing rising debt and worsening conditions for farmers, their statement (handed to me by a party member) included the following criticism of the government's antiterrorism actions:

> The *Shoora* ['committee'] felt that the implementation on the NAP [National Action Plan] against terrorism in the wake of the Peshawar Army Public School [attack] was negligible and the government had failed to make any progress on most of the points of the NAP including the arrests of the culprits involved in the Peshawar tragedy. On the other hand, it said, the government had spent most of its time in an uncalled-for campaign against the mosques and madrassahs, which was aimed at harassing the religious circles instead of wiping out terrorism.

They further reported:

> The JI Shoora renewed its commitment to stand by the masses especially against the problems of poverty, price hike[s], load shedding, lawlessness, and terrorism. It said that the JI would organize the oppressed and downtrodden masses in line with its people's agenda for the enforcement of the Islamic system with the ultimate aim to establish a truly Islamic welfare state.

Similarly, PAT has been rallying to 'revolutionise' the current system to create a truly Islamic welfare state based on 'participatory democracy'. PAT's current manifesto, called 'Green Revolution', developed in 2014 after mass protests against government corruption and electoral rigging, promises to bring free housing to the homeless, unemployment allowances to the unemployed and free education and health facilities for the population. It specifically takes aim at elimination of corruption to achieve its goals. The newly formed TLP lists similar objectives on its website. The TLP's mandate focuses on nine points: accountability, implementation of law, justice, free health, free education, security for all, freedom for Kashmir, utilising the media's role, a strong economy and friendly foreign relations. The TLP calls itself an 'Islamist political party' with an overall objective 'to make Pakistan an Islamic state, governed by Shariat-e-Mohammadi ['Muhammad's Sharia'], through a gradual legal, and political process'. Both PAT and TLP have also been known to condemn terrorism.

A review of these political parties' manifestos shows that a stand against corruption and distancing their Islamist agendas from terrorism are common features. Another common agenda item for these parties, as will be demonstrated in the discussion below, is to ensure that blasphemers are punished. While TLP was formed with an explicit aim of defending the honour of the Prophet, the other two parties also support the killing of blasphemers and have been active in anti-blasphemy campaigns. However, while they agree on certain agendas, they are also competing with each other for power and influence within the political sphere. How, then, do they establish their legitimacy and gain supporters when they are all rallying for the same causes? How does the rivalry play out with their shared goals and agendas?

It comes down to who can establish themselves as the rightful guardians of these causes. To do that, they need to make sharper and more aggressive claims than the others. Their politics involve asserting authority and legitimacy by taking *ownership* of a cause and making absolutist, aggressive claims to outdo each other. They fight over the *ownership* of a cause by claiming that they are the ones who care the most about it and *represent* it on the *national* stage. For example, a senior member of JI talked to me at length about how they were trying to bring all religious groups and parties together for the cause of protecting the honour of the Prophet. They organised a *national* conference on the issue of blasphemy in May 2016 after Mumtaz Qadri's execution and invited all other groups and parties to join them. The JI member complained:

> Everyone saw that masses came to Qadri's funeral and made it obvious that they love the Prophet Muhammad, and Mumtaz Qadri due to his association with the Prophet. These masses and their leaders include people belonging to all schools of thought. We in Jamaat-e-Islami have been trying to bring [together] all religious groups and sects in the same forum on this issue. We believe in solidarity and we should all work together on this. We held a convention earlier this year where we invited all sects and groups and formed a joint action committee. However, some Barelwi groups do not want to come together with us because they want to use this issue for their own political gains. They do not come to the joint forums. Even though Mumtaz Qadri's father did not make them the custodian of the campaign, they have been pretending it is only their issue. Some other Barelwi groups come. But Allama Sarwat Qadri, Khadim Hussain Rizvi, etc., are not willing to come with us.

PAT and TLP have also been organising similar national conventions where they represent *themselves* as the ones most concerned with, and the legitimate guardians of, the honour of the Prophet. JI and PAT both have significant women's wings and, in the past, their women members have also organised conferences on the honour of the Prophet. TLP does not have an active women's wing so far, but it has held rallies and conventions across the country and protests, including major sit-ins in Islamabad in March 2016 and November 2017. So, different religious political parties strive to outdo each other by competing for the ownership of issues such as blasphemy, which has gained tremendous symbolic power in the Pakistani political sphere.

Some of the older religious political parties, such as JI, relied on the strategy of using charity to amass support. They have an established charitable organisation called Al-Khidmat Foundation that provides health, education, disaster relief and other free community services. Similarly, Minhaj Welfare Foundation is the charity wing of Minhaj-ul-Quran organisation. The more charismatic leaders of PAT and TLP are also engaged in giving public sermons to attract support. Tahir-ul-Qadri has gained the support of an urban educated population due to his textual approach: he delivers his sermons with stacks of books in front of him, reading out references from those books in Arabic, translating and sharing references to the 'sources' with the public on the spot. His approach is based on discursive reasoning and rationality. Allama Khadim Hussain Rizvi of TLP, on the other hand, was known for his passionate speeches in the Punjabi vernacular, appealing to rural, less-educated and lower socioeconomic sections of society. The fact that he was a disabled man who travelled across the country in a wheelchair, giving lectures on the love of the Prophet, often reciting verses in Arabic, added to his credibility and legitimacy. Moreover, he dissociated himself from worldly benefits to prove his altruism to the cause. For example, in one of his sermons, he said:

> A police officer came to me and asked if I wanted money, political position, visa for abroad, etc. I told him that I am not concerned with any of these things they use to lure me. I am here only for the love of the Prophet.[10]

---

10   Available from: www.youtube.com/watch?v=axCwC-pywJk&t=1185s. Note this video is now private, when accessed in October 2020 it was still a publicly available video; it is possible that it was made private after the passing of TLP chief Rizvi in November 2020, or because the Pakistani government banned TLP as a terrorist organisation in April 2021.

He further said at another point in his sermon:

> My only purpose is to bring the system of *Nizaam-e-Mustafa* ['Muhammad's system'] into practice. Once this mission has been accomplished, I will be happy to serve as a sweeper at the graves of the lovers of the Prophet—who have died defending the honour of the Prophet.[11]

It must be noted that the term *nizaam-e-mustafa* in the Pakistani political sphere is at least as old as Pakistan itself. Different political parties, including JI and PAT, have used it at various points to make their political claims. It has, however, more recently been associated with defending the honour of the Prophet. Since 2011, many religious parties have raised the call for *nizaam-e-mustafa* to counter the offence of blasphemy in Pakistan. Despite the widespread use of the term, all religious political parties claim they are the true custodians of *nizaam-e-mustafa* and that they are the only ones who can bring this system to Pakistan. Once again, we see the battle for the public imagining of the nation underlying this debate. Khadim Hussain Rizvi of TLP proclaimed while addressing a crowd of his followers in Karachi in January 2017:

> There is only one way of achieving a prosperous state of Pakistan, and that is by defending the honour of the Prophet. Those who speak against me are in fact speaking against the honour of the Prophet. Now is the time that every Sunni should vote for us, to bring the religion of the Prophet, *Nizaam-e-Mustafa*, to the throne. It is the responsibility of every single Sunni in this country.[12]

In this statement, again, we see absolutist claims made to evoke support from the masses by suggesting that they are either with TLP or against the honour of the Prophet. These claims are further legitimised by the spiritual experiences attributed to Khadim Hussain Rizvi, by himself and his followers. For example, when he was arrested in early January 2017 for celebrating the murder of Salman Taseer in Lahore, there were stories going around on Facebook about his spiritual powers (Tanveer 2017). His followers claimed that:

---

11   Ibid.
12   Available from: www.youtube.com/watch?v=6mP8WlKg3qc. Note this video is now private, when accessed in October 2020 it was still a publicly available video; it is possible that it was made private after the passing of TLP chief Rizvi in November 2020, or because the Pakistani government banned TLP as a terrorist organisation in April 2021.

as Maulana Khadim Hussain Rizvi entered the prison cell, which was a really abject part of prison full of cockroaches, he gestured to the cockroaches and told them to stay away from him as he was there for the love of the Prophet. And no cockroach dared to come close to him.

Spiritual authenticity is attributed to religious and political leaders through such stories.

In addition to miracle-based charismatic authority, Rizvi also established himself as one who took a 'tough stand against the forces of evil'. He was known for being particularly aggressive and using swearwords against his enemies: the West, liberals, secularists, the government, the police and anyone who did not support his cause. His style of gaining legitimacy by asserting his authority in absolutist and violent terms set him apart from JI and PAT, whose tones are softer. Interestingly, while TLP has emerged relatively recently compared with JI and PAT, it became the fifth-most popular political party in the 2018 general elections. Thus, Rizvi's absolutist and more aggressive stance, his use of strong colloquial language, his disability and his pretentions to humility were some of the major factors that contributed to his popularity and legitimacy.

This is not to say that a particular party or religious scholar has won the competition to establish themselves as the most legitimate defender of the honour of the Prophet. The struggle is alive and will predictably remain so. New religious scholars and parties may emerge, the older ones may revive themselves with better strategies and techniques, but it is the process of the contestation itself that has led to the sharpening of the dominant religious discourse concerning blasphemy and the articulation of punishment in absolutist terms over time.

Conclusion

Over the past few decades, the dominant religious discourse around the punishment of blasphemy in Pakistan has become increasingly homogeneous despite the rising heterogeneity of its promotors. Amid the uncertainty created by the multiplicity of claimants to religious authority, the religious political parties have turned to competitive absolutist claims within this discourse to consolidate their own power and legitimacy. The homogeneity and absolutism of the discourse lend it a symbolic power within the religious-political sphere that becomes the focal point of competing claims to legitimacy by various players within this sphere. The symbolic power of the issue of blasphemy rests on its *affective meaning*, which appeals to people's imaginations and rouses their passions. The recent political events in Pakistan manifest the symbolic power of the absolutist discourse concerning blasphemy and its centrality to politics in contemporary Pakistan.

In November 2017, two Sunni Barelwi political parties, TLP and Sunni Tehreek, took to the streets to protest the alleged blasphemy committed by the law minister Zahid Hamid when he changed the wording of the declaration of faith in the parliamentary oath (Hasan 2017).[13] The government retracted the change after the outcry from religious groups and explained it away as a clerical error. However, the religious parties were not satisfied and demanded the minister's resignation and an inquiry into who was responsible for the attempted change. The abovementioned Barelwi parties organised a rally, culminating in a sit-in at Faizabad interchange in the capital, Islamabad. The sit-in by the parties' religious leaders and thousands of their supporters continued for almost three weeks, interrupting the normal life of residents and holding the city hostage.[14] In the final week of November, the government decided to disperse the protestors, which led to clashes with the police. Several people including police personnel died and hundreds were injured (Hasan 2017).

As a result, protests by infuriated religious groups spread across the country. The government had to eventually call in the army, which refused to use force against the protestors. However, the army arbitrated a peace agreement between the protestors and the government.[15] As per the agreement, the law minister had to resign and the government had to accept a number of the protestors' demands, including the release without charge of arrested protestors. The law minister not only resigned but also had to issue a public statement reaffirming his faith and his firm belief in the finality of the Prophet Muhammad. In fact, the government, the military and protestors were all using the same language of their faith and love for the Prophet Muhammad to legitimise their respective positions (Wasim and Azeem 2017).

---

13 The declaration was changed from 'I solemnly believe in the finality of the Prophet Muhammad' to 'I believe in the finality of the Prophet Muhammad'.
14 Due to a road blockage, a child died in an ambulance, unable to reach hospital in time. Residents of the city had extreme problems commuting to schools, offices and so on.
15 The army's role as an 'arbiter' was later challenged by the Supreme Court of Pakistan.

A small number of analysts and intellectuals saw these events as a compromise of democracy and surrender of power to agitating religious groups. While this is not something new in the history of Pakistan—as those in power have always tried to appease religious groups to amass support and legitimise themselves—the enormous political currency, and symbolic power, gained through the issue of blasphemy and the massive number of people who came out in support of the issue were astonishing for many. The dominant religious discourse has successfully engaged ordinary people, who are the primary agents involved in blasphemy accusations at the microlevel. Widespread uncertainty due to the multiplication of religious authority and religious leaders' sharpening discourse inculcates further moral anxieties among ordinary people.

Part II

3

Blasphemy accusations: Power, purity and the enemy within

During my fieldwork, I studied more than 50 incidents of blasphemy accusations closely and surveyed many others from a distance. One striking commonality between almost all the cases I came across was that they started within microlevel interpersonal relationships between people known to each other. While wider religious and nationalistic narratives that enable blasphemy accusations and punishments to take place are constructed and promulgated at structural and societal levels, it is within everyday interpersonal relationships that these narratives are acted out—relationships characterised by prior familiarity and hierarchical power relations, built on symbolic and conceptual boundaries. I focus on the everyday and the interpersonal to answer two interrelated questions: 1) what triggers blasphemy accusations; and 2) why are certain people targeted with these accusations? The discussion will show that accusations of blasphemy are often triggered by perceived transgressions of hierarchical symbolic boundaries and are made against expendable familiar others.

Most studies of blasphemy in Pakistan have argued that blasphemy accusations are usually a result of personal rivalries, and that blasphemy laws are used instrumentally ('abused' or 'misused') to settle personal scores (see, for example, Dobras 2009; Hoffman 2014; Khan 2015; Siddique and Hayat 2008; Uddin 2011). I argued in the Introduction against the law-centric understanding of blasphemy accusations and subsequent chapters will further elaborate on that. In this chapter, I want to expand the understanding of the motivations behind blasphemy accusations regardless of whether or not they are referred to authorities. While a substantial number of blasphemy accusations do indeed arise from personal rivalries and grievances between people—as the 'instrumental use' thesis posits—this explanation is too simplistic and does not take into account other contributing factors. I found a complex combination of motivational factors at play in most instances of blasphemy accusations—including personal piety, a desire for power and the purification of society, as well as local cultural and moral frameworks.

The purely instrumentalist explanations are often defensive and given in response to arguments describing blasphemy accusations as rooted in the religious beliefs and passions of Muslims. In my research, I found that, in most cases, it is impossible to distinguish between and neatly categorise the motivations as *either* instrumentalist *or* rooted in religious piety. Instead, more often than not, the accuser is both a *vengeful person* and a *becoming Muslim*—to use Naveeda Khan's (2012) term. The *vengeful person* is driven by a violation that may not be religious in nature but is still considered a transgression of social hierarchies or norms. The violation may be an aberration of character with respect to expectations, nonconformity with expected roles and behaviour or a transgression of the established social hierarchy. The *becoming Muslim* is motivated by a sense of guilt and sin and is living in a state of moral torment, constantly striving to be a good Muslim, the benchmark for which is set by the modern nation-state of Pakistan and the dominant religious rhetoric and continues to be raised higher. I argue that most accusations are driven by elements of both vengeance *and* personal piety *at the same time*.

The transgression: Purity and social hierarchy

The concern for purity is central to understanding how certain transgressions lead to blasphemy accusations in Pakistan. To understand the transgression as an impurity that needs to be removed, it is helpful to see it as a *violation* of conceptual categories and symbolic boundaries. Conceptual categories are preconceived notions of the right order of things in society—also described as a 'mental map'—the alteration of which is considered a violation (Krohn-Hansen 1994: 372). Symbolic boundaries are 'group-making social processes' that consist of meaningful classifications, cultural patterns and social practices that allow social actors to perceive a symbolic order of reality concerning their group identity (Hartmann 2015: 166–69). The *violation* of conceptual categories and symbolic boundaries can lead to physical *violence* in society (Hartmann 2015). It is this dual nature of *violence* with which I am concerned. Bowman (2001: 25) explains the etymology of the word 'violence', which is derived from 'violate', implying an 'integral space broken into and, through that breaking, desecrated'. Thus, Bowman (2001: 25) argues, in its passive grammatical sense, 'violate' indicates something 'characterized by impurity or defilement'. From this perspective, the transgression of social hierarchies and moral codes of conduct constitutes the primary instance of *violence*. Corbin (1976: 108) employed Douglas's (1966) concept of 'dirt' as 'matter out of place' to make a similar point about *violence* as a disturbance in the normal order of thoughts and ideological categories. The violation of conceptual categories of purity can lead to physical violence against those deemed transgressive.

Anthropological studies of violence have shown that discourses about purity/impurity are frequently invoked in violent conflicts and genocides around the world. Purity discourses were conjured in some of the most violent moments in recent history, such as the Holocaust (Hinton 1998), the Khmer Rouge genocide in Cambodia (Hinton 2005), the Hutu–Tutsi conflict in Rwanda (Malkki 1995) and Hindu–Sikh violence in India (Das 1996). However, while notions of 'pure' and 'impure' are employed in a wide range of violent contexts, 'the meaning of such conceptual categories' always takes on 'distinct local forms' (Hinton 2002: 19). The Holocaust, for example, drew on ideas of race and genetics, blood, soil, bodily aesthetics, and so on, to construct ideals of purity, whereas the Khmer Rouge employed agrarian metaphors and Buddhist notions of purity and impurity (Hinton 2002). Hinton thus argued that the broad conceptual categories of us/them and purity/impurity draw on local cultural patterns and refer to ideas that already have some symbolic value for the specific group of people.

Other scholars have argued that the cultural patterns and local forms on which the purity discourses draw should not be seen as given or fixed in time. Duschinsky (2013) argued that the categories of 'pure' and 'impure' are discursively constructed within specific sociopolitical circumstances. Appadurai (1998: 231) also argued, while acknowledging the importance of Douglas's ideas about 'purity and category-mixture' in understanding violence, that the categories of pure and impure are not 'culturally given'. Instead, in his explanation of ethnic violence, he demonstrated how notions of purity and impurity are contingent on subjectivities constructed within specific contexts (Appadurai 1998).

According to Appadurai (1998: 236), 'purity is a matter of moral coherence'; a lack of moral coherence leads to moral anxiety, and deviant acts and thoughts can be perceived as transgressions. I have demonstrated in earlier chapters how the present moral anxieties of Pakistani Muslims are a consequence of specific historical and political circumstances. At the microlevel, ideas of purity and impurity are contingent on Pakistan's social hierarchies and the sensibilities of those in power when it comes to blasphemy accusations. Bail (2008: 39) argued that it is important to pay attention to how symbolic boundaries or notions of purity and impurity are often chosen, 'policed or made permeable' depending on the 'interests of majority groups'. In the light of this conceptualisation, I argue, blasphemy accusations are triggered by transgressions that disrupt the symbolic boundaries and moral coherence of the majority groups and those who are in power. Transgressions are perceived subjectively depending on the relationship between the accused and the accuser. The power structures within these relationships determine who is perceived as a transgressor and which 'cognitive, affective and cultural resources' are mobilised against them (Hartmann 2015: 166). The aim is often to punish the transgression of social hierarchies—perceived as an impurity—to reassert the moral order of the society.

The underlying ideals of purity and impurity that define a transgression also vary depending on the respective places of the accused and the accuser(s) in society. For example, the religious identity of the accused is an important factor that determines the perception of purity and the transgressions thereof. To demonstrate this, I will use a variety of examples: the first case is an accusation against a Muslim woman, the next two cases are against Christians and the last case is an accusation against an Ahmadi. The narratives of purity invoked are different in each case; however, there are certain underlying themes that run through most of the narratives of purity presented here. The most significant of these common themes is the gendered understanding of purity. The transgressions are often conceived in terms of the sexual purity of women, even when the immediate violation is not at all sexual and the accused is a man. In the following examples, we shall see in further detail how narratives of purity are tied to women and their moral character.

The first case is of a Muslim woman, Marium, who was accused of blasphemy. She lived in a small, overcrowded *mohalla* ('neighbourhood') with narrow streets on the periphery of Lahore. She was the principal of a small school in the locality and offered religious sermons to the women of the area in her free time. She conducted these meetings at her house, where she preached religious teachings and also sometimes shared her own writings. She was accused of blasphemy for her allegedly deviant views, such as saying that 'singing the praise of the Prophet was not allowed' and the 'Prophet was simply another human being'. It must be noted that these views are already held by some groups and subsects within Sunni Islam in Pakistan. Marium, however, not only presented her 'deviant' views, but also challenged the existing hierarchical structure of the society. In her sermons and writings, she not only questioned mainstream interpretations but also asserted her own right as a woman to interpret and preach religion. It was the imam of the local mosque who officially accused her of blasphemy. The key witness presented against her was another religious cleric who used to teach the Quran to Marium's children. I met both of them (the accuser and the primary witness) several times and attended some of their court appearances as well. The imam who became the complainant against Marium told me:

> She came to me one day with a copy of Quran and asked me to read certain verses from it. I told her that I had already read those and asked her what she wanted to say. She said that the 'Quran itself has walked to you'. I asked, 'How can the Quran walk to me?' She said that she is Syed, belonging to the Quraish bloodline [the Prophet's lineage] and has received revelations from God. I rebuked her by saying that she was telling a lie and that she should go away.

When I asked the imam whether it was then he accused her of blasphemy, he surprisingly said, 'No'. He explained to me that the women of the locality (including his wife) who used to attend the religious sermons at Marium's house had been telling their menfolk (including himself) about Marium's deviant (according to him) interpretations of religion for some time. He admitted that, despite the fact he had heard of the 'blasphemy' originally through women, no action could be taken against Marium because 'the women can't become complainants and witnesses in the court; it would require them to visit court every week and that would not be suitable for them'. Besides, men are the ones who are expected to be the protectors of religion and in effect the eligible claimants of spiritual purity. He also acknowledged the delay between the occurrence of the offences—which, according to him, continued for weeks—and the invocation of legal authority against the accused. Moreover, before the legal action was initiated, violent crowds besieged Marium's house, roused by some pamphlets containing 'deviant' interpretations of religion that she had allegedly published and distributed. It was under pressure from the violent crowd that police eventually arrested Marium and initiated formal proceedings against her. The imam claimed that it was he who had urged the police to intervene, 'otherwise there would have been destruction and bloodshed'.

Having talked to the accuser and other witnesses and followed the case closely, I am of the opinion that the story about Marium visiting the imam and sharing 'blasphemous' words, as alleged, was fabricated after the fact. In my view, there were two reasons behind this: first, to enhance the legitimacy of the blasphemy accusation, and second, to boost the religious authority and personal piety of the imam—in his own eyes as well as in the eyes of the public. The second point is demonstrated when he himself said:

> The complainants generally stop appearing for trials because it requires a lot of commitment and religious passion to visit the court every week. Therefore, I myself became the complainant, as I did in another case that is also undergoing trial at the moment, to ensure that it is seen through to the end. Pursuing these cases provides me with a holy purpose in my life.

His religious authority in the eyes of others also increased, as one of his friends who had become closer to him after this case told me:

> It is because of people like him that our society is surviving in the face of such atrocious sins [as blasphemy]. These people are like an embankment protecting the society from the flood of sins. It is due to these holy men holding up the society that, despite the tremendous increase in grave sins such as blasphemy in the present day, the Muslim community is still intact.

While the narrative of protecting society from 'impurity' caused by a 'flood' of blasphemy provides legitimacy to the role and authority of religious clerics, it also reinforces the idea of the presence of impurity and evil in society and the constant need to purge it. One of the lawyers who took up the imam's case against Marium in court reflected on the state of 'sin' (blasphemy) in society:

> Too many cases of blasphemy these days—what a shame! This is such an unfortunate time to be alive when so many people are committing blasphemy every other day. We should not even be alive. We should die from shame for having seen so many cases

of blasphemy in our lives. I feel more pain for these cases than even for murder cases. There was a time when a murder used to shake everyone, but nowadays so many people are dying every day in brutal circumstances that we have become desensitised to the cruelty of murder. However, we cannot get desensitised to the issue of honour of the Prophet. Blasphemy will always remain the most heinous crime in society.

Hence, in Marium's case, we see as the motivational factors behind the accusation both the strategic instrumental use of the blasphemy laws to punish the perceived transgression of a woman challenging the imam's authority by providing alternative religious interpretations and an aspiration for personal piety by removing 'sins' and 'impurity' from society. *Purity* in this instance is the purity of the correct religious beliefs and of religious authority according to the accuser and his supporters. Alternative interpretations of religion are a norm among lay people in Pakistan, as discussed earlier. However, Marium was a woman and her claim to religious authority represented a challenge and hence an impurity for the existing hierarchy. By punishing her transgression, the imam reasserted the ideal moral order of society according to him, and also established the purity of his own self. This is how blasphemy accusations grant social legitimacy to the accusers' endeavour to punish perceived transgressions, whether they are of social, moral or religious codes of conduct or the established hierarchy. Blasphemy accusations, hence, hold dual symbolic power: the power to legitimise violent action against one's rivals or those considered transgressive, and the power to grant social legitimacy, moral authority and a licence of spiritual purity to the accusers.

The second case is that of Sara, a young Christian woman from a poor family. It had rained heavily all morning one hot and humid day in the early monsoon when I met Sara and her family. I travelled by car to her small town, some 200 kilometres from Lahore. Sara's brother came to a mutually agreed landmark in the town to receive me so that he could direct me to their home. He was riding his Honda CD70 motorbike and told me that I would have to leave the car at a certain point beyond which the streets were too narrow for any vehicle except bicycles or slim motorbikes to get through. He led the way to a market area close to his neighbourhood where my car could be parked. We then entered a convoluted area of extremely narrow streets; I gave up after a few turns trying to memorise the route to be able to find my way back. The streets were paved but had open sewerage pipes running along both sides. The rain had made the mud and garbage mixture on the streets slippery. Despite that, there were tens of children of all ages, some barefooted, and a few little ones even bare-bottomed, playing on the streets. They all stared as we passed—Sara's brother on his bike, at a speed less than 5 km/h, and me walking carefully behind him to avoid slipping off the slimy path. We passed a mosque and a church—within a few hundred metres of each other—as we made our way to Sara's house.

The neighbourhood was inhabited by both Christian and Muslim working-class families. While there was some spatial segregation, as some of the streets were occupied by Christians or Muslims only, the residents interacted with each other regardless of their faith. There were certain limitations to those interactions, as in other parts of Pakistan—for example, Muslims do not eat at Christians' homes and there is no intermarriage. Everyday interactions include trade, the provision of services and even attending weddings and funerals of people from the other community. Rubi, a middle-aged Muslim woman who lived a few metres from the neighbourhood mosque and had good relations with the local imam's family (who lived next to the mosque), used to sew clothes for women in the neighbourhood. Sara's Christian family had been her customers for several years. Rubi was the one who accused Sara of blasphemy, when on her visit to Sara's house she saw some political banners with the names and pictures of politicians spread on the floor. She accused Sara of having insulted the Islamic names (of the politicians) and their beards (a symbol associated with the Prophet) printed on the banners by using them as floor mats. Rubi reported this to the imam of the mosque, who gathered a crowd of men and boys from the village and incited them to attack Sara and her family.

Sara's family had been living in that neighbourhood for 35 years. Rubi and her family, the imam and a majority of those who gathered to set Sara and her family on fire had also been living in the same neighbourhood for decades. The two families interacted with each other regularly, but their relations and interactions were the very basis of conflict. Rubi's sister-in-law had eloped with one of Sara's cousins. While they had both returned to the community and denied the elopement, no-one in the neighbourhood believed them. Regardless of whether it was merely a rumour or the truth, there were several perceived transgressions within that scandal: a Muslim woman eloped, the man she eloped with was a Christian and they returned to the community without acknowledging any guilt or responsibility.

The first retribution was against the man who had dared to commit such a transgression. All I heard from different people was that 'he could not stay in the neighbourhood anymore'. No-one said what would have been the consequence of him coming back to stay in the neighbourhood, but as has happened in other similar cases, he could have been killed by the woman's family. However, the transgression did not stop there, as the man stealthily returned to the neighbourhood for his father's funeral and stayed with Sara's family. Since it is hard to keep secrets in such a closely linked community, some people in the neighbourhood found out about this visit. This rumour upset Rubi's family and created friction with Sara's family. Rubi made the blasphemy allegations against Sara soon after this. Hence, in this case, while the violation was not essentially religious in nature, it was transgressive enough, and was seen as polluting and corrupting—an effect that had to be undone by active reinforcement of purity.

Similarly, in another case, Nadir, a Christian man, had an affair with a Muslim woman in his village. His brother told me that their relationship had been going on for about 15 years and was a constant concern for the village. The imam of the village's mosque, along with other Muslims, tried to convert Nadir to Islam a few times. They asked him several times to convert and marry the Muslim woman, to which he did not accede. The imam tried implicating him in false police cases related to the sale of alcohol, but he managed to evade the charges. Eventually, when he would not concede to any offence, he was accused of blasphemy by his Muslim friend Aslam. People from their village told me that Nadir and Aslam had known each other for years and were often seen together. Aslam accused Nadir of sending blasphemous text messages to his phone. They had been hanging out together even the night before the accusation. In this instance, the whole case may be a conspiracy against Nadir, triggered by the perceived transgression on Nadir's part and his defiance of all disciplining methods employed by the community. He was thus perceived not simply as an impurity himself, but also as an ongoing threat and danger to the purity of the society.

Sara's and Nadir's religious identity as Christians is key to understanding the perceived transgressions in both cases. In cases of accusations made against Christians, I suggest that the physical impurity embedded in South Asian understandings of caste is central to the perception of transgressions. I have written elsewhere about perceptions of local Christians as being filthy—polluted as well as polluting—bodies, and the physical and spatial segregation between Muslims and Christians in Pakistan (Ashraf 2018: 59).

Most Christians in Pakistan belong to lower socioeconomic strata and are relegated to menial, 'dirty' jobs: cleaning toilets, removing animal dung, collecting garbage and so on. The physical segregation of Muslims and Christians ranges from the existence of specific Christian 'colonies' in the residential landscape to the use of separate utensils and crockery for eating and drinking. The treatment of non-Muslims as a 'threat to the health and purity of Muslims' has been documented in premodern Muslim societies as well (Emon 2012: 133). For example, non-Muslims were required to distinguish themselves from Muslims when attending communal baths so that they could not 'pollute the water unbeknownst to the Muslims therein' (Emon 2012: 133).

In present-day Pakistan, however, Christians are considered more polluting than other non-Muslim minorities such as Sikhs. They are treated with exceptional disgust due to a combination of factors, including their usually darker skin colour and their lower socioeconomic status compared with other religious minorities. The treatment of Christians as 'untouchables' can also be attributed to the persistence of 'caste ideology' with its inherent ideas of bodily purity and impurity (Fuller 1976: 68). Christians in Pakistan are believed to have converted from lower castes of Hindus, and continuing discrimination against similar groups of converts has been documented as the residue of the Hindu caste system (Dumont 1980: 203; Mosse 1996). While Pakistan's Christians are a religious minority, they are also categorised as a caste group in official documents. In fact, the police reports and court documents that I studied identified 'Christianity' as a *zaat* ('caste') rather than a religion. Thus, Christians are considered dually inferior in the social hierarchy, as a religious minority and as a lower-caste group.

Christians can thus transgress the social hierarchies and moral codes of conduct in both these domains: religion and the caste-based social hierarchy.[1] In practice, however, the boundaries between religion and caste are not fixed and thus physical transgressions in the non-religious domain can also be framed as religious transgressions and punished accordingly. In the cases of Sara and Nadir, for example, the transgressions

---

1   I have discussed other examples of blasphemy accusations against Christians based on caste-based ideals of purity elsewhere (Ashraf 2018). Such examples include accusations following a Christian woman drinking from a Muslim woman's cup, Christians spreading decorative sheets featuring Quranic verses on one of their saint's graves and a Christian woman returning the 'polluted' butter she had bought from a Muslim woman. I came across many other examples during my fieldwork in which improper physical contact with Christians led to accusations of blasphemy.

were physical and sexual in nature—even though Sara was substituted for the initial transgressor. Therefore, under threat were not only the ideals of purity based on social hierarchy and caste ideology but also the ideals of sexual purity, which are associated with honour. Das (1996: 62) argued in the context of Indian Punjab that 'two values, purity and pollution on the one hand, and honour and shame on the other, are particularly important for the regulation of sexuality' in Punjabi society. Pakistani Punjab shares the same cultural values: purity and pollution, honour and shame. Physical transgressions of the social and sexual boundaries are thus extremely offensive in themselves and the religious identity of Sara and Nadir as Christians added to that intensity. Hence, the accusations of blasphemy against Sara (in the absence of the man who was the real transgressor) and Nadir were a symbolic response to perceived acts of transgression of the social hierarchy, of the ideals of sexual purity and of religious boundaries—all at the same time.

In the case of Christians, therefore, caste ideology becomes a distinct factor in determining purity, impurity and transgression in social interactions. However, the types of transgressions seen as blasphemous are considered a form of impurity even in relation to Muslims. Interestingly, the ideals of sexual purity are invoked to prove the impurity of the accused even when the accused is a Muslim. A common belief repeated to me by supporters of blasphemy-related violence, from laymen to clerics and lawyers, was that 'whoever commits blasphemy does so because they are literally bastards; it had been forewarned by the Prophet himself that anyone who commits blasphemy would reveal his questionable ancestry'.

One of these people said to me with unshakeable conviction:

> You can use modern science to determine the truth of the Prophet's saying. Go and test the DNA of any of the blasphemers and you will find that they were illegitimate children, impure by birth.

By calling blasphemers 'illegitimate children', the accusers are questioning the moral character—linked to sexual purity—of their mothers rather than the moral character of their fathers. Thus, it is women whose character determines whether one is pure or impure. Das (2007: 112) remarked in the context of Sikh militant discourses in India that 'the concern with establishing "pure ancestry" with the accompanying doubts about illegitimacy and true paternity are male doubts'. She argued that such an imagining of purity revealed that the community being constructed was a 'masculine nation' (Das 2007: 113). The tendency to question the ancestry of alleged blasphemers demonstrates that the purity discourses invoked in accusations of blasphemy are also embedded within a masculine and patriarchal imagining of the nation. The fact that masculine ideals of sexual purity are conjured in relation to Christians, Muslims and other groups also suggests that patriarchal notions of purity are widely applicable to Pakistani society. In addition to questioning the ancestry of the accused, the accusers and their supporters often also highlight the 'sexual impurity' of the accused in terms of *zina* ('illegitimate sexual relations'). In a high-profile case of blasphemy by a woman, I was told by those who supported the death penalty for her that 'she was sleeping with her sister's husband' before she was accused of blasphemy.

While the use of sexually insulting words against those one disapproves of is common in most cultures around the world, the strong association between being blasphemous and being sexually impure—through deviant sexual conduct or by virtue of being born to a sexually impure mother—is of curious concern here. The offence of blasphemy and the offence of sexual transgression (or sexual impurity) appear to reaffirm each other. One is likely to be accused of being a blasphemer when one transgresses norms of sexual conduct (violates women), and a blasphemer is deemed inherently sexually impure. It appears to be a circular argument where the offence itself is used as evidence of its commission. However, it is significant as it offers us insights into two important arenas of thought: the moral values that are central to the culture and the power of language. As far as moral values are concerned, I have already argued for the centrality of the value of purity in the lives of Pakistani Muslims, and more generally in South Asia. The emphasis on sexual purity is also a reflection of strongly patriarchal concerns for control over sexuality in both the South Asian and Islamic ideals to which South Asian Muslims ascribe. More important here, I argue, is the power of language as a 'social performative' through which social identities are called into being (Pennycook 2004: 14). The use of words is not merely to signify something, but also to *do* something. Hence, by asserting that a blasphemer is sexually impure, a socially sanctioned identity is called into being. The performative function of the language is thus 'the discursive constitution of the subject as inextricable from the social constitution of the subject' (Butler 1999: 120). The sanctions of sexual and religious impurity corroborate each other to construct the social identity of an alleged blasphemer. It can therefore be argued that moral sanctions are superimposed on one another to effectively and definitively dismiss what is perceived to be transgressive or impure in society.

The final example I want to discuss is the case of an Ahmadi man named Rashid. He was in a relationship with a Muslim woman, Nida, whom he met at an after-school academy they both attended. They had been talking to each other for about two years and had developed feelings for each other. Rashid wanted to marry Nida and sent a marriage proposal to her family. Nida's mother was doubtful about whether Nida already knew Rashid, so she asked Nida to tell her everything about their relationship. It was then that Nida told her mother that Rashid was from an Ahmadi family but had 'converted to Islam in front of her'. Nida's mother was suspicious and told Nida not to trust Rashid because 'Ahmadis lie about being Muslims'. Nida did not have any doubts about Rashid's sincerity, so she was devastated to hear her mother's judgement. When Nida continued to insist on marrying Rashid, her mother took her to a religious scholar for an 'expert opinion' on the matter. The religious scholar, who was friends with one of the lawyers with whom I was meeting regularly for my research, invited the lawyer along to one of his meetings with the mother and the daughter. The lawyer, who supported punishment for blasphemy, invited me as well. Thus, I met Nida and her mother in the presence of the legal and religious experts on the matter.

Nida's mother told me how her daughter had been deceived and led astray by Rashid. She told me that she was very thankful to Allah that she found out the truth in time and brought Nida to meet the religious scholars, who told her 'the realities of the Ahmadis'. She claimed that her initiative and the religious guidance from the scholar had dissuaded Nida from 'following a crooked man to hell'. She claimed that her daughter was now much safer. Tears rolled down Nida's cheeks as she nodded and said:

> It is hard for me. I believed in Rashid and had developed a strong emotional attachment with him. But I guess my mother is right. I guess it is all in my better interest. After all, I do not want my kids to be born in a false religion. Maybe it is all good for the purity of my own faith. But it is very hard to accept at this time. I have started praying regularly to deal with the trauma. Allah will help me. I will be better soon.

Later, there was a suggestion by someone in the room that Rashid had 'posed' as a Muslim, which is a crime (according to Pakistani law) and a serious transgression that should be punished. They contemplated how best to make Rashid pay for his crime. Everyone in the room tried to convince Nida to lodge a formal complaint against Rashid to ensure that he did not fool any other Muslims. I did not meet them again due to some unexpected developments in my fieldwork, so I do not know whether they followed through with the complaint. But what I witnessed was a blasphemy accusation in the making. In this case, the main concerns were the purity of the nation and the purity of their faith.

In the cases of accusations against Ahmadis, the theme of deception forms a key concern in perceptions of purity and transgression thereof. Appadurai (1998: 234) pointed out the 'tropes of deception, treachery, betrayal, imposture, and secrecy' that are sources of 'cognitive paranoia' about the identity of the enemy. He suggests that fear of deception, linked to uncertainty about the identity of the other, is inherently also linked to the desire to achieve and maintain the purity of society (Appadurai 1998: 236). Deception is thus an impurity that is considered an even more dangerous transgression by the very virtue of its indistinguishability from the pure. Therefore, Ahmadis, for most Pakistani Muslims, are transgressive by the very fact of their 'hidden' identity because they claim to be Muslims. The possibility of the corruption of society is thus seen as materialising in the very existence of the Ahmadis. Hence, the purity of the nation (based on the religious identity of Muslims) is at stake in instances of blasphemy accusations against Ahmadis.

Through different examples of blasphemy accusations in this section, I have highlighted various underlying ideals of purity—of religious belief, authority, caste, sexual behaviour, women, ancestry, nation and of the self—the transgression of which may trigger accusations of blasphemy. The cases have shown that, despite the frequent instrumental use of blasphemy accusations against one's rivals, the explanation for these accusations cannot be reduced to instrumentality. In most instances, the accusations are driven by personal vengeance as well as underlying concerns about the purity of conceptual categories. The notions of purity are based on social hierarchies and boundaries—not only of religious identity but also of caste and other systems of stratification. Depending on the context of the case, various ideals of purity and respective moral sanctions can be superimposed on to each other to effectively discipline the transgressors. The transgressions or violations committed by an individual are often seen as transgressions against the community and the moral order of the whole society. In many cases, those 'violated' (for example, Rubi's sister-in-law or Nadir's Muslim girlfriend) do not perceive the violation as such; rather, the defenders of society—imams or other men—are the ones who step in to determine the transgression and punish it. Thus, transgressions arise within interpersonal relationships but are then transformed into acts of communal and national shame.

The accused: Familiarity and the enemy within

Prior familiarity between the accused and the accuser(s) is a common characteristic of most blasphemy accusations in Pakistan. The cases I have discussed so far involved people who already knew each other and had an ongoing interactional relationship. The accuser(s) and the accused can be neighbours, colleagues, linked through trade and/or exchange relationships and sometimes even friends. Violence among neighbours and familiars is not a unique or new phenomenon. Some of the most violent moments in the recent history of humanity have seen 'familiar' people turning against each other (for example, in Poland during the Holocaust[2] and in Punjab and Bengal at the time of Partition of the Indian Subcontinent). Studies of witchcraft accusations in modern-day Indonesia have also highlighted the 'familiarity' of the accused as a significant factor contributing to the phenomenon. Herriman (2006: 363) writes about witchcraft being a primarily local phenomenon in which neighbours accuse each other and the whole village then violently purges the accused. Siegel, in his book *Naming the Witch* (2006: 188), argues that the uncanny other (the witch) emerges from the familiar. In his large-scale comparative study of communal violence in societies, Tambiah (1996: 276) contended that:

> assailants and victims are frequently not strangers to one another. They have been 'neighbors' in the loose sense of having lived in the same towns, or resided intermixed or side by side.

Similarly, Appadurai (1998: 238) showed through various examples 'the transformation of neighbours and friends into monsters' as a common feature of ethnic violence. He argued that it was because of the 'uncertainty' and 'cognitive paranoia' associated with those *others* within the community that they were pinned down as 'the enemy within' (Appadurai 1998: 234).

Žižek, in his 'Neighbors and Other Monsters' (2006), also showed how neighbours and other familiar people occupy an ambivalent and uncertain place in society. He identified a spectrum of otherness that ranges from: 1) the other, as in 'other humans like me'; 2) the other as the symbolic 'Big

---

2 As Gross (2001) demonstrated in his groundbreaking study of Jedwabne, Poland.

Other'³—that is, the rules of our social coexistence; to 3) the 'Other qua Real', the 'impossible thing, the inhuman partner, the other with whom no symmetrical dialogue mediated by the Symbolic order is possible' (Žižek 2013: 143). He argued that in the image of the neighbour as 'the other like me' always lurks the other extreme: the unfathomable, monster, radical Other (Žižek 2013). Hence, the people who are known and familiar but occupy the position of the non-specific 'other' are the ones who can be transformed into the 'absolute other', against whom violence is then justified. It is the very quality of familiarity that implies some degree of 'sameness' due to which the enemy within must be forcibly expelled and objectified as 'the total other' (Tambiah 1996: 276). In so doing, the 'difference' with the enemy, or the transgressions that turn them into the enemy, must be exaggerated to an extent that the 'other' is 'degraded, dehumanized, and compulsively obliterated' (Tambiah 1996: 276).

In the case of blasphemy accusations in Pakistan, I argue that familiarity is significant because it informs the perceptions of the character of the accused in the minds of the accusers. These perceptions are not pieces of neutral or benign information; rather, they impact on the likelihood of being 'offended' by the words/actions of the person in question. They shape and impact on how a person's certain actions and behaviours are received and the reactions they generate. My broad survey of blasphemy cases—both officially registered and unofficial rumours leading to violence—reveals that blasphemy accusations overwhelmingly take place in physical and social spaces with identifiable characteristics. The physical space can be a neighbourhood, village, mosque, school, workplace or market. However, in most of the cases, these spaces are inhabited by people from lower socioeconomic strata, with highly cohesive social networks, unlike those in affluent urban areas. These are the areas where social policing of individuals and families is generally very high, whether it is the clothing choices made by one's neighbours or colleagues, the company one keeps, the food one eats or the social interactions in which one engages. There are indirect ways of controlling people's behaviour, such as gossip and reputation-based social relations, as well as direct ways such as accountability to local moral authorities (religious clerics, elder men of the community or other influential members) or the mob. Such

---

3   The symbolic 'Big Other' is 'the "substance" of our social existence, the impersonal set of rules that coordinate our coexistence' (Žižek 2013: 143).

close monitoring of social behaviour sets these places apart from more affluent and urbanised areas where social policing (along with communal solidarity) has been in decline in recent decades.

Hence, in most cases of blasphemy accusations, people are generally familiar with one another's social identity, behaviour, family background and networks. This familiarity means that those with lesser power in social relations are more likely to be accused. The accusers make accusations when they *know* they can mobilise support against the person they are accusing. Moreover, familiarity means that the accusers know which parts of the accused's identity and behaviour can be marked as transgressive to mobilise support against them. The accusers in most incidents of blasphemy accusations are not only familiar with the names and faces of the accused beforehand, but also target major markers of their social identity (for example, Christian, Muslim, Shia, Ahmadi, liberal, secular, Deobandi, Sunni) and personal conduct. It is this information that determines what will be deemed offensive and transgressive. For example, in his iconic statement before the court after killing Salman Taseer, the Governor of Punjab, Mumtaz Qadri proclaimed:

> The personal life of Salman Taseer shows that right from early times he proved himself as an infidel. He married three times. One of his wives was 'Sikh' by religion. He arranged his so-called marriage in a secret way with that lady in New Delhi in India. His lifestyle, faith and living with a lady of non-Muslim faith, reflecting his act of living in constant state of *Zina* ['adultery'] under the pretext of marriage [which is not permissible in Islam] speak volumes about his character and associated matters.[4]

While Qadri did not know Taseer on a personal level, he had been working as Taseer's bodyguard. Moreover, this is a rather exceptional case because Taseer was a public personality and his personal traits were well-known, as was his vocal stance against the blasphemy laws. In addition, he was seen to represent the lifestyle and political position of the Westernised elite—a whole subsection of Pakistani society. Thus, in this case, the general vilification of the alleged blasphemer's character becomes a magnified symbolic act. In many other cases, familiarity with the 'character' of the accused can determine whether the accusation even occurs. Asad and Zain, the accusers in another case of blasphemy against

---

4   *Malik Muhammad Mumtaz Qadri vs The State* (2015) Criminal Appeals No. 210 and 211 of 2015, Supreme Court Islamabad: 6.

a Christian man with whom they used to work, told me that the accused was training to be a pastor. They asserted that he used to study the Bible and other religious texts of Christianity, and thus they merely expected he would insult one of the Islamic books (a publication by a local religious leader) that belonged to the accuser. In yet another case, a man who accused one of his neighbours, a Muslim woman, of blasphemy, said to me in an interview:

> Have you looked at the way she dresses? She wears jeans and goes around with open hair and so much make-up on her face. Can you expect people like her to respect our religion? She was always unobservant of Islam and one day crossed the limits.

Thus, we see the familiarity of the accusers with the accused is of immense significance in determining the 'offence' or 'violation' that leads to an accusation of blasphemy. However, it is not *just* that familiarity that leads to blasphemy accusations; it is also a transgression through which the familiar others cross the prescribed limits of the given relationships. In other words, it is proximity and a delicate balance of intimacy in those relationships that may tip one from being a familiar other to the 'absolute Other'—the enemy who has crept in and, by so doing, transgressed the normal order of things.

The *other* is an existential issue for the one who, in constructing the *other*, identifies and legitimises the *self*. The *others* thus created are 'containers of one's disavowed aspects' (Kakar 1990: 137). The disavowed aspects are 'unacceptable, condemned parts of the self' that are 'projected outside' (Kakar 1990: 137). The *other*, in this sense, 'is a transgressor of deeply-held taboos' (Kakar 1990: 138). In pointing out the *other* as the enemy, the *self* substitutes 'the enemy one harbors within oneself' (Tambiah 1996: 277). One's personal piety cannot be questioned if one accuses someone else of being impure. One's authority must be pure and legitimate if one calls those who question it impure. A similar argument is made by Siegel (2006) with regard to witchcraft accusations in Indonesia. He suggested that the fear that anyone—including one's own self—could be a 'witch' is what drives people to find the 'witch' in others. He writes:

> The witch is always a dual personality. One can say that the witch is the other of the self as it goes ordinarily unexpressed. Precisely for this reason, he is unacceptable. Witchcraft is the 'proof', when the possibility is pressing, that one cannot take the place of the other.

> That one is not oneself what one accuses the other to be; one is not him and one cannot find oneself in his place. Once the witch is expelled, the world works again as it should. (Siegel 2006: 203)

Thus, it is the possibility of the impurity of the self that leads to pointing out transgressors of symbolic boundaries and social hierarchies as *others* outside the *self*. While individuals accuse one another of blasphemy, driven by individual concerns for piety and purity, the figure of the blasphemer represents more than an individual. Even though accusations are made against specific individuals, those individuals symbolise something greater than themselves: the sin, the impure, the undesirable difference, the unacceptable change in society. The accused are thus chosen either from the margins of the society or from those who transgress the conceived boundaries within that society. They are familiar but not known, they are the ones who can be condemned and dismissed as killable bodies—'bare life'—with the sanction and support of the community (Agamben 1998). As Siegel (2006: 137) suggested, the witch is, 'underneath his appearance as neighbour, the embodiment of a foreign force'. Blasphemers, similarly, are the face of the haunting evil and the impure in the individual and collective identities that are steeped in moral anxiety, as we saw earlier. It is the abstract speculative evil that is bigger than their individual experiences of evil and sin around them. Hence, blasphemy accusations can also be called an 'attempt to give the uncanny a face' (Siegel 2006: 147).

Conclusion

Blasphemy accusations in Pakistan take place within everyday interpersonal interactions between people already known to each other. The accusations are a manifestation of existing tensions and hierarchies within these relationships. They are triggered by perceived transgressions of symbolic boundaries and the moral order of society. The motivations behind such accusations are neither purely religious nor entirely instrumental in nature. They are embedded in local power structures and ideals of purity based on various religious and cultural moral frameworks. The accused are the expendable familiar others against whom power and support can be mobilised. Once accused, they become the face of the uncanny evil and sin in society.

At a structural level, accusations of blasphemy are also a result of complicated, interconnected social, political and historical processes. In the previous chapters, I have highlighted the conception of the 'idea of Pakistan' as a qualitative change in the course of historical events that continues to impact how the self, the community and the other are understood and constructed in Pakistan. Moreover, the reformist movements within South Asian Islam, in response to British colonisation, shaped not only the movements for Pakistan, but also the public religiosity of Pakistani Muslims. While these movements began with various groups of elite Muslim scholars who were influenced by modernity's ideals of individual responsibility and who were aspiring to return to the assumed purity of an idealised bygone era, they have come to increasingly shape the religious sensibilities of ordinary Muslims in Pakistan. Nevertheless, despite the undeniable significance of the historical contingencies and the role of the state of Pakistan in enabling the issue of blasphemy to become a destructive force in society, the aim of this chapter has been to demonstrate how the larger religious and political trends are acted out by people at the local level.

Thus, notwithstanding the institutionalisation of the ideals of piety, purity and exclusivity by the state of Pakistan, and the popularisation of absolutist religious discourse, this chapter has shown 'the ways in which the conceptual boundaries of the state are extended and remade' in the everyday lives of its citizens (Das and Poole 2004: 20). However, as Das and Poole (2004: 22) warned, everyday lives or 'local worlds' do not stand in binary opposition to the state; rather, they are enmeshed with the state. I see this correlation in terms of what Foucault (1982: 785) called the 'political "double bind", which is the simultaneous individualization and totalization of modern power structures'. It means that the exclusivist tendencies driving the need for purification are simultaneously ingrained in individual lives and state structures; it is not simply a top-down application of power. Instead, ordinary people also have the power to shape what will then become the focal point for mobilisation to agents vying for power in the political sphere. My account of blasphemy accusations with an emphasis on the microlevel relationships between the accused and the accuser(s) demonstrates how 'the state is continually formed in the recesses of everyday life' (Das and Poole 2004: 23). It is not merely the conception of the idea of Pakistan as 'the land of the pure' that enables the use of blasphemy accusations as a mechanism of purification in society. The practice of the same at the local level also contests and continually redraws the metaphorical borders of 'the land of the pure'.

4
Violence in the making: The politics of escalation from accusation to punishment

News such as that of the lynching of Mashal Khan in April 2017, the burning of Christian couple Shama and Shahzad in November 2014, the torching of the Christian neighbourhood of Joseph Colony in March 2013 and other incidents of 'mob violence' following blasphemy accusations make headlines, invoking shock and horror among humanitarian circles both nationally and internationally. However, we rarely get to hear how the accusations of blasphemy led to the violence. What happened between the accusation and the punishment? As discussed in the previous chapter, an accusation is usually made within microlevel interpersonal relationships. In this chapter, I will demonstrate how interpersonal conflicts—already intensified by blasphemy accusations—are transformed into collective violence. Not all blasphemy accusations lead to collective violence, but when they do, that violence can differ based on the identity of the accused. When the accused is a Muslim, as in the case of Mashal Khan, the collective violence is targeted at the individual. When the accused is a non-Muslim, there is a potential for collective violence to take the form of communal violence in which the whole community or neighbourhood of the accused is targeted. In both scenarios, there is an escalation of the conflict from the interpersonal to the collective, and from a single incident to a communal concern. I argue that blasphemy accusations do not inevitably lead to violence; rather, various factors and individuals come together in the process of escalation to *make* the violence possible.

The potential for conflict is embedded within interpersonal relationships in the form of ideals of purity and hierarchy, the transgression of which may lead to violence. Blasphemy accusations are often a response to a culmination of factors that are seen as impurities and challenges to the existing moral order of society. Veena Das (1990: 14) argued that, for the:

> diffused hostilities to translate themselves into violent conflict, a contiguity has to be established between specific, concrete, and local issues on the one hand, and a master symbol on the other, in terms of which the conflict is viewed in the public consciousness.

In the case of blasphemy accusations, the 'master symbol' is created in the very moment a transgression is framed as blasphemy. Face-to-face relations are thus stripped of 'the concreteness of relationships' and replaced with 'imagined identities' within the instance of the accusation (Das and Kleinman 2000: 9). The escalation that follows further sharpens the symbolism and generalisation since the crowds are concerned not with the nature and details of the original offence but with the symbolic figure of the blasphemer. While the accusations are driven by individual concern for power and purity, they are quickly turned into a communal urge to remove the threat of impurity to achieve the idealised 'pure' society. Stanley J. Tambiah (1996: 192), in his work on collective violence, proposed the concepts of focalisation and transvaluation to understand the process of escalation. Focalisation is 'the process of progressive denudation of local incidents and disputes of their particulars of context and their aggregation' and transvaluation is 'the parallel process of assimilating particulars to a larger, collective, more enduring, and therefore less context-bound, cause or interest' (Tambiah 1996: 192). The processes of *focalisation* and *transvaluation* are crucial to the *making* of collective violence against those accused of blasphemy in Pakistan.

I call it the *making* of collective violence because a blasphemy accusation—despite all the symbolism attached to it—does not automatically lead to collective violence. In fact, the journey from accusation to punishment may take several courses, depending on the circumstances and the inclinations of those who become involved in the situation. The accusation may lead to invocation of state laws against the accused, nonstate violence or both. In rare cases, the charges may be dropped and a resolution reached without any serious punishment. I argue that the outcome of the conflict—the form of punishment delivered—is determined by various *actors* who are involved at different stages of the conflict. Das and Kleinman (2001: 2) emphasised the significance of:

> the entanglement of various social actors, ranging from global institutions to modern states on the one hand and small local communities inhabiting [an] increasingly uncertain world on the other, in the production and authorization of collective violence.

Having discussed the role of the state earlier, in this chapter, I focus on the local-level actors such as police officers, imams and religious leaders, politicians, local government representatives, NGOs, activists and journalists. Through an emphasis on the role of the actors who are involved in the *production* and *making* of the violence, I argue that the course of action chosen after an accusation of blasphemy is not entirely arbitrary. Nor is collective violence—when it happens—a *sudden* outburst or eruption of emotionally charged crowds. At every step of the process, the individuals involved have a range of choices available to them and it is through the successive culmination of those *choices* that violence becomes possible.

Some of these actors, such as local imams and other religious leaders, play the most vital role in the 'authorisation of collective violence'. They are 'propagandists'—key to the process of escalation—'who appeal to larger, more emotive, more enduring (and therefore less context-bound) loyalties and cleavages' such as those of religion and national identity (Tambiah 1996: 192). Paul Brass (2003b: 32–33), in his study of communal violence in India, also identified some key actors who play crucial roles in the orchestration of violence, such as informers, propagandists, recruiters of the mob, rumourmongers, fire-tenders and conversion specialists. Brass (2003b) found 'fire-tenders' and 'conversion specialists' to be of key significance in the making of collective violence. The fire-tenders are those who keep 'the embers of communal animosities alive' and the conversion specialists 'decide when a trivial everyday incident will be exaggerated and placed into the communal system of talk, the communal discourse, and allowed to escalate into communal violence' (Brass 2003b: 32–33). Local imams and religious leaders act as both fire-tenders, through dissemination of absolutist religious discourse, and conversion specialists, by turning a specific incident of transgression into a communal issue and instigating violent emotions among the wider community. Similarly, other actors—particularly the police, government representatives, politicians, NGOs and journalists—play important roles in either constraining or enabling violent action. I will discuss the motivations of these actors and the impact of their choices on the outcome of conflict.

An exclusive focus on the role of actors in the production of violence has been criticised as an instrumentalist approach. One of the strongest critics of this approach, Sudhir Kakar (1996: 151), argued that it:

> underplays or downright denies that there are 'instigatees', too, whose participation is essential to transform animosity between religious groups into violence. The picture it holds up of evil politicians and innocent masses is certainly attractive since it permits us a disavowal of our own impulses toward violence and vicious ethnocentrism … [allowing] a projection of the unacceptable parts of ourselves onto 'bad' politicians.

Blom and Jaoul (2008: 4), in their critique of Brass's theory, also argued that he presented an instrumental approach that ignored the 'popular agency and meanings that are actively involved in the production of communal violence'. They further contended that an exclusive emphasis on how the actors 'manipulate, manage and organize' the feelings and emotions of people understated the role of emotions (Blom and Jaoul 2008: 14). Instead, they argue, emotional and affective aspects are as significant to mobilisation for collective violence as are the cognitive ones (Blom and Jaoul 2008: 13). Not only are people's emotions powerful in their own right, rather than being simply a resource to be 'mobilised' by their leaders, but also the 'entrepreneurs' of violence might themselves have an emotional stake in the issue (Blom and Jaoul 2008: 14). Reason and emotion are therefore mutually constitutive and work together in the production of collective violence.

While the role of actors in the *making* of violence is important, it is equally important to understand that violence is *meaningful* and draws on shared emotional and symbolic repositories. As Das (1990: 28) contended:

> [T]here is no contradiction between the fact that, on the one hand, mob violence may be highly organized … and on the other that crowds draw upon repositories of unconscious images.

Crowds are 'disciplined', 'have clear objectives' and 'are often fighting for the restoration of a moral order' (Das 1990: 27). At the same time, they draw on 'powerful symbolic images' and exhibit 'states of heightened emotion' (Das 1990: 25). Similar arguments have been made by other scholars with regard to the simultaneously organised and passionate nature of crowds in the *making* of collective violence (see, for example, Sidel 2006: 13; Tambiah 1996: 270). Paul Brass—often criticised for his instrumentalist approach—himself acknowledged that instances of collective violence:

> combine objective and intentional factors, spontaneity and planning, chaos and organization. They are best conceived as dramatic productions in which the directors are not in complete control, the cast of characters varies—some of them being paid, some of them acting voluntarily for loot or fun—and many of the parts have been rehearsed, but others have not. (Brass 2003b: 32)

Similarly, according to Horowitz (2001: 12), ethnic and communal violence are a 'bizarre fusion of coherence and frenzy' and 'an amalgam of apparently rational-purposive behaviour and irrational-brutal behaviour' (p. 13). While I disagree with the characterisation of emotional and affective aspects of collective action as representing 'chaos', 'frenzy' or 'irrational-brutal behaviour', and see them instead as manifestations of symbolic structures, it is important to emphasise that collective action is both premeditated and passionate.

Therefore, in understanding the process of escalation that leads from blasphemy accusations to violent nonstate punishment, I employ an integrative approach in which I explain the *organisation* of violence as well as what it *means* to those involved. Violent action against those accused of blasphemy draws on certain repertoires of action, symbolic structures or a 'web of signifiers' (Das 1990: 9) and wider moral narratives. At the same time, various actors exercise their agency and derive their own meanings from the situation once it has turned into a societal and communal issue and, in so doing, they determine the outcome of the conflict. It is the contiguity established through the decisions and actions of various actors that enables violent action to take place. However, it should be kept in mind that individual actors, while exercising their agency, are also limited by the wider structures and religious and national narratives within which they operate (Das and Kleinman 2000: 16–17). Hence, collective violence against those accused of blasphemy is produced within the struggle for collective *as well as* individual identities, economic and political interests and moral concerns.

The process of escalation

In most cases of blasphemy accusations followed by some form of collective mobilisation and/or violence, a rough pattern can be drawn. The events that follow the accusation usually involve the stages identified in Figure 1.

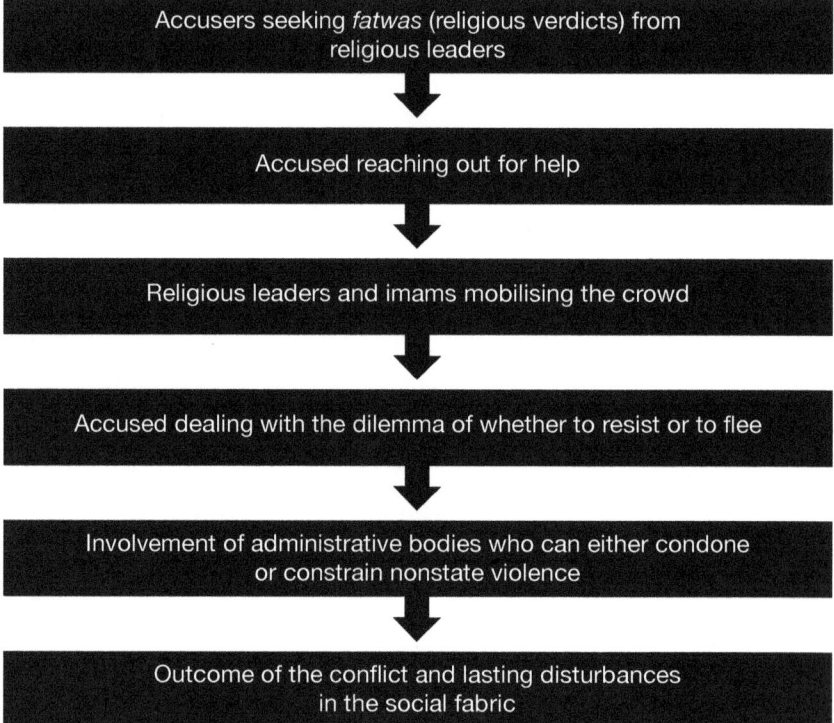

Figure 1. The process of escalation from accusation to punishment
Source: Author.

It is important to stress here that this process, as a complete unit, is not inevitable. As already mentioned in the Introduction, of more than 1,500 cases of accusations between 1987 and 2017, only 75 led to nonstate killings. Some of those nonstate killings were carried out by individuals such as police officers, security guards and other nonstate actors. Thus, the number of times an accusation leads to collective violence is more of an abnormality than a norm, making it even more vital to understand the specific factors that *enable* collective violence in those specific cases. Moreover, there are cases in which mobilisation for violent action occurs, following some of the phases identified in Figure 1, but does not lead to a killing. There may be other forms of damage incurred in those cases, such as looting and burning of property, but violent killing of the accused does not take place. There are also instances in which the primary individual accused manages to escape violence but someone close to them is punished in their place. Even in cases in which the collective action follows through to the violent killing of the accused, there may be an overlap or reversal of order between the stages identified above. Therefore, the process identified in Figure 1 should be seen as fluid and fragmented at best, and the actual form in each case is contingent on the specific context of that case.

Nevertheless, these stages roughly form a repertoire of collective action—a concept first introduced by Charles Tilly (1986: 390). A repertoire of collective action is the usual form taken by an instance of collective violence in the given context. In the case of blasphemy accusations leading to subsequent violence in Pakistan, the above stages have become a common course of action, even though most cases do not go through every stage. Each stage further draws on certain repertoires of action and cultural symbols. Tambiah (1996: 296) presented a rather comprehensive list of sources that may be included in these repertoires:

> The repertoire and capacities that constitute the cultural capital and arsenal from which the component units and phases of collective violence are drawn include the following: the calendar of festivals, the stock of performances, processions, orations, and public protests; stereotyped labelings and rumors, formally recognized insults, triggering actions, and shamings; and the array of communications media (newspapers, posters, television, VCRs, tapes, etc.) available and deployed. All these help shape the swirls, cumulative rhythms, and phased transitions, in the rise and fall of collective violence in public arenas.

Some of the sources—corresponding to the categories identified by Tambiah—commonly drawn on in episodes of violent action following blasphemy accusations include Friday prayers and sermons, mosques and their loudspeakers, mobile phones and social media. The case studies in this chapter will elaborate how these sources are employed. I divide the rest of this chapter into the six phases I have highlighted in Figure 1. Different actors take lead roles in different phases, even though the stages may be occurring simultaneously or in a different order, as already pointed out. While I focus on specific actors at different points in my discussion, it must be kept in mind that several actors may be concurrently active.

The following discussion will demonstrate how contingency between certain actors and their actions at certain points is established in a way that leads to collective violence.

Seeking *fatwas*: Authorisation of violence

In most cases of blasphemy accusations, the immediate step taken by the accuser(s) after they have framed a transgression as blasphemous is to reach out to local imams or religious scholars. Even in the most abrupt-looking instances of collective violence, such as the lynching of Mashal Khan, the accusers approached religious scholars to seek their *fatwa* ('religious verdict') on the matter. The verdicts from the imams or religious scholars affirm that 'the offence' was committed and that it was blasphemous. They also suggest the subsequent courses of action to be taken—whether the case should be reported to the police or the accused killed outside the state legal system. Local imams and religious scholars thus have the authority to legitimise violence against the accused. In almost every case I studied, the accusers had approached religious leaders to prove the legitimacy of the accusation. In a particularly extreme case, the accusers consulted several major religious centres of their sect to seek their verdicts on the matter. In other instances, the opinion of the cleric from the local mosque was considered sufficient to prove that blasphemy had been committed. Nevertheless, some form of religious authority is called on to legitimise violence against the accused. The following two examples will demonstrate how religious scholars were approached by the accusers and the impact their verdicts had on the escalation of the conflict.

Saleem is a poor Christian man who worked as a sweeper at a rural health centre in a small town about 4 kilometres from his home village in central Punjab. He was accused of blasphemy by his co-workers who had allegedly found a video derogatory of the Prophet Muhammad on his phone. He was beaten up by his co-workers from the health centre pharmacy following the accusations, but management dispersed the group. The next day, Saleem returned to his job as usual, hoping that his colleagues' anger had subsided and things would be back to normal. There was very little activity besides the regular work routine, but Shahzad, the prime accuser, who had been the most angry, was suspiciously absent from the scene. On the third day, Saleem went back to the health centre pharmacy and apologised again to the men who worked there. They told him that they had forgiven him but that Shahzad, who was still absent, was very angry with him. They advised him to talk to Shahzad over the phone and ask him for forgiveness.

They dialled Shahzad's number and when Saleem spoke to him, Shahzad told Saleem that he had gone to a nearby town to fetch a *fatwa* from a mufti declaring that Saleem had committed blasphemy and must be killed. Shahzad told Saleem that he would not be spared for his crime. On hearing this, one of the men at the pharmacy advised Saleem to return to his village. He acknowledged that the situation was out of their control with the issuing of the *fatwa*. It should be noted here that while some of Saleem's colleagues were forgiving and willing to help him, it was the uncompromising wrath of one person (Shahzad) that led to further developments in the case. It is important because at most stages of the escalation, all it takes is one person in a certain position of power taking a particular decision to push the conflict in a violent direction. Saleem quit his job and went back to his village but the *fatwa* led to a violent mobilisation against him. Once the *fatwa* was issued stating that Saleem had committed blasphemy, by having an allegedly blasphemous video on his phone, the details and authenticity of the accusation were no longer important. The word that went around was the 'established' claim that Saleem had committed blasphemy and must be killed.

Similarly, in another case, the accuser obtained a *fatwa* from his religious leader and told the accused's apologetic relatives that 'it was too late' for them to seek peaceful resolution. Asad, a Sunni Muslim man, worked as a delivery driver at a glass shop in a busy market area in Lahore. The shop was owned by a Christian man and the accountant at the shop was also a Christian. One day the accountant was absent and his brother, Rahim, who was training to be a pastor, was filling in for him. Asad accused Rahim of writing insulting remarks about the Prophet Muhammad on one of the Islamic books Asad had left in the shop 'to read in his free time'.[1] After the accusation, Asad took the allegedly desecrated book to the Jamaat-ud-Dawa *markaz* ('religious centre') in Township, Lahore, where he was

---

1   There were a few copies of the Bible in the shop. One of the other books present, which belonged to Asad, was an Urdu publication titled *Mainay Bible se poocha Quran kyun jalay* (*I Asked the Bible Why Quran Was Burnt*) by Maulana Amir Hamza, a self-proclaimed religious scholar who is also one of the founders of the banned militant organisation Lashkar-e-Taiba. Asad, along with his Muslim friend Zain, came into the shop and saw Rahim studying Hamza's book alongside a copy of the Bible. Asad claimed that he ignored Rahim, thinking 'he might be interested in learning about Islam and may get inspired to convert'. Asad claimed that the next day he found some comments scribbled in the margins of the book cursing the author of the book, Muslims and the Prophet Muhammad.

a member and visited regularly. His religious leader, 'Hafiz Sahab', as he called him, affirmed that Rahim had committed blasphemy and must be punished. The owner of the shop and Rahim's brother kept calling Asad to persuade him to sit down with them and 'sort the issue out by talking'. They sought forgiveness for Rahim. However, in Asad's words, 'it was too late', as he had already obtained a *fatwa* on the matter, which meant that no compromise was possible. In this instance, the offence was eventually reported to the police and a state trial was initiated. However, before that, the *fatwa* was used to mobilise a crowd that vandalised the shop where Rahim worked and pressured police to arrest Rahim and register a case against him.

In both cases, the *fatwa* legitimised the punishment of the accused regardless of the state court's verdict. Blom and Jaoul (2008: 9), adopting French author Jeanne Favret-Saada's concept, asserted that the 'mechanism' of an outrage involves three parties: 'someone who denounces', 'a referent denounced as "outraging"' and 'a given authority called upon to intervene'. The fact that local imams and religious scholars are often approached *before* the police or any other governmental authority suggests that they have as much, if not more, authority as the state to legitimise violence. Religious scholars may refer the case to police or become complainants themselves, but the fact they are sought as an authority on the matter is important. It shows that, for the accusers and their supporters, the state of Pakistan, its laws and law enforcement bodies are not the only—or even primary—sources of authority. In cases of blasphemy accusations, religious scholars have the power to stamp legitimacy on the accusations and any subsequent violence. The religious scholars approached for *fatwas* have the power to direct the conflict towards either state or nonstate punishment, a violent or a peaceful solution.

Moreover, as Fox (2000: 15) suggested, the 'clergy and other religious elites' are 'the most visible and authoritative arbiters of religious legitimacy' as they can grant 'the aura of religious legitimacy' to even the most secular of conflicts. Through their *fatwas*, imams and religious scholars strip away the mundane details of the perceived transgressions, which may not always be religious in nature, and establish the accusations as definitively religious offences. This is a major step in escalation, as it sets the processes of focalisation and transvaluation into motion with great force. Once a *fatwa* has been issued, the word that circulates is void of the interpersonal contextual details of the accusation. It is a rumour in Das's sense of the term insofar as its 'form of language, its force, its lack of signature' and 'its appeals to the uncanny' are concerned (1998: 125). It creates the figure of a blasphemer, the *Other*, who must be punished to purify the society.

Reaching out for help: Opportunism and mistrust

As soon as the accused realise that they will not receive forgiveness for their perceived crime, they turn to their neighbours, family, religious community, NGOs and sometimes the police for help. These relationships are, however, rife with various tensions and mistrust. When Shahzad told Saleem that he had attained a *fatwa* according to which he must be killed, Saleem went back to his village and shared his story with Daniyal, his neighbour and friend. Daniyal, a security guard by profession and a socially active man in his Christian neighbourhood, was the head of the local church committee. I met him two months after the incident, when he was himself living in hiding because he had enraged the accuser and the Muslim community by helping Saleem. He recollected his response on hearing about the blasphemy accusation against Saleem:

> Our Christian community is generally not organised, and we do not have any formal way to consult each other. Due to lack of proper organisation, I had taken the initiative and brought a few young men from our community together to form a small church committee. I was the president of that committee and we operated under the church of the nearest urban centre.[2] But the priests and fathers in the church are very weak. They are either cowards or work for their own interests. They do not stand for the Christian community. I called the father in our church, but he told me not to get involved with the matter [the blasphemy accusation] in any way. He suggested not to help Saleem or his family and to stay away from them; he said: 'Don't go to his house even if the Muslims kill him.'

While Daniyal was worried for his friend Saleem, he was extremely disappointed in the church and his religious leaders. He went on:

> See, we are common people, but the fathers always wear the robes of piety and spirituality, regardless of which they are so self-serving. I told the father that I will help Saleem because he is a part of my community. I said to him that he can keep his

---

2   Name of the city intentionally removed from the account.

> 'fathership' to himself; I will do my duty. I also knew the father in another town where my brother-in-law lives. I decided to contact Father Anthony from my brother-in-law's city. I went to see Father Anthony along with three other men from our Christian community. I was aware that Father Anthony was also not to be trusted as we had had troubles with him in the past. We see the fathers as a shadow of Jesus, but they have absolutely none of the qualities of Jesus Christ. They are an embodiment of Satan instead. Even Muslim clerics are better than the Christian priests. They are selfish and greedy. Father Anthony agreed to give shelter to Saleem but later it turned out that he was also working in his own interests. He wanted to 'sell' the issue and make money off it. He thought he would present Saleem as a victim and receive money from church organisations outside Pakistan.

The expression of disappointment with the local Christian priests remained an important part of my subsequent conversations with Daniyal. He felt deceived and betrayed by his own people—the people of the same faith who, in his view, were supposed to look after each other. Daniyal's sentiments reflect the unravelling of the true nature of social relations, described as a key characteristic of social crises by Turner. Turner (1980: 151) suggested, 'in social dramas, false friendship is winnowed from true communality of interests; the limits of consensus are reached and realized; real power emerges from behind the facade of authority'. While the crisis unearths the true loyalties (or absence thereof) of specific individuals, the underlying tensions in social relations are already present in the form of widespread mistrust and conspiracy theories among the people. Every incident strengthens these widespread fears and perceptions, but the disappointment of individuals in each situation is unique to their subjective experiences.

Feelings of mistrust were expressed by my other Christian participants as well, who blamed the Christian clergy, whom they looked up to, of being self-interested and cowardly. However, it was not only the priests and other religious leaders whom they mistrusted; they had similarly critical opinions of Christian NGOs and human rights organisations whom they turned to for help. They complained about the insensitivity of these organisations and the way they exploited situations of crisis, such as blasphemy accusations, to make money and receive foreign donations. Daniyal explained that most Christian social workers, who are supposed to work for the welfare of the Christian community in Pakistan, are least concerned with the plight of the Christian minority. They visit the sites of incidents of blasphemy accusations and violence against Christians, take pictures with the accused and their families, post those pictures on various media platforms, but never return to help those in vulnerable situations. In fact, by exposing their faces to the world through various media, they contribute to the vulnerability of the accused instead of helping them. A young girl accused of blasphemy in another case echoed this concern when she complained:

> Some people from this NGO visited me right after the accusation. They have now put my pictures on the internet, asking people to pray for me. But everyone in our neighbourhood has seen my pictures and if I ever go out, they can recognise me and tell others that I am the one who committed blasphemy. That is why I cannot live in my neighbourhood anymore, even though the accusations were proven to be false and the case against me was dropped by police.

NGOs aim to receive donations from foreign funding organisations in the name of humanitarian aid. Similar concerns were highlighted by various other participants of my research including other minority group members accused of blasphemy, lawyers representing them in the courts and even social workers themselves, some of whom accused *other* social workers of being dishonest and corrupt. These social workers also complained about the accused *themselves* conspiring to be *victims* of blasphemy accusations, to 'sell' their stories to get attention from foreign media and be 'rescued' by seeking asylum in a Western country.

Interestingly, the affected persons from different religious backgrounds also accused one another of concocting their own tragic stories of blasphemy-related violence. For example, Christians complained that Ahmadis—proportionally the largest group among those accused of blasphemy—intentionally had themselves implicated in blasphemy cases so they could flee the country. They also lamented that such self-serving conduct by certain people compromised the chances of receiving help for the *real victims* (themselves). Even more striking were the complaints from accusers who supported killing the alleged blasphemers and argued that there were certain cases in which the accused intentionally and deliberately provoked Muslims (by insulting their religion) so they could pose as *victims* in front of the international community and escape the country. I believe the suspicions of corruption among social workers and the wider mistrust of other people by the accused reflect to some extent the general attitudes of Pakistanis, whose country is mired in corruption and economic uncertainty. Due to widespread corruption, Pakistanis are generally mistrusting of other people, the government and NGOs when it comes to the distribution of limited resources.

While those complaining of dishonesty among the accused pointed out specific cases to me in which they thought the accused had ulterior motives, I did not find any evidence to support these suspicions. However, in my own interactions with the accused, a desire to seek asylum in a foreign country and/or receive financial help from foreign donors did come up several times. Given that these people knew I had some connection to Australia, even though they were unsure of my capability to help them, it was not surprising that they quite frequently brought up the idea of receiving any possible help through me. One of my respondents, a Christian man accused of blasphemy, asked me whether I could talk to church organisations in Australia on his behalf. In another extreme case, the accused, also a Christian man, told me of his plans to cross the border illegally to get to Europe. He hoped to be able to seek asylum there and 'raise the issue of the plight of the Christian minority in Pakistan with the European Union'. He also exclaimed that he was quite hopeful that, once Donald Trump came to power, he would save all the world's Christians, including the Christian community of Pakistan, from their fate at the hands of Muslims.

While most of these assumptions and speculation among various groups are based on widespread mistrust, there is certainly some opportunism operating around the issue of blasphemy in Pakistan. Das and Kleinman (2001: 25) suggested that:

> the media and the human rights organizations play an important role not only in representing the violence but also in becoming actors in the anticipations of local communities on how their suffering is to be addressed.

In terms of representing violence, photos of the victims are shared 'as if their experiences were commodities that were being advertised' (Das and Kleinman 2000: 4). In doing this, NGOs aim to receive funding from foreign donor bodies, for which they compete against a host of other local NGOs. As Cottle (2008: 149) noted: 'Aid agencies now co-exist and compete for media attention and donor funds within an increasingly crowded field'. Within this competitive environment, representations of violence—and of the victims of violence—are geared towards 'exactly what the media require' (Cottle 2008: 151). In terms of shaping the expectations of victims of 'how their suffering is to be addressed', NGOs establish the ideas of seeking asylum and receiving financial help as desirable outcomes for the victims. While there are some NGOs and social workers who are genuinely working to aid those accused of blasphemy, the majority of those accused end up feeling frustrated and left out because of this system of limited resources and high expectations.

Regardless of the actual help that the accused seek and that those with resources and power can provide, the wider perceptions, as well as actual experiences, of betrayal among individuals give rise to a widespread mistrust that complicates the possibility of seeking and receiving help for the victims. It leaves the accused in a vulnerable position without any reliable sources of legal, financial and social support. In times of crisis, the accused often experience a sense of powerlessness as friends, neighbours, religious leaders and social workers let them down, and *other* victims—or 'fake' victims—usurp the limited resources available. NGOs and social workers are key actors who can determine the course of action the conflict will take. A few of the accused thanked the NGOs and social workers who had stepped in at the right moment to help them and their families flee the conflict and save their lives. Nevertheless, most of the accused felt left out and frustrated because they did not receive appropriate help. The failure of religious leaders, NGOs and social workers to provide appropriate help may be due to limited resources or their own political and economic interests. Nevertheless, actions taken by these actors also contribute to determining the fate of the accused. While the accused struggle with finding reliable sources of support in the face of threat, accusers can usually mobilise multiple sources of patronage within a short time through established religious organisations, mosques and local leaders.

Mobilising the crowd: The role of mosques, local imams and religious organisations

While Daniyal managed to find temporary shelter for Saleem to protect him from Shahzad's wrath, soon it was not only Shahzad who was after Saleem's life. He was joined in his fury by hundreds more. A few days after the initial accusation, Shahzad shared the news of Saleem's blasphemy with Akbar, a Muslim resident of Saleem's village. Akbar shared it with two other Muslim members of the community. The three of them discussed the matter and took it to the mosque committee. The mosque committee included a chairman and 11 other members. They were respected (due to their religiosity), economically well-off and socially influential. They were not formally involved in politics but had an active role in their community. The mosque committee discussed the matter among themselves and decided to escalate the matter further by encouraging the residents of their village to punish the 'blasphemer'. The committee's decision is another example of *deliberate* decisions taken to influence the outcome of the conflict. The members of the mosque committee shared the news that blasphemy had been committed by a resident of their village with local Muslims in the mosque, who started looking for Saleem and keeping an eye on who was visiting his house and meeting his family.

The use of the mosque as the sociopolitical public space where the masses are mobilised and roused for collective action is another feature common to most instances of blasphemy-related violence. Sidel (2006) found a similar pattern in his study of religious riots in Indonesia. He notes that, 'in virtually every case, the "assembling process" involved mosques ... and other sites of Islamic worship and schooling as key locations for mobilization in defense of the faith' (Sidel 2006: 103). Veena Das (1990: 9) highlighted the key role of 'symbolic space' in the mobilisation for collective action. Mosques are communal spaces that bring the residents of a village or neighbourhood together on a regular basis and also hold symbolic value as a sacred space in Islam. Mosques also allow the use of their loudspeakers to inform people—even those who do not attend the mosque regularly—of blasphemy accusations and incite them to violent action. The 'call' to violent action, when coming from a mosque, has a symbolic affinity with the 'call to prayer'—a call to display one's loyalty to Allah. The sound of the 'noisy propaganda—such as through orations and speeches amplified through loudspeakers' also has a capacity to generate visceral and affective responses (Tambiah 1996: 232). The use of the mosque and its loudspeakers, however, depends on the inclinations of the imam, who, as I have already mentioned, is the key actor in the mobilisation of violent crowds.

On a few exceptional occasions, imams have played a positive role by trying to appease the community and prevent violent action (Sirajuddin 2017). In some other cases, imams and clerics have referred the accused to the police and the courts, to be dealt with through accepted legal channels. In such circumstances, local clerics may be playing a dual role: of inciting the public to violence while also handing the case over to the police. The galvanised crowds are in fact used as a threat to pressure the law-enforcement bodies. The imam of a small neighbourhood in Lahore told me that, while he 'publicly condemned the offence committed by the accused and incited the attendees in his sermons', he called the police himself when the crowd resorted to vigilantism. He said:

> As I saw the crowd getting violent, I called the police and told them that if they do not arrest the accused soon, there will be acute violence because people are so ferocious; they are uncontrollable.

Thus, while he provoked the masses against the accused in the first place, he withdrew from responsibility for the potential violence by calling the police at the last moment. There are also a considerable number of cases in which imams have used their position to amplify the conflict by actively provoking local Muslims to punish the accused (and their communities) themselves, instead of resorting to the power of the state. Depending on the specific context and the inclinations of the imam, the course of action chosen may be in the personal interests of the imam, such as strengthening his religious authority and enhancing his legitimacy in the eyes of the public. The imam may also be driven by his own sense of moral anxiety and desire to achieve purity. Whatever the individual motivations, the role of 'professional Muslims', as Sidel (2006: 103) calls them, is crucial 'in stoking the fires of religious tension and providing interpretive frames for the extrapolation of local disputes into larger, interreligious issues'. Thus, imams play the role of fire-tenders in galvanising crowds (Brass 2003b: 33).

In Saleem's case, the imam played that role and used the mosque pulpit to deliver sermons riling up Muslims against Christians. Daniyal told me that the imam framed the issue as part of an eternal war between Christians and Muslims. He claimed: 'The Christians are the same people who threw stones at the Prophet Muhammad, and it is time to finish them now'. There is an advanced level of transvaluation happening here in which the imam replaces the everyday relationships between Christians and Muslims living in the same village with imagined identities and broad moral narratives. Through this process of transvaluation, the people who were engaged in everyday interactions with each other 'end up as particles of a large, homogenized, and organized avalanche' (Tambiah 1996: 193). This effect is achieved through 'mytho-historical clarion calls that recall their past, explain their present, promise a rosier future, and justify and exonerate punitive violence' (Tambiah 1996: 193). By calling on the 'mytho-historical' story of Christians attacking the Prophet Muhammad with stones—establishing a literal image of the offence of blasphemy—the imam presented Christians as the aggressors and Muslims as the victims. Once 'the subjectivity of experience has been evacuated' in the construction of imagined identities of self and the symbolic Other, the 'aggressors can see themselves as if they were victims' (Das 1998: 109). Seeing themselves as the victims of Christian attacks—through attacks on the personality of the Prophet, who is central to their Muslim identity—Muslims justified punitive violence against the whole Christian community.

The imam and the mosque committee directed the crowd, inflamed by punitive passion, to torch all Christians' houses and the local church, along with Saleem's house. They agreed on a time to carry out this action: after Friday prayers—part of the 'temporal structure of riots' (Das 1990: 9). Friday prayers are a symbolic event as well as a 'strategic checkpoint' for religious rallies, protests and even social activism in Pakistan and other Muslim countries (Butt 2016; Sidel 2006). The period after Friday prayers is therefore not an arbitrary time chosen to perform violence; it has traditional religious and communal significance. The religious significance draws on the emphasis on Friday prayers in Quranic and prophetic traditions; the communal significance lies in the fact that it is the biggest regular social gathering for Muslims. Friday also has symbolic significance as the day of purification for Muslims—religious traditions and local customs recommend washing, cleansing the body, trimming one's nails, and so on, on Fridays. It is no surprise, then, that Friday becomes the day of symbolic purification of society as well. In addition to the symbolic significance of Friday, the delay in carrying out the punishment is strategic, too, as it gives clerics and other religious leaders time to recruit the 'mob' and reach out to an audience wider than those who attend the local mosque regularly or live in the immediate vicinity. Daniyal, who saw the mob in his village very closely, asserted:

> People who were part of the crowd were the lowest [socioeconomic] ranks of people. They were lower-caste professions like shoe-repairers, barbers, etc. Many of them were not residents of our village. They had joined from the neighbouring villages. The big influential people—the mosque committee and the imam of the mosque—incited the crowds and themselves watched the show. They also got the religious organisations involved, who riled up the crowds even more. Sunni Tehreek and other Sunni organisations [and political parties] gathered the mob and provided them with combustible material.

The religious organisations become involved through their connections with local religious leaders and imams. They facilitate further politicisation of the issue and mobilise resources from across various villages and cities. During my fieldwork, I also followed the social media pages and subscribed to SMS groups of some key religious organisations actively engaged in anti-blasphemy campaigning. News about incidents of blasphemy accusations is widely spread via social media and mobile phones. Thus, conflicts escalate from interpersonal incidents of perceived transgressions to meta-issues concerning the Muslim community as a whole. The escalation to this point and the mobilisation of the crowds are brought about by key actors or 'recruiters': the clerics and religious organisations who have vested political interests in the issue. Nevertheless, those who join the mob are driven by their own insecurities, fears, frustrations and passions. The 'recruiters' themselves have both emotional *and* political/strategic interests in mobilising crowds against the accused. The violence is planned and crowds are recruited following certain patterns. At the same time, the experience of *being in the crowd* allows individuals to transcend their individuality, submerge themselves in a collective identity and generate 'unimaginable brutality' (Kakar 1990: 143).

To resist or to flee? Agency in powerlessness

What does one do when one sees a crowd of angry men ready to attack? The natural response would be to run for one's life. However, the decision to flee also presents an emotional dilemma. News of Muslims' plans to torch the Christian neighbourhood reached Daniyal and other Christian residents of the village through loyal friends. On the Friday chosen for the torching, a wedding was also scheduled to take place in the Christian neighbourhood. The father of the bride-to-be, along with four other Christian men, went to see a local influential Muslim man on the Thursday to seek permission to hold the wedding ceremony. The Muslim man told them:

> Don't marry your daughter in this village because we are going to burn your houses tomorrow. If you want to conduct the wedding ceremony, go to a close-by village or do it with no more than 10 people here.

He also told them that, if they wanted to avoid the torching, four Christian men had to be handed over to the Muslims—the four who had helped Saleem run away and had assisted his family. Daniyal was one of the four men named.

The Christian men's delegation returned and warned the whole village, and refused to surrender the four men. However, to escape the consequences, most Christians fled the village that day. Daniyal decided to stay in the face of imminent danger—an experience he described as spiritual. For months after the incident, he reflected on his experience 'of looking death in the eyes' and drew his self-worth, amid all the chaos, from the fact he had resisted. He explained his decision:

> The purpose of the Muslims warning us beforehand was in fact to scare us and make the Christians leave their properties behind and flee the village. On Friday, I told Saleem's family to go to some safe place and they left. Almost 90 per cent of people moved out of the village. My family also fled. They were worried for me and asked me to go to some safe place, but I refused and told them that I could not leave the village because God, my lord, had given me the power to face this. I also said that if I ran away, then what would happen to our people? I was ready to die for my people. I did not care about my life. Seeing my stubbornness, my parents stayed with me and the rest of the family left. That night, God gave me so much power that I cannot tell you. I could have easily fought off even a thousand men single-handedly. I praise God for this. This is a secret between me and God. God told me not to leave; he told me that if I left, everything would be ruined. I had two guns and seven cartridges with me at my house. I fed the cartridges into the guns and got ready for a fight. I resolved that, first, I would stop the crowd with words and ask them to solve the problem through talk. If they still attacked me, I would fight them.

This is an example of how the accused and those close to them exercise their agency, while making decisions in risky circumstances. Acting in faith was not merely a way of gaining psychological refuge for Daniyal; it was also his moment of self-actualisation, allowing him the possibility to believe that he had some 'power', despite his powerlessness in the circumstances. In a similar incident, a Christian woman, Sara, who was accused of blasphemy, refused to flee while a crowd of Muslim men was gathering outside her house. In a tone of defiance, she told me: 'If I had run away, that would have meant I actually committed blasphemy. I was innocent. So, I wanted to stay and tell the truth (at the risk to my life)'. Both Daniyal and Sara had to eventually escape, despite their resolve to stand firm in the face of the threat. However, that brief period of 'resisting' allowed them the opportunity to feel that they had some agency in the circumstances. As Daniyal relied on his presumed spiritual prowess with the determination to 'fight' when he stayed back, it gave him a sense of purpose and meaning long after the episode was over. Mashal Khan also continued to defend his position and kept attending university after he had been accused and suspended with a warning to not be seen on campus—until the day he was lynched by his fellow students. While most of the accused never get a chance to fight back in the face of violence or even truly contest the accusation, they must live through the dilemma of whether to defend themselves or flee the threat of violence.

Victims and survivors are not usually seen as significant *actors* in the production of collective violence. However, the decisions of the accused in the face of threat can also determine the eventual outcome of the conflict. If Mashal Khan had fled, he could also have been a survivor—even though not all of those who flee survive. There have been cases in which, despite an attempt to flee, the accused was followed, captured and brought to violent punishment. In fact, attempts to flee further fan the flames and may lead to even more intense forms of punishment. Nevertheless, *it is possible* to escape violent punishment if the accused manages to find appropriate ways to escape and safe places to go. This is dependent on their resourcefulness. Saleem avoided death at the hands of the violent crowd because he managed to escape in time. I argue that, while the accused are the weaker actors with the least amount of agency to determine the outcome of the conflict, their decisions may save their lives in some cases. Moreover, regardless of the effective impact of their choices, *the subjective experience of agency* shapes their self-image and self-worth and helps them cope with the adverse consequences of the conflict. As Das (1990: 31) suggested, survivors are not passive beings 'completely controlled and moulded' by circumstances beyond their control; rather, the 'assault and the threat of annihilation' bestow 'a heroic dimension to the task of surviving'. I would like to extend Das's concept of 'heroic dimension' to the victims as well, to those who choose to resist but who do not survive.

Constrain or condone? The role of police and administrative bodies

When Friday prayer time approached, Daniyal's friend Kashif—a man who had converted from Christianity to Islam—went to the mosque. The imam was rousing the passions of the crowd with his sermon and preparing them to attack. Daniyal recalled:

> As the mob started gathering after Friday prayers, Kashif told me to contact the police and whomever else I could. I called 15 [police] and the person on duty arrived within a few minutes and controlled the whole situation by dispelling the crowd. The police asked me why I hadn't called them earlier. I told them that I thought I could handle the situation myself, but I realised at the last moment that I could not.

The police dispersed the crowd by convincing the Muslim leaders to discuss the matter in the presence of the police. In this rare, fortunate event, they managed to contain the violence by forming a peace committee with three representatives from each side (Muslims and Christians). In the presence of the police (deployed in numbers in the village for weeks after the incident), the Muslims calmed and retreated from their intention to torch the Christian neighbourhood. It must be noted, however, that, by the time the mob gathered and Daniyal called the police, an NGO worker whom he had contacted earlier had spread the news among influential activists who got local and international media coverage for the incident and managed to pressure higher-level police officials to attend the site and control the situation.[3] Some human rights activists began spreading the contact details of senior government members and police officers from the relevant district on social media, encouraging people to push them to ensure peace in Daniyal's village. These activists were affiliated with

---

3   While we see a positive impact of the media in this case, in other cases it may be counterproductive. For example, due to their extensive coverage of blasphemy cases, news reports reach greater numbers of people prepared to be violent than would have been possible without such exposure. Asia Bibi's case was highlighted by the media to an extent that it led to mass demonstrations at the national level; Muslims from across the country demanded the death penalty for her. Similarly, media coverage had an immense role in making a hero out of Mumtaz Qadri for hundreds of thousands of Pakistanis. Moreover, the media coverage of blasphemy cases has also contributed to a rise in the number of such cases across the country. This is because common people who were never aware of the existence of the blasphemy laws now have a convenient tool at their hands if they want to take revenge on their rivals or redress a personal grievance.

powerful politicians and managed to gain the authorities' attention just in time. However, this is not always the case. In many other incidents, police and administrative bodies failed to contain the violence.

It is widely known that police were informed and were present at the time of the Joseph Colony incident, Mashal Khan's lynching and several other cases, but could not (or were unwilling to) prevent violent action. The role of local government representatives, who have a certain influence over the public in their areas, has also been noted as being mostly unhelpful. Let us consider a specific example of police and government failure to contain violence. In December 2016, in a village in Chakwal District, local Muslims orchestrated an attack on an Ahmadi mosque resulting in a few casualties and vandalism of property. A couple of weeks before the attack, the Muslims had posted a letter with 580 signatories to the district coordination officer and copied it to several other government representatives, including ministers and the prime minister himself. In the letter, they declared their grievances against the Ahmadis for occupying a mosque in their village and warned that, if the government did not take action against the Ahmadis, they would be compelled to take extreme measures themselves. The Ahmadi community also wrote to the local administrators, seeking government protection due to threats from the Muslim community. The government representatives failed to respond and deliberately stayed out of the matter. There have been various other incidents in which the police and government officials failed to restrain violence despite prior knowledge and warnings. Ian Copland (2010: 147) argued that, to successfully curb collective violence, 'the state must want to act, and have the will to do so, even at the cost of offending some of its supporters'. He further contended that 'modern states clearly have the capacity to contain outbreaks of communal violence. They must also, of course, want to do so' (Copland 2010: 150). There are several reasons police and local government representatives *do not want to* act.

The interests of local government representatives lie in maintaining their voter support, hence they try to avoid getting involved in situations in which the majority is engaged in violence, even though they are not actively condoning violence. Similarly, the police's 'reluctance to use force may be an expression of solidarity with those against whom the police or the army is being asked to use force' (Das 1990: 23). After all, 'policemen are part of society' and may themselves subscribe to the ideas under contestation (Das 1990: 24). Das (1990: 23) pointed out that the state—and its subsidiaries, such as the police—has its own repertoire of action for managing situations of violent conflict. Police action may be deliberately delayed so the crowd can 'inflict considerable damage before they are brought under control' (Das 1990: 24). This is not only because of police sympathy with the majority, but also because the state's legitimacy is at stake when using force against the perpetrators of violence.

Thus, while the police and administrative bodies have the capacity to contain violence, they may instead condone it to gain moral legitimacy or because of their own personal beliefs. They can also choose to deliberately stay out of the conflict to pursue their political interests. Hence, the conflict is not politically neutral, as the actors involved have their political interests at the fore. Turner succinctly pointed out how social dramas are essentially political processes:

> Social dramas are in large measure political processes, that is, they involve competition for scarce ends—power, dignity, prestige, honor, purity—by particular means and by the utilization of resources that are also scarce—goods, territory, money, men and women. Ends, means, and resources are caught up in an interdependent feedback process. (Turner 1980: 152)

The decision of the police and government representatives to act to control violence or to stay out of the matter is also political. The course of action to be taken is sometimes decided according to the political goals of those on the frontlines; at other times, it is according to the political goals of the higher-ups, such as ministers, who are not physically present at the site of the conflict. Despite the various possible sources of motivation—emotional, political, strategic—the decisions of police and administrative bodies can determine whether or not violent action takes place.

Lasting hostilities and wider disturbances in the social fabric

Despite having reached a peace agreement with the local Muslims, Daniyal did not see the situation in his village as peaceful. He continued to interact with various news media. He was interviewed by journalists from Britain, France and Germany. His proactive role in communicating with NGOs and media outlets agitated the local Muslims even more. Due to their growing hostility towards Daniyal, he had to eventually flee the village. He explained:

> The Muslims still had grievances against us because there were police in the village. NGOs were visiting every day. The Muslims thought they were being attacked by the Christians. They felt like a bald man whose head is being picked by birds. They started blaming me for the whole situation. They said that I was responsible for the police and the NGOs taking up the issue and coming to our village. Peace has apparently been restored in my village, but the eyes of the Muslims are still waiting for me. They believe that the Christians succeeded due to my efforts and that I gave the whole story to the news agencies. They think that I am the mastermind behind the success of Christians over them. So, the Muslims continue to look for me and Saleem. They were saying they would not spare the two of us. Therefore, even now, I, Saleem and his family are not safe. We are all living in hiding [separately].

While the conflict had been resolved formally, the grievances remained and found alternative outlets of expression. The local Muslims—particularly the landowning caste (Jatt Biradri)—decided to boycott the Christians socially and economically. The village consists of about 3,000 Muslim homes and 30 homes belonging to Christians. Muslim residents of the village are economically stronger than the Christians as they own land and have family members working in the Gulf and Middle East sending money home. Wheat growing is the mainstay of sustenance and economic activity in the village. Working on the crops of the landowners is the major source of livelihood for most Christians who belong to the working class of the village. They earn about Rs200 (~$2) per day for working in the landowners' fields. Some Christians are bonded labourers living under conditions of slavery. They serve their Muslim overlords 24 hours a day and get a meagre amount in return for their services. They are 'bonded' to certain families/landowners as labourers in return for money they or their ancestors may have borrowed from the landlords but could not return. Daniyal lamented the economic dependency of the Christians on Muslims and the misery that ensued following the boycott:

> To be honest, most of us live all our lives indebted to Muslims. We can never pay off the money they may have lent to our previous generations at some point in time. But after this incident, the Muslims stopped hiring us [Christians] for labour on their lands. It was the wheat-harvesting season. They stopped giving us grain (as many of us get our payments in grain). Christian women who worked in Muslim houses (as household help) could not work anymore. So, we had no grain and no money. The Muslims

threatened us that if we did not pay their debts back, they would capture our houses as well. We own the houses because they were allocated to us by the government a long time ago. However, the Muslims said they would grab our houses if we failed to pay their charges back. It was impossible because they were not giving work to Christians anymore. There was a primary school in our community but even that has been closed because of this issue.

In the months following the incident, relations between the Christian and Muslim communities slowly returned to 'normal'. The school was reopened and Muslims started hiring Christians again. However, full rehabilitation of the society after serious episodes of violence when 'perpetrators, victims, and witnesses come from the same social space' and engage with each other in their everyday life is almost impossible (Das and Kleinman 2000: 2).

No glib appeal to 'our common humanity' can restore confidence to inhabit one another's lives again. Instead, it is by first reformulating their notions of 'normality', much as the experience of disease changes our expectations of health, that communities can respond to the destruction of trust in their everyday lives (Das and Kleinman 2001: 23).

Healing and rehabilitation, therefore, mean transformation of society to a different state in which the relationships among people are permanently altered (Das and Kleinman 2001). The aggressors reinhabit the same world with an enhanced sense of their moral purity and power. Tambiah (1996: 230) noted that the perpetrators of collective violence are not 'burdened with concerns and reactions that impede their return to everyday life'. In fact, engaging in violence against those deemed to be transgressors of religion further consolidates the perpetrators' sense of self and morality by helping them achieve 'purification', even if they are tried and/or punished by the state later on. In cases of communal violence, having demonstrated their power and superiority against an already weaker and inferior community, the aggressors are further emboldened in their exploitation of the marginalised.

For the survivors, on the other hand, the violence lays bare 'the artificial order of normal times' and alters the way they see themselves in relation to others (Das 1990: 32). For Daniyal and Saleem, the transformation was extreme because they had to permanently relocate and reconstruct their lives in the shadow of constant threat. Once accused of blasphemy, it is practically impossible to get rid of the label and resume life as before, which was the case for Saleem. The case of Daniyal, however, is unusual because he was not the primary accused. Nevertheless, through his defiant actions, he antagonised the Muslims in such a way that no peace with them was possible. Some form of peace could be established with those who conformed to the existing social hierarchies even within the conflict—such as those who went to the Muslims to seek permission for the wedding. Daniyal, however, not only defied the hierarchies but also tried to turn them around by bringing the village to the attention of NGOs and the international media. Therefore, no peace was possible with him.

Permanently altered are the relationships not only between the two communities, but also among the members of the same community. Relationships with friends and relatives who refuse to support the accused and their families in times of crisis are also permanently deformed, if not severed. Sara, the young woman accused of blasphemy, told me that her fiancé broke off their engagement after the accusation and her relatives stopped visiting. Most of the accused (survivors) to whom I talked during my research had similar complaints about their relatives abandoning them in the face of violence. They often expressed how the crisis had 'laid bare the truth of their social relationships'. Thus, the moments of violence reveal not only the true extent of (potential) hatred between communities that already share uneasy relationships with each other—such as Christians and Muslims—but also the illusions inherent in relationships of loyalty and solidarity. Through the moments of violence, the victims and survivors also realise the full extent of the indifference to and/or prejudice against them of the state and its administrative bodies. Thus, as Veena Das (1990: 32–33) put it, the survivor learns to see 'how the microcosm of violent space and time that s/he inhabits is a reflection of the macrocosm of the violent modern state'. The outcome of the conflict, therefore, 'is no clear-cut victory, no definitive crossing over to safety and renewal' and also 'no complete defeat, no ultimate breakdown and dissolution' (Das and Kleinman 2001: 24). The social fabric of the society is permanently affected, 'and yet in the midst of the worst horrors, people continue to live, to survive, and to cope' (Das and Kleinman 2001: 1). The conflict may come to an end, but violence lives on within the intimacies of everyday interactions and may surface at some other point, in some other form.

Conclusion

I have demonstrated in this chapter how things escalate from interpersonal accusations of blasphemy to communal outrage and which mechanisms determine the form the punishment will take. I have argued that, in cases where violent action takes place, the process of escalation draws on certain repertoires of action such that legitimation is sought from religious authority rather than state authority, crowds are mobilised by local imams and mosques, and the administrative bodies take sides based on their own strategic interests in the conflict. On the other hand, the accused seek help from their communities, their own religious organisations, NGOs and other civil society actors—all of whom have their own interests in and fears about the situation. Thus, subjective decisions from a number of actors determine the course of action to be taken and the eventual outcome of the conflict.

Following Veena Das's conception, I argue that, for violence to occur, a certain 'contiguity' has to be established not only between the specific issues and the collective symbols, but also between the decisions taken by various actors at different stages of the conflict. Thus, the occurrence of collective violence following blasphemy accusations is not inevitable; it is within the power of the key actors, such as religious leaders and imams, the police and administrative bodies and the invisible hand of the higher-ups in the state, to quell or contain the potential for violence. However, it is not the same balance of factors—a set formula—that leads to collective violence in each case. On the contrary, the key drivers, the tipping point and the most significant players may be different in each case. Therefore, whether an accusation will lead to collective violence is contingent on the decisions of key actors as well as the specific context of the case. I have further contended that collective violence—when it happens—is both organised and meaningful. It is both premeditated (as Paul Brass argued) and emotionally significant (as Blom and Jaoul proposed). Collective violence is organised and planned by the key actors and also draws on emotional and symbolic repositories that render the violence meaningful to the perpetrators.

Part III

5

Legitimate punishment of blasphemy: Contestation between the legal system and popular justice

On 31 October 2018, the Supreme Court of Pakistan passed its landmark judgement in the case of Asia Bibi, a Christian woman accused of blasphemy who had been on death row, in solitary confinement, since 2010 (Hashim 2018). The highest court of Pakistan acquitted Bibi, but the decision led to widespread protests around the country and the threat of violence by thousands who did not accept the court's decision (Hashim 2018). The protest organisers—the senior leadership of TLP—demanded that the three Supreme Court judges who had acquitted Bibi be killed, along with Bibi herself. Protestors blocked key roads in major cities, causing schools and offices to shut for two days. The government finally reached an agreement with the protestors, promising the Supreme Court decision would be reviewed and that legal measures would be taken to put Asia Bibi's name on the exit control list to prevent her leaving the country (Bilal 2018). Through public demonstrations and threats of violence, the protestors made it clear that they did not accept the Supreme Court's decision. They wanted Bibi to be hanged, but the legal system failed them by not delivering the desired punishment. The Supreme Court's decision was, therefore, not legitimate in the eyes of the protestors as it clashed with their ideals of justice and the legitimate punishment for perceived blasphemers.

Earlier, in 2011, Salman Taseer, then governor of Punjab, and Shahbaz Bhatti, then federal minister of minority affairs, were assassinated for publicly lending their support to Asia Bibi (Dawn News 2011a). Taseer—accused of blasphemy for supporting an alleged blasphemer—was killed by his official bodyguard, Mumtaz Qadri, who has since been revered as a hero by his supporters (Nasir 2016). Qadri was sentenced to death for murder and was hanged in 2016 (Nasir 2016). His funeral was attended by tens of thousands of devotees—again, a clear message that the court's decision to punish Qadri was not accepted as legitimate. In 2016, I talked to one of Qadri's devotees who was present during the final hearing of Qadri's appeal by the Supreme Court. He exclaimed:

> I was sitting there in the court, on a front bench, as the judge sentenced Mumtaz Qadri—may blessings of Allah be upon him. The judges are misguided to think that they can use the law of this country, the Islamic Republic of Pakistan, to go against Islam. It is not the law that decides who is right. In this case, the law was definitely on the wrong side as it sentenced Mumtaz Qadri, the lover of the Prophet, to death. Qadri only ascended in his spiritual rank as he embraced martyrdom eventually. It is the law that has lost here by not upholding the sovereignty of Allah's commands. Such a sad state our country has come to despite being an Islamic state!

This statement unequivocally contests the legitimacy of the state legal system and points to a higher system of legality and legitimacy based on the sovereignty of Allah's commands. The disapproval of the two key Supreme Court decisions—*Asia Bibi vs The State* (2018) and *Mumtaz Qadri vs The State* (2015)[1]—indicates that, in the eyes of the people, state laws are not the ultimate sources of legitimacy and authority to determine the appropriate punishment for blasphemy. In the case of Asia Bibi, the protestors were demanding that *the state* hang her. In the case of Mumtaz Qadri, his supporters approved of the *nonstate* killing of the alleged blasphemer. Thus, *legitimate punishment of blasphemy* in Pakistan can be carried out by the state or by nonstate actors but only as long as it conforms to the perceived sovereignty of Allah's commands, which corresponds to the competing ideas of the state of Pakistan, as already discussed. However, there is no consensus on the ideal state of Pakistan

---

1   *Asia Bibi vs The State* (2018) Criminal Appeal No. 39-L, Supreme Court Islamabad; *Malik Muhammad Mumtaz Qadri vs The State* (2015) Criminal Appeals No. 210 and 211 of 2015, Supreme Court Islamabad.

and, by corollary, no unanimous agreement on the sovereign will of Allah. The legitimacy of the appropriate punishment for blasphemy is therefore continually contested between the state and nonstate actors.

In the Introduction, I argued against law-centric approaches to understanding the issue of blasphemy and suggested employing the framework of legal pluralism for a more nuanced approach. Legal pluralism is the theory that societies may have multiple coexisting, overlapping or clashing systems of legality based on different notions of morality, authority and legitimacy (Benda-Beckmann 2009; Fitzpatrick 1983; Griffiths 1986). Following this conception, I argue that the *legitimate punishment* of those accused of blasphemy is based on multiple sources of legality and legitimacy, mainly the state legal system and wider narratives of popular justice. While the state's legitimacy is *institutionalised* in its legal system, comprising courts, jails, and so on, popular justice is more a source of *ideological* legitimacy. Nevertheless, both the state legal system and the ideals of popular justice draw on Islamic law and the dominant religious discourse about blasphemy (discussed in Chapter 2). The legal system claims to represent Islamic law, at least with respect to the punishment of blasphemy, and the Western legal framework of positive law at the same time. Popular justice, on the other hand, draws on Islamic law, glorifying narratives embedded in collective memory and a local history of public punishment as spectacle. The two sources of legitimacy—state law and popular justice—may in many cases align with each other in their interpretations of the will of Allah. On other occasions, they are in contest over the interpretation and implementation of the sovereign will of Allah. In instances of clash, state law may be totally dismissed by religious groups as representing Western law rather than the will of Allah. Nevertheless, in most instances, the state coopts ideas of popular justice and nonstate actors coopt ideas of the state's legality to establish their respective legitimacies.

There are a range of opinions on the issue of the punishment of blasphemy in Pakistan, with various levels of acceptance of the state. Most Pakistanis believe the state enshrines the appropriate Islamic laws to punish blasphemers and that they should be implemented. I focus mainly on those who reject outright the legitimacy of the state, at least in some cases. When speaking of popular justice, I refer to the discourse of religious leaders, who are the key actors contesting the state's legitimacy and authority. The contestation for the legitimate punishment of blasphemy must be seen as a domain of political competition between the state and nonstate figures of religious authority, each with their own ideas of the 'Islamic state' of Pakistan. I will start with a discussion of the state's claims to legitimacy and the ways in which they are challenged. I will then discuss the popular sources of legitimacy on which nonstate claimants of justice draw. I argue that, while the state's crisis of legitimacy creates space for the ideas of popular justice propagated by nonstate figures of religious authority to take hold, the popular narratives concerning the punishment of blasphemy shape the standards against which the state's legitimacy is measured. The ideas of popular justice determine whether or not the state's right to decide on the fate of the accused will be accepted as legitimate. Hence, it is a vicious cycle in which the state is expected to act in a certain way, linked to popular narratives of justice and the state's claim to represent them, but in its failure to do so it cedes more legitimacy to the ideas of nonstate justice.

Contesting the state's monopoly over 'legitimate' violence

The claim to represent Islamic law and the institutionalised modern legal framework are the key sources of legitimacy for the state of Pakistan. However, the legitimacy of the state is challenged on two salient grounds: disagreement with the state's interpretation of the higher will of Allah and the ineffectiveness of the state in implementing the will of Allah. The former is a challenge to the state's claim to transcendence and sovereignty as a law-giving entity. The latter is a challenge to the state's ability to uphold and implement its own laws.

What gives legitimacy to state law?

The modern state has been widely characterised as the sole arbiter of the 'legitimate' use of violence. Max Weber (1946: 77) regarded 'the legitimate use of physical force within a given territory' as a defining feature of the modern state. René Girard (1977) distinguished between state violence and nonstate violence by calling these public vengeance and private vengeance, respectively. According to Girard (1977: 16), public vengeance—the state's use of violent punishment to avenge an offence through its judicial system—is an exclusive feature of well-policed modern societies, 'which serves to deflect the menace of vengeance' by limiting it to 'a single act of reprisal'. He argues:

> [A]s long as there exists no sovereign and independent body capable of taking the place of the injured party and taking upon itself the responsibility for revenge, the danger of interminable escalation remains. (Girard 1977: 18)

In his view, public and private vengeance are the same in principle, but private vengeance is often described as taking the 'law' into one's 'own hands' (Girard 1977: 17). According to Girard, what gives the state's public vengeance legitimacy is its quality of 'transcendence'—that is, being impartial and above the parties involved. He writes:

> As soon as the essential quality of transcendence—religious, humanistic, or whatever—is lost, there are no longer any terms by which to define the legitimate form of violence and to recognize it among the multitude of illicit forms … There are as many legitimate forms of violence as there are men to implement them; legitimacy as a principle no longer exists. (Girard 1977: 26)

Thus, the state's monopoly over 'legitimate' violence derives from 'the essential quality of transcendence' attributed to it. The 'transcendence' of the state of Pakistan as a modern state with its claim to monopoly over the right to exercise physical force within its territory is rooted in the Islamic system of social justice, as per the Constitution. The first sentence of the preamble to the Constitution of Pakistan (1973) posits that 'sovereignty over the entire Universe belongs to Almighty Allah alone' and the representatives of the people of Pakistan must uphold the 'sacred trust' and 'the limits prescribed by Him' in exercising their authority. The constitution further prescribes that the state is to be run in accordance with the principles of Islamic social justice. The judges appointed by the state also draw on the Quran and prophetic traditions in making their decisions. The legal system, and its right to deliver legitimate punishments to those accused of blasphemy, is hence embedded within a modern religious and national framework. The transcendence and sovereignty of the state are accepted to some extent as most cases of blasphemy accusations are indeed taken to the legal system, as was the case of Asia Bibi. The verdicts of the state's courts of law, however, are not *always* accepted as legitimate. Moreover, the accused may be punished by nonstate actors without any recourse to the law. Even when cases are taken to the legal system, the accused can be punished privately while a trial is under way or even after acquittal. Thus, the state does not have a monopoly on delivering punishment to those accused of blasphemy. The transcendence and sovereignty of the state of Pakistan are, therefore, neither absolute nor universally accepted.

Beyond transcendence: Multiple sovereignties

Theories of natural law, such as Girard's conception of transcendence as an essential quality of state law, provide a 'founding myth from which the absolute status of law' is derived (Harris 1996: 4). However, when the transcendence of state law is not absolute, such as in the case of Pakistan, the state is not the only law-giving entity. In such cases, nonstate actors may also hold 'the capacity to suspend both laws and norms and thus create a conceptual ethical zero point from where "the law" can be given' (Hansen 2005: 170). For example, Khadim Hussain Rizvi, the TLP leader heading the protests against the Supreme Court judgement in the case of Asia Bibi, proclaimed in one of his early sermons: 'We do not believe in any "courts". "Courts" are a Western concept. We Muslims have *adaalat* where our Islamic laws are applied, and blasphemers are punished'.[2]

Rizvi criticised the English word 'court' and used the equivalent word in Urdu to express his dissent. This criticism highlights a deeper sense of disapproval in which the sovereignty of the state and the state's position as the lawgiver are challenged. Through this conception, an alternative system of transcendence is established, which draws on the same religious system of justice as the state but does not acknowledge the state's right to interpret and implement religious commands. Thus, the religious system transcends and subsumes the modern judicial system but may not be limited to the same. It can be understood as a hierarchy of systems, where the state's punishments are considered legitimate as long as they conform to the higher system of transcendence, religious justice, but this higher system can also legitimise punishments outside the state legal system. In Hansen and Stepputat's words, a 'de facto sovereignty' is thus created, which grants nonstate actors 'the ability to kill, punish, and discipline with impunity' (2006: 296). On the basis of this de facto sovereignty, the Supreme Court's decisions are challenged and alleged blasphemers are consequently killed without reprisal outside the courts of law.

---

2   Available from: www.youtube.com/watch?v=axCwC-pywJk&t=1185s. Note this video is now private, when accessed in October 2020 it was still a publicly available video; it is possible that it was made private after the passing of TLP chief Rizvi in November 2020, or because the Pakistani government banned TLP as a terrorist organisation in April 2021.

The existence of de facto sovereign powers, along with the formal state, is not exclusive to Pakistan. Hansen and Stepputat (2006) argued that the roots of fragmented sovereignties lie in the colonial past of postcolonial states. They write:

> A key feature of the colonial world was that different kinds and registers of sovereignty coexisted and over-lapped. Most modern states claim effective legal sovereignty over a territory and its population in the name of the nation and the popular will. Although this is always an unattainable ideal, it is particularly tenuous in many post-colonial societies in which sovereign power was historically fragmented and distributed among many, mostly informal but effective, forms of local authority. (Hansen and Stepputat 2006: 297)

In Pakistan, religious leaders are usually the local authority to assume the role of de facto sovereign power in legitimising violence against those accused of blasphemy through their *fatwas* and religious verdicts. Sovereignty is, therefore, a 'tentative and always emergent form of authority' that is claimed through performance of violence by the state as well as by nonstate actors (Hansen and Stepputat 2006: 297). Comaroff and Comaroff (2006: 35) have similarly argued that 'postcolonies tend *not* to be organized under a single, vertically integrated sovereignty sustained by a highly centralized state. Rather, they consist in a horizontally woven tapestry of partial sovereignties'. It is through these partial sovereignties and dispersed religious authority that the legitimate punishment of blasphemy is contested. With various claimants over sovereignty, including the state, competing against each other, it is hard to establish a single source of legitimacy for the punishment of those accused of blasphemy.

Ineffectiveness of the legal system

While the existence of multiple sovereignties and systems of transcendence challenges the state's exclusive position as the lawgiver in society, the legal system is still the most popular route chosen to punish alleged blasphemers. In fact, the state is expected to uphold and implement its legal system in accordance with Islamic law. The state's legitimacy is therefore also challenged when it fails to function efficiently and effectively to punish blasphemers according to the people's ideas of justice. One of the most common arguments made by my research participants who supported punishing blasphemers outside the law was related to the 'ineffectiveness of the state legal system'. In this section, I will discuss why and how the state is perceived to be incapable of delivering justice effectively. It is pertinent to understand, first, how the legal proceedings work in cases of blasphemy. For the rest of this section, the terms 'law', 'legal' and 'courts' refer to the state legal system unless otherwise specified. The information regarding the courts and legal procedures is based on my primary fieldwork when no other sources are cited.

As already mentioned, most cases of blasphemy accusations are taken to courts of law. However, the police are generally not the first point of contact after an accusation. It is usually the religious leaders of the accusers who determine whether and when a case will be reported to the police. In many cases, the religious leaders, in collaboration with local influential persons, use the threat of mob violence to get the police to register cases of blasphemy and to arrest the accused. In my discussions with them, the police themselves claimed that they arrest the accused for their own safety due to the threat of nonstate violence. As per the procedural requirements, introduced by an amendment to the Criminal Procedure Code in 2004 to prevent misuse of the anti-blasphemy laws, a case of religious offence cannot be registered without investigation by a police officer of at least the level of superintendent. However, as several people including police and lawyers told me, the procedural requirements are rarely implemented in practice, as pressure from local religious leaders and their supporters does not allow proper and impartial investigation.

Once the first information report (FIR) has been registered on the application of the complainant(s)—who in some cases are the religious leaders themselves, who take over cases from the accuser(s) to emphasise their own piety and authority—a police report is prepared. The police report includes evidence in the form of statements from the accusers, witnesses and the accused—usually verbal testimonies. In some cases, physical objects such as desecrated copies of religious books are also collected. As far as the statement of the accused is concerned, it is often a *confession* of the offence, which is used to claim the merit of the complaint and to initiate formal court proceedings against the accused. A curious phenomenon is the common discrepancy between the initial statements of the accused in the form of a confession in front of police officers and their later statements in front of the court, where they deny having committed the crime. This is because, initially, due to lack of legal counsel, the accused are not aware of the legal implications of confessing and, in their desperate attempts to escape prosecution, they confess and ask for forgiveness or are forced into confessing. Nevertheless, once the police report (usually referred to as a Challan form) has been prepared, it is taken to the Sessions Court. In the Sessions Court, a charge-sheet is framed based on the police report and the accused is notified and given time to respond to the accusations.

As per the PPC, blasphemy is an offence against the state, even though it is usually reported by private complainants. Hence, there is always a state prosecution lawyer. The accused/defendants are also entitled to state lawyers; however, due to pressure from religious groups, accusers and the community of lawyers themselves, state lawyers are often scared of representing the accused. It is even harder for the accused to appoint a private lawyer due to threats against and intimidation of anyone who dares to represent a person accused of blasphemy. There have been incidents in which the defence lawyers of the accused have been openly threatened in court rooms, and even murdered (BBC News 2014). The accusers, on the other hand, are supported voluntarily and free of charge by many influential lawyers who claim to be doing so for love of the Prophet. Hence, from the very beginning of the legal proceedings, there is a power imbalance between the accused and the accusers, already tipping the judicial system in the favour of the latter.

Once the trial begins, it usually takes several years for the Sessions Court to decide on a case. Nadeem, a young Christian man, was accused of blasphemy in 2013 for allegedly desecrating a religious book. He was arrested following threats of violence from the accuser, his religious leaders and the crowd they had managed to gather. A complaint was registered against him under Sections 295-A and 295-C of the PPC. In 2016, when I met Nadeem, the court still had not recorded his statement. Nadeem's brother, who was the primary relative following up on his case, told me that he had been coming to court hearings every second week since 2013. He said he had been unable to find work since the accusation against Nadeem and his arrest, due to the stigma attached to the family of a 'blasphemer'. Moreover, the fact that he had to take time off every other week to visit Nadeem in jail and attend the court hearings meant employers were not interested in hiring him. Nadeem's brother and mother—the only other members of his family—had already been forced out of their house and neighbourhood due to threats of violence. They moved in with some relatives and lived as dependants, which Nadeem's brother found humiliating yet unavoidable. Nadeem's lawyer had applied for his bail, but the court proceedings were so slow, it was not until early 2017, towards the end of my fieldwork, that Nadeem finally received bail. When I subsequently met his lawyer, he told me they were facing two major challenges: first, finding a safe place for Nadeem to stay, and second, breaking to him the news of his mother's death a few months earlier. Nevertheless, they were gleefully celebrating their 'success' because bail is rare for those accused of blasphemy while the trials drag on for years.

One major reason for the delay is the generally slow pace of legal proceedings in Pakistan and the massive backlog of cases waiting to be heard. According to a recent report by the Law and Justice Commission of Pakistan (2020), more than 2 million cases were pending in the country's courts in June 2020.[3] The report includes statistics from the Supreme Court, high courts and district courts. Many of these cases have been pending for decades. One common cause of delay is the insufficient human resources in the judicial system—a situation compounded by frequent strikes by lawyers (an average of four to five working days every month during my fieldwork) and the absence of judges. Within this context, blasphemy cases are no exception; however, there are various additional factors that contribute to even longer delays in cases of blasphemy.

I attended Sessions Court for a few months, following cases of blasphemy under trial. In most of the cases I followed, neither the complainants nor the witnesses appeared for the court hearing. After a few weeks of observation, I asked the prosecution lawyers (private lawyers prosecuting cases of blasphemy voluntarily) about the absence of the complainants. They hesitantly explained to me—rather disappointedly—that the complainants register cases due to their anger at the time of the incident, but then get busy in their lives and do not pursue the cases, which shows 'their shaky faith and weak resolve to punish the blasphemers'. Nor do they drop the cases, ensuring prolonged suffering for the accused, who remain imprisoned during their trial—sometimes for decades. Further delay is caused in cases of blasphemy by judges and lawyers leaving due to threats made against them. The accused will likely spend years going through the trial process.

When Sessions Court judges eventually decide on cases, they usually convict the accused and award a harsh sentence, including the death penalty. Surprisingly, many of the decisions of the lower courts in cases

---

3   These numbers are for all legal cases (not just blasphemy cases) and are updated fortnightly on the website of the Law and Justice Commission of Pakistan: ljcp.gov.pk/nljcp/home#1.

of blasphemy are reversed by higher courts after appeals, which also take years to be processed (Amnesty International 2016: 13). The number of people accused who are acquitted by the higher courts after appealing their sentences in the lower courts is significant, and shows the different dynamics of threat and pressure operating at the two levels. Sessions Court judges are more easily intimidated, leading to decisions in favour of the accusers. The judges of the higher courts usually have more power and security at their disposal and thus can afford to acquit the accused. However, this does not mean that the higher court judges are not threatened or punished for deciding in favour of the accused. There have been incidents in which even higher court judges were attacked or had to flee for their lives after deciding in favour of the accused (DW 2011; Walsh 2011). The recent public wrath against Supreme Court judges in the case of Asia Bibi is another example of the pressure under which the judges operate.

Thus, initiation of legal action ensures at least several years in prison for the accused while they go through the trial process and wait for the court's decision. Regardless of whether they are convicted and punished or acquitted, the initiation of legal action itself is effective in putting an end to the normal life of the accused. Even if—and when—they are acquitted, they cannot resume their previous lives. In most instances, they have to live the rest of their lives in hiding, adopting a fake identity. Very few of those accused have been able to escape this fate by fleeing to another country. Hence, even if they escape death at the hands of the mob and at the gallows, they are effectively denied a normal existence and social life. Nor does the acquittal absolve them of the label of blasphemer. There have been several incidents in which those acquitted were subsequently killed because they had not been absolved of the offence they had committed *in the eyes of the people*. Legal action against the accused, therefore, causes them to suffer in many ways regardless of whether they are proven guilty or innocent. They suffer due to the power imbalance between the two parties from the beginning of the proceedings, the long delays in court decisions and their life prospects after the decision.

All of this suffering, however, is not counted as an effective punishment for their crime. Recall that none of those sentenced to death for blasphemy so far has been executed by the state. Thus, legal action is deemed ineffective in bringing the accused to justice in the eyes of the accusers and their supporters. Many of the people to whom I talked, including lawyers representing the accusers, argued that people were forced to 'take the law into their own hands' because the legal system was not effective in delivering the desired punishment. This argument reflects a much wider pattern of justifications given by proponents of nonstate justice in other places and contexts. Berg and Wendt (2011: 14) contended in their study of vigilantism and mob violence across the globe:

> The justifications for popular justice sound strikingly uniform across cultures, namely that the people must take the law into their own hands because legal institutions are either non-existent or too weak. Some apologists argue that the laws are not tough enough to deter criminals; others believe that the punishments prescribed by the law are inadequate to satisfy the popular desire for swift and harsh retribution.

While state law in Pakistan promises harsh punishments—typically the death sentence—for blasphemers, these punishments are not implemented in line with people's expectations. Hence, the law fails to provide the 'swift and harsh retribution' imagined by the proponents of nonstate punishment of blasphemers. The legal system is therefore deemed *ineffective* in delivering the justice desired. Berg and Wendt (2011: 7) also demonstrated that, by complaining about the ineffectiveness of the legal system, the proponents of popular justice principally challenge the 'modern state's efforts to monopolize criminal justice and to institute an "abstract, rational, detached, and antiseptic legal process"'. They further argued that the prevalence of nonstate punishment in a society questions the state's claim to a monopoly over legitimate violence, denies 'the popular acceptance of this claim' and demonstrates a lack of faith in the state's capability to enforce its laws effectively (Berg and Wendt 2011: 14). Similarly, in the case of the punishment of blasphemers in Pakistan, the state's claim to transcendence and sovereignty and its ability to implement its laws effectively are questioned. The state's legitimacy is thus challenged on the grounds of its incorrect *interpretation* as well as its ineffective *implementation* of the sovereign will of Allah.

The ineffective implementation of state law is also attributed to the malice of Pakistan's Westernised elite, who control the state and the judiciary and represent Western interests rather than the will of Allah. Otunnu (2016: 17–18) identified rule by economic and political elites and chronic dependence on other states and international regimes as some of the characteristics of states that are undergoing a 'crisis of legitimacy'. These characteristics are relevant to the case of Pakistan. In 2016, during my fieldwork, several of my research participants expressed their angst at the fact that the state was 'so swift in hanging Mumtaz Qadri but had delayed hanging Asia Bibi for years'. For them, the failure to hang Asia Bibi demonstrated the state's unwillingness to act, which they attributed to the 'influence of Western powers'. In 2018, when the Supreme Court acquitted Bibi, protestors rejected the decision, claiming it was a result of corruption among the judges and the government, who were colluding with Western governments and NGOs to undermine Islam. Protestors perceived the acquittal of Bibi as an attempt by the government to appease Western states and gain favour as Pakistan was going through an economic crisis at the time. Even when the state's actions cannot be linked to immediate economic and political interests that may force it to go against the perceived 'will of Allah', Pakistan's ruling elite is seen as a representation of corrupt and un-Islamic values. The erosion of the legitimacy of the state in Pakistan is therefore aided by the fact that the ruling elite are seen as Westernised and serving the interests of Western governments and other entities who seek to undermine Islam. Pakistan's 'crisis of legitimacy' is thus cumulative as it derives from the state's lack of absolute sovereignty, its perceived ineffectiveness in delivering justice and its corruption through representing the interests of Western powers rather than the will of Allah.

Popular justice: Legitimacy of the nonstate violent punishment of blasphemers

Thurston (2011: 80) noted that 'communities try to erect and operate alternate [sic] means of judgement' when they sense that the legal mechanisms are failing them. Along similar lines, Otunnu (2016: 1) argued that states that are going through crises of legitimacy are more prone to nonstate political violence. Pakistan's crisis of legitimacy lends space to the development of 'alternative means of judgement' and 'political violence' by nonstate actors when it comes to the punishment of blasphemy. Having discussed the grounds on which the state's monopoly over 'legitimate violence' is challenged, I will now discuss the ways in which the legitimacy of the nonstate punishment of blasphemers is established. There are various sources that lend legitimacy to nonstate violent punishment of blasphemy, a major one of which is the dominant religious discourse, which establishes the act of killing a blasphemer as an expression of a true Muslim's love for the Prophet. In this section, I will discuss popular narratives that glorify individuals who have committed such an act in the past. Drawing on the collective memory of past events and imbuing it with religious symbolism, these narratives construct models of desired action and appropriate ways of dealing with a blasphemer. I will further discuss how the spectacle of public punishment lends legitimacy to acts of collective violence against the accused. It must be kept in mind that the sources of legitimacy—popular narratives that glorify acts of private vengeance as well as the symbolic power of the spectacle of collective punishment—reinforce each other and are components of the same 'violent imaginaries' (Schröder and Schmidt 2001: 9). It is within these violent imaginaries that 'swift and harsh' punishment of alleged blasphemers is imagined and carried out (Berg and Wendt 2011: 14).

Constructing heroes through glorifying narratives

In an Urdu book titled *Shaheedan-e-Namoos-e-Risaalat* (*Martyrs of the Honour of the Prophet*), the editor Muhammad Mateen Khalid (2007) has put together a number of essays about 18 heroes. The essays are short biographies, discussing the lives, character, personalities and heroic deeds of the said martyrs. All 18 are considered heroes of Islam because they killed alleged blasphemers and were themselves executed by the state for murder. Hence, they are believed to have offered their lives to the cause of defending the honour of the Prophet Muhammad.

The first on this roll of honour is Ghazi Ilmuddin, who is one of the most legendary lovers of the Prophet Muhammad for present-day Muslims in Pakistan. He was the 21-year-old who in 1929 assassinated the Hindu publisher Mahashe Rajpal, who had published a book allegedly containing insulting remarks about the Prophet Muhammad. He was hanged for murder under the British government in 1931. Since then he has been revered by the Muslims of the Subcontinent for his display of true love for the Prophet. Discussions of the honour of the Prophet and blasphemy frequently reference his personality. Ilmuddin's name itself symbolises the pinnacle of love and passion for the Prophet Muhammad. In a dedicated biography of Ilmuddin, Rehman Maznab writes:

> Ghazi Ilmuddin was only a year old and his mother was nursing him when a beggar knocked at the door. She carried baby Ilmuddin to the door and opened it. She saw the beggar standing there and gave him some money. When she was about to close the door, the beggar glanced at the baby in her lap. The beggar addressed the mother and said, 'He is a lucky child and will bring a lot of fame to

his parents.' He further said, 'Allah has blessed you with a special gift in the form of this child. Look after him and always dress him in green.' (Maznab 2007)

Green is a colour associated with the Prophet Muhammad, as the dome of his mosque in Medina is painted green. In the story narrated above, the author is hinting at the special spiritual characteristics of Ilmuddin by birth. It is implied that he was chosen to be a successful lover of the Prophet. There are many other similar stories that exalt and glorify someone who carried out punishment of an alleged blasphemer even though the person in question was not well known before the act. Thus, it is in the narration of the act and the association of glorifying narratives with the person who committed the act that the public acceptance of such punishment is established. These glorifying narratives are a powerful source of legitimacy for not only the specific instance of punishment of a blasphemer, but also all future such events.

Ilmuddin is revered not just by marginalised or fringe sections of society. He was praised by Allama Muhammad Iqbal, the national poet and visionary of Pakistan. He was defended in the British court by Jinnah—some people believe, for free—who also threw his weight behind Ilmuddin's nonstate punishment of Rajpal. Thus, the founder of the nation and some of its most respected heroes supported Ilmuddin (Rumi 2018). More recently, on 15 January 2018, then Chief Minister of Punjab, Muhammad Shahbaz Sharif, named the newly constructed block of a public hospital after Ilmuddin, calling it 'Ghazi Ilmuddin Shaheed Block' (Pakistan Today 2018a). Thus, Ilmuddin is widely accepted as a hero of the nation, of Pakistanis and of Muslims.

There is an abundance of literature glorifying Ilmuddin, and even movies have been made by Pakistan's mainstream film industry. These films, which were not censored, depict explicit scenes of the killing of Rajpal by Ilmuddin. The literature and films portray a narrative of Ilmuddin's life that attributes to him spiritual powers and saintly characteristics.[4] Ilmuddin's shrine is in Lahore and an annual *urs* is arranged at the shrine. *Urs* is a Sufi concept that means the union of the lover (a human) with the

---

4 It was common for Muslims to turn offenders executed by the state during British rule into saints and heroes. Anderson (2015) wrote about this as a reason why, in some states, British judges preferred imprisonment and transfer to other colonies as punishment over execution.

beloved (God). The death of a Sufi is not lamented because it is a spiritual union and is to be celebrated. The caretaker of Ilmuddin's shrine in Lahore said in an interview:

> Ghazi Ilmuddin taught the whole humanity a lesson that no-one should mock others' religions. He made himself an example for the followers of Islam throughout the world by demonstrating that every devoted follower has the responsibility of protecting their religion. One should not fear death when it comes to fighting for the honour of the Prophet because that fight is for Islam, and if one dies while fighting for Islam then he becomes a Ghazi, and Ghazis have a very high place in *Jannat* ['heaven']; it is the greatest gift one could receive from God.

While historically Ilmuddin was the most celebrated 'martyr' and 'Ghazi' of the 'honour of the Prophet', there are many others like him. At present, Mumtaz Qadri is the most celebrated lover of the Prophet who delivered punishment to an alleged blasphemer and was himself punished by death. His personality has also been enormously glorified. Before Qadri was hanged, the religious leader of the mosque he used to regularly attend, Hanif Qureshi, published a book. In his statement in the court, Qadri declared that he had made up his mind to kill Taseer after attending one of Qureshi's sermons at the mosque. In the book, Qureshi recounts a 'miracle' that Mumtaz Qadri's father told him about. The miracle took place a few years before Qadri was born. Qureshi quotes Qadri's father as saying:

> We had a dedicated corner for prayer in our house where a prayer mat was always laid. I used to get up in the middle of the night to pray. One night, as I woke up for my prayer and reached that corner of the house, I saw a *Naurani shaksiyat* [a spiritual being made of light], dressed in white, praying on the prayer mat. I saw him finish his prayer and silently move towards the door. Before leaving, he told me: In the southern corner of this house, a friend of God will be born who will raise the flag of Islam's honour in the whole world and make you proud. Qadri was born two years later. I kept that spiritual encounter a secret until the day Qadri fulfilled his spiritual duty by killing the governor. (Qureshi 2012: 36–37)

Once Qadri was executed, more spiritual stories were associated with him. A few days after Qadri's funeral, a religious scholar claimed that he went to Qadri's grave and saw Qadri's hand emerge from the grave holding a sword. Qadri now has a shrine near Islamabad where his devotees go to offer prayers. While the killers who are still alive are also highly honoured by their supporters, it is after they die for the cause and become 'martyrs' that their spiritual journey is seen as complete and their status as saintly figures fully realised. Thus, the killers of alleged blasphemers are glorified themselves and at the same time shape the narratives of the ideal punishment for a blasphemer. In the interpretation and representation of punishment, heroes and legends are constructed, and more material is generated for the legitimation of future punishment of blasphemers.

Historicity plays a major role in the legitimation of violence; the present violence is justified against past violence and generates symbolic value for future violent action (Schröder and Schmidt 2001: 9). Experiences of violence imbued with cultural meanings are stored in society's collective or social memory and are an important resource on which to draw in the legitimation of future violence (Schröder and Schmidt 2001: 8–9). While drawing on the glories of past heroes provides meaning for the present, the heroes who are created in contemporary acts of violence become symbolic icons for future reference. They contribute to the construction of 'violent imaginaries' in which future acts of violence are imagined before they are performed (Schröder and Schmidt 2001). Thus, through representational strategies such as narratives, performances and inscriptions, the legitimacy of the nonstate punishment of alleged blasphemers is established. However, the narratives that glorify acts of violence do not automatically drive people to imitate those actions. At an individual level, the glorifying narratives and the wider religious discourse are interpreted and acted on differently by different people. One of Mumtaz Qadri's supporters, already quoted, described to me his experience of attending the hearing of Qadri's appeal in the Supreme Court of Pakistan:

> I was angry and wanted to throw my shoe at the judge's face, but I couldn't. I was not Mumtaz Qadri, who killed a blasphemer without any second thoughts, even though I am a Muslim and love the Prophet Muhammad. Mumtaz Qadri did what only chosen Muslims can do upon hearing of blasphemy against the Prophet Muhammad—peace be upon him.

He acknowledged that, while he saw Mumtaz Qadri as a hero for killing a blasphemer and embracing martyrdom, he could not do that himself. He saw it as a weakness of his own faith but proclaimed that, in principle, he supported the nonstate punishment of blasphemers. Similarly, most people who believe in the glorifying narratives are inspired to different degrees. For many, participating in collective violence rather than individual acts of heroism is an acceptable form of action. Nevertheless, the narratives that glorify nonstate violence against blasphemers are a key source of legitimacy on which to draw when such incidents do happen.

Staging legitimacy: The spectacle of public punishment

The instances in which individuals carry out punishment of blasphemers seldom take place in public. It is often *after* the act of killing that the killers claim the motivation behind their act was love of the Prophet, and it then becomes a public affair in which glorifying narratives are generated. In cases of mob violence, however, the punishment is carried out in public spaces where the act is visible to a large number of people. With advances in technology, that visibility is further increased, as videos and images are recorded and circulated, such as in the lynching of Mashal Khan. The public visibility, or spectacle, of such punishments is another key factor lending legitimacy to nonstate violence against blasphemers. The spectacle is created by the staging of power, as Schröder and Schmidt (2001: 6) argued:

> Violence without an audience will still leave people dead but is socially meaningless. Violent acts are efficient because of their staging of power and legitimacy, probably even more so than due to their actual physical results.

The power of staging is particularly important when the punishments are delivered by nonstate actors. Hence, the qualities of nonstate violence that make it effective as a practice include its highly visible and sensual nature, which makes it powerful enough to stage an ideological message before a public audience (Riches 1986: 11). Sidel (2006: 14) also argued that violence is 'performative and representational' by definition, as it seeks 'recognition in the—imagined—gaze of a broader audience'. Thus, collective violence against blasphemers is a potent means of communication employed by the perpetrators to convey several messages, including ideas of popular justice and their legitimacy. Through public violence, the state's claims to a monopoly over legitimate violence are also contested as the core purpose of violence often stems from contradictions over claims of legitimacy and justice (Krohn-Hansen 1994: 370–71). The ideas of popular justice that regard mob violence or vigilante action as a legitimate way of punishing blasphemers are embedded within the specific local historical context of Pakistan.

Vigilante justice is not exclusively applied to the punishment of those accused of blasphemy, although it has become a lot more frequent in such cases. In 2010, two teenage boys, Mughees and Muneeb, were lynched in Sialkot by a mob, in the presence of police, after being accused of robbery and murder (Dawn News 2011b). In 2014, after the terrorist attack on a school in Peshawar, there were widespread demands from the public—even progressive sections of society who condemn mob violence in cases of blasphemy—for public execution of the terrorists (Boone 2014). In response, the government lifted the moratorium on the death penalty, leading to the execution of hundreds in the following months to appease public anger (BBC News 2015). In January 2017, several bloggers, activists and university professors 'disappeared' in what were later revealed to be extrajudicial abductions by intelligence agencies (BBC News 2017; Hashim 2017a). A Facebook page called 'Pakistan Defence', with more than 8 million followers, accused the 'disappeared bloggers' of having engaged in anti-Islam and anti-Pakistan propaganda (Hashim 2017a). The public, at least on social media, was again demanding public punishment of those accused. In January 2018, a seven-year-old girl was raped and killed in Kasur, after a series of similar incidents over the previous few years in the same town (Dawn News 2018). People were once again furious and called for public execution by lynching, hanging or burning the culprits (Dawn News 2018). This time, a senate standing committee even proposed a bill seeking public hangings of rapists of young children (Pakistan Today 2018b). The bill was rejected by the National Assembly (Pakistan Today 2018b). However, if the bill had passed, it would not have been the first time in the history of Pakistan that public hangings were carried out.

In the 1980s, under the rule of military dictator General Zia-ul-Haq, public hangings were attended by thousands of spectators (Mehdi 2013). The practice was abandoned in 1988 with the return of democratic government. Thus, the idea of public punishment is not uncommon or new in Pakistan. There is a long history of public executions (either by the state/rulers or at the hands of the public) on the Indian Subcontinent more generally. During British rule, public hangings and execution by cannon were used to deter crime and control citizens (Anderson 2015). Public executions using elephants were common during the Mughal era (Schimmel 2004: 217; Weiss and Garfield 2017). The public acceptance or legitimacy of public punishment varied depending on the wider legitimacy of those in power, but the visual and performative aspects of public punishments were normalised.

The relationship between state and nonstate public executions requires some attention. There are different levels of legitimacy, legality and acceptability associated with the two. However, the fact they are both a *public spectacle* is of significance for the sake of my argument. When people accept and expect the spectacle of public punishment and believe in the legitimacy that goes beyond the legality and sovereignty of the state, nonstate public punishments are not an aberration. Thus, while public executions by the state in the past differed from the nonstate punishment of blasphemers in contemporary Pakistan, there are certain underlying similarities. Amy Wood (2009), in her book on lynching in America, illustrates the connection between public executions and nonstate public violence. In her appropriately titled chapter 'They Want to See the Thing Done', she argues that, while the lynchings of African-Americans that began in the 1880s were a new phenomenon, they were:

> firmly rooted in the traditional social performance of public executions. At public executions, white southerners learned what hanging a person looked like and that watching such a spectacle was socially acceptable. Lynch mobs even appropriated many rituals of public executions—the declarations of guilt, the confessions, the taking of souvenirs and photographs—to confer legitimacy on their extra-legal violence. They saw themselves not as criminals or defilers of the law, as their critics saw them, but as honorable vindicators of justice and popular sovereignty, fulfilling their rights as citizens to punish crimes against their communities. (Wood 2009: 24)

Thus, the two forms of public punishment are inherently similar as far as their performative and symbolic values are concerned. Wood (2009: 3) calls it 'the cultural power of lynching', which 'rested on spectacle: the crowds, the rituals and performances, and their sensational representations in narratives, photographs, and films'. Similarly, the spectacle of mob violence against alleged blasphemers is what makes it a powerful mode of punishment that derives legitimacy from the history of public punishment and shapes ideas of popular justice. Together with the glorifying narratives and dominant religious discourse concerning the punishment of blasphemy, the spectacle of punishment sends a message that 'the community has endorsed the killing' and that the perpetrators 'need not fear the sanction attached to killing' (Tambiah 1996: 278). It is therefore in the communal acceptance of violence—whether it is carried out by the state or by nonstate actors—that its legitimacy is established. Incidents of public violence are also 'performative representations' of 'antagonistic relationships' (Schröder and Schmidt 2001: 10). Nonstate violence against blasphemers represents an antagonistic relationship between the state and the claimants of religious authority within society. It is through the *public performance of violence* that the state's claim to a monopoly over legitimate violence is contested.

Conclusion

Nonstate punishment of those accused of blasphemy must be seen as political violence, contesting the state's claims of a monopoly over legitimate violence. Contestation for the *legitimate punishment of blasphemy* happens within the wider context of competing ideas of the Islamic state of Pakistan. The wider religious framework of the state—its claim to be an Islamic state and to represent the will of Allah—is what makes it vulnerable to challenges from within society about the correct interpretation and implementation of Islamic law. The state's monopoly over the exercise of legitimate violence is challenged because it is unable to deliver the ideals of Islamic justice as perceived by certain religious leaders and their followers. It is therefore a contest between the state and the religious authorities as to who more authentically represents the will of Allah and the Islamic justice system. The state of Pakistan, therefore, loses legitimacy due to the existence of multiple claimants of sovereign authority within society. In addition to the lack of absolute sovereignty, the failure of the legal system to effectively deliver the desired punishment to alleged blasphemers, and the perceived Westernised outlook of the ruling elite, as well as judges, contribute to the crisis of legitimacy of the Pakistani state. Due to this crisis of legitimacy, the proponents of popular narratives glorifying the nonstate violent punishment of blasphemers gain legitimacy and establish their authority to decide the fate of the accused. However, ideas of popular justice are what shape the standards of legitimacy against which the state's performance is judged in the first place. I argue that it is a vicious cycle in which the narratives of popular justice and the state's crisis of legitimacy mutually constitute and reinforce each other.

Within this system of mutual reinforcement, the state and nonstate actors have to constantly position themselves as legitimate in relation to each other. One way of establishing legitimacy is by placing the blame on the other party such that the state blames the people for 'taking the law into their own hands' and the proponents of nonstate justice blame their actions on the state's inability to deliver justice (Sundar 2010: 114). Thus, nonstate actors make their claims of legitimacy with reference to the state legal system. Nonstate punishments do not operate in complete opposition to the state; rather, they simultaneously accept and contest the state's legitimacy. Similar trends have been shown in other contexts where vigilante action or nonstate punishment demonstrates a desire for inclusion in the state justice system and, at the same time, a willingness to enforce punishments outside that system (Goldstein 2003: 33). It has also been shown that vigilantes are 'both antagonistic to the state and co-opted by it' (Smith 2004: 449).

On the other hand, the state also has to make a dual engagement with the ideas of popular justice—by dismissing those who take the law into their own hands and by itself coopting popular narratives. Those who represent the state of Pakistan (judges and officials of the government and other affiliated entities) have to constantly appeal to the religious discourse and popular ideas of justice to reestablish and sustain their legitimacy. For example, the day after the acquittal of Asia Bibi, the Chief Justice of Pakistan, Mian Saqib Nisar, made a separate statement in response to the widespread protests against the verdict. He declared:

> I and the bench [members] are all lovers of the Prophet (peace be upon him). We are ready to sacrifice ourselves for the Prophet's (PBUH [peace be upon him]) honour. But we are not judges only for Muslims. If there is no proof against someone, how can we punish them? (Bhatti 2018)

Judges had to justify their decision with reference to the popular ideals of justice rather than the legality of the state justice system. Similar statements have been made in the past by various others representing the state—including prime ministers—regardless of which party is in power. While these statements are meant to appeal to popular sentiment to garner legitimacy for the state, there are also occasions when parts of the state not only appeal to but also believe in and act on the popular narratives themselves. During my research, I learnt about incidents of the accused being killed while in police custody by members of the police themselves.

Other state actors—intelligence agencies with links to the military—have also reportedly been engaged in extrajudicial abductions and torture of persons accused of blasphemy (BBC News 2017). Thus, it is hard to draw boundaries between the state and society, and consequently between state and nonstate punishment of blasphemers. As Sundar (2010: 114) pointed out:

> Vigilantism by definition presupposes a state against whose monopoly over violence (cf. Weber) vigilante violence is measured. However, when practised by dominant groups in society or by a state against whose monopoly over violence (cf. Weber) vigilante violence is measured or by agents of the government itself, it questions the very contours of the state, making it hazy as to where the power of a legitimately constituted state ends and that of powerful groups in society begins.

Similarly, by demonstrating that the state's legitimacy and popular ideas of justice are not all that different from each other, I argue that the 'the very contours of the state' are obscure when it comes to the legitimate punishment of blasphemy in Pakistan.

6

At the nexus of state and society: Continuities and discontinuities between the legal system and popular justice

Nonstate punishment of, or vigilante action against, those accused of blasphemy is usually seen in stark opposition to the state legal system. However, there are many people who do not see state and nonstate punishments as expressions of two distinct systems of justice. Instead, they have a coherent worldview in which both state and nonstate punishments are simultaneously justified. There are also those who distinguish between the law and vigilante action, but even in so doing, they coopt the popular narratives that glorify acts of nonstate violence against those accused of blasphemy. In this chapter, I will demonstrate the continuities and discontinuities between the legal system and popular justice from the points of view of two groups of people who I believe are located at the nexus of the state and civil society. The first group is an organisation of lawyers who voluntarily represent the accusers in court to ensure that the state punishes the accused for their alleged offence of blasphemy. These lawyers also represent nonstate punishers in the courts, advocating that they should not be held culpable by the state. Therefore, this group of lawyers supports both state and nonstate punishment of alleged blasphemers. The second group are the state judges deciding on the cases of blasphemy. While the lawyers stand truly at the nexus of state and society as they mediate between the two, the judges officially represent the state but are also a part of the society. My discussion of the lawyers is based on my ethnographic fieldwork with them over several months, and the discussion of the judges' discourse is based on publicly available court judgements.

In the first section of this chapter, I will discuss the discourse of a specific group of lawyers. These lawyers engage with multiple arguments and narratives to construct a coherent worldview in which they simultaneously support state and nonstate punishment of alleged blasphemers. I will discuss the major narratives with which they engage, such as reason-based justifications, Sufi ideals of devotion and passionate love in which they actively defy reason and textual interpretations of religious sources. This section will demonstrate how they believe in multiple sources of legitimacy and strategically construct their arguments in various circumstances. I argue that the multiple and apparently dissonant narratives provide the lawyers with meaning as well as resources for strategic argumentation. I contend that the lawyers' discourse demonstrates a continuity rather than a dissonance between reason and passion as they construct a coherent worldview in which both state and nonstate punishments are justified.

In the second section of this chapter, I will discuss the discourse of judges. Judges also draw on multiple sources of legitimacy—state law and Western legal concepts, textual sources of Islamic law and popular narratives such as that about the heroic figure of Ghazi Ilmuddin—in constructing their arguments. An analysis of court judgements will show that these sources can be used in different ways. For example, religious sources are referred to in judgements both in favour of *and* against the accused. The lower courts, sessions courts, usually refer to religious sources (Quran and *hadith*) and popular narratives when making decisions *against* the accused. Higher court judges may employ the same sources to reach the opposite decision, *in favour of* the accused. Hence, judges exercise discursive reasoning to reach various decisions while drawing on the same set of sources. Nevertheless, even in the boldest of the judgements in favour of the accused, judges have to appeal not only to the textual interpretations of religious sources, but also to popular narratives concerning nonstate punishment. Hence, I suggest the legal system and popular justice should be seen as extensions of each other rather than two distinct and competing domains. Through an analysis of the discourse of lawyers and judges, I argue against the dichotomies of reason/passion and state/nonstate in understanding the legitimate punishment of blasphemy in Pakistan.

The discourse of lawyers: Reason, passion and strategic argumentation

Mustafa Chaudhry, a soft-spoken middle-aged man with a short greying beard, wearing a black suit that is the uniform for lawyers, enters the Lahore Sessions Court every morning. Most days he is accompanied by three or four male lawyers, all in their black suits, and a female lawyer wearing a hijab over a black coat and a traditional white dress. This is his core team but on occasions there may be many more lawyers accompanying him. Sitting on benches in tin sheds in the concrete yards of the Sessions Court, their day starts with cups of tea. The 'tea boys' highly regard Chaudhry and his team, as do other lawyers passing by, who stop to pay their respects. As they sip tea, they also organise the files for the cases they are to attend that day. Every day, they appear in several cases of blasphemy as volunteer private prosecution lawyers for the complainants. Sometimes, their daily agenda also includes attending hearings as volunteer defence lawyers for those who have carried out violent punishment of alleged blasphemers outside the legal system. They believe they are doing so for love of the Prophet Muhammad, as is their religious duty. According to them, each and every blasphemer from around the country must be punished harshly, and those who punish the accused outside the law are the epitome of the passionate love and devotion that a Muslim should have for the Prophet Muhammad.

Chaudhry heads Khatm-e-Nabuwwat Lawyers' Forum (KNLF), an 800-member organisation of lawyers on a dual mission to prosecute all cases of blasphemy across Pakistan and defend those who punish the alleged blasphemers outside the law. The founding members of the KNLF, which is based in Lahore, claim they are all professional lawyers who offer their services voluntarily for the sake of *namoos-e-risaalat* ('honour of the Prophet') in the path of Allah. They have a women's wing as well that assists the forum especially with cases of blasphemy in which the accused are women (recall that the officially named accusers or complainants are rarely women). The KNLF lawyers claim that whenever there is an allegation of blasphemy, anywhere in Pakistan, they visit, meet the accusers and the accused and assist in the prosecution. They assert that they 'conduct proper research' as to whether or not the offence was actually committed before offering their legal assistance to the complainants. However, during my five months of regular interaction with them, I came across many instances in which they decided to support the accusers the moment they heard of the incident, before verifying the details of the case being reported. Nevertheless, they always maintained their claim that they work without bias or prejudice against the accused, and that they fight only for the love of Allah and his Prophet. For cases outside Lahore, they assist and support local lawyers from the relevant areas. Many of those local lawyers are members of the forum, too.

Besides the registered members, many other lawyers also join the KNLF when they appear before the courts for blasphemy-related trials. KNLF has a communications team that is responsible for circulating messages among the lawyers' community about the time, date and location of blasphemy-related trials. When I asked Chaudhry about the purpose of non-member lawyers attending the trials, he said: 'Every Muslim lawyer wants to register his presence in the court of Allah'. It is worth noting that these lawyers refer to the courts of law as the 'court of Allah', but they are not accepted as the *only* courts of Allah. In the previous chapter, I mentioned that religious leader Khadim Hussain Rizvi did not accept the 'courts' of the modern state of Pakistan as the places where Islamic justice is delivered. For the KNLF lawyers, however, the state courts represent courts of Islamic justice in most cases.

KNLF members have appeared in hundreds of cases of blasphemy since the 1990s. During the period of my research with them, they appeared in multiple trials for blasphemy (sometimes as many as half a dozen) every day. I accompanied them to many of these trials and spent the remainder of my time with them either at their bench in the Lahore Sessions Court or at the personal office of the KNLF president, Mustafa Chaudhry. The two most iconic cases they have represented in the Supreme Court of Pakistan are *Asia Bibi vs The State* and *Mumtaz Qadri vs The State*. In the former, they supported punishment according to state law for a woman accused of insulting the Prophet Muhammad. In the latter, they supported the perpetrator of the nonstate killing of Salman Taseer, who was accused of blasphemy for his criticism of Pakistan's blasphemy laws. Thus, they support state and nonstate punishment of alleged blasphemers at the same time.

My first meeting with the KNLF's founding members was an uneasy one, with suspicion and mistrust on both sides. I was afraid they would disapprove of me and my personal ideas (if they found out what they were) as not conforming with their religious understanding. I was uncertain of the consequences of such an evaluation from their side. They, on the other hand, were suspicious of my motives. I had Chaudhry's phone number and called him to ask for an interview. I told him I was a PhD student researching the blasphemy laws in Pakistan. When I arrived at his small third-floor office in an old, tattered building on a very busy street just behind the Lahore High Court, he and a few other members of his team, including the head of the women's wing, were present. It was a hot September afternoon and they cheerfully offered me tea and soft drink. However, before I could start talking to them, they asked me several questions. They asked me about my religion and sect, my 'school of thought', the reason I was interested in the blasphemy laws, why I chose it as my research topic and my take on the issue of blasphemy. I hesitantly answered their questions about my religious and sectarian background. They were somewhat relieved to hear that I was from a Shia family as Shias are considered much closer to the Sunni Barelwis when it comes to reverence of holy personalities and objects—compared with Sunni Deobandis, who criticise both the Sunni Barelwis and Shias for veneration of persons and objects. Nevertheless, I told them that, as a researcher, I was interested in understanding the viewpoints of different parties on the issue of blasphemy and that I had formed no opinions on the matter. Naturally, they were suspicious of me and thus gave very calculated responses to my questions in that first meeting.

It is important to see how the lawyers' answers in the first meeting differed from the opinions they shared in my later meetings with them, when they had become more comfortable with my presence. During my interactions with them, they went from defending the state law to arguing that there may be exceptional circumstances in which punishment can be delivered outside the legal system, to presenting nonstate punishers as the epitome of devotional and passionate love even in the absence of 'exceptional circumstances'. I will begin by discussing their initial responses in which they defended the law concerning the punishment of blasphemy. These responses shed light on how the KNLF members engage in a dialogue with a legal framework that claims to embody Islamic law but is also embedded in Western legal concepts and structures. Such an engagement is a persistent concern for them and shapes their ideas and responses. In my first meeting with them, when I asked them about the appropriate punishment for a blasphemer, Chaudhry replied:

> When the law is present, we should refer the cases [of insult to Islam and the Prophet Muhammad] to the law. The purpose of law in any society is to maintain order. If people get up and start punishing other people on their own, there will be no peace left in the society. Rule of law must always prevail.

He further asserted:

> If we did not have the blasphemy laws in place, can you imagine what would have been the fate of all the accused in these cases? The justice would have been served in the streets and neighbourhoods. So, the blasphemy law is indeed a great blessing for the blasphemers. It gives them a chance to clarify themselves in case there has been a misunderstanding or false allegation. In the absence of this law, Ghazi Ilmuddin's law would be implemented. There are so many cases currently being heard in the courts. The trials are going on. These are our courts; we must support them. People should be made aware of the existence of the blasphemy laws and their right usage. The appropriate way is to bring any incident to the court's notice and support it with evidence.

Not only did he justify the need for the blasphemy laws, but also he praised the procedures required for registering a case, the trial methods and even the court judgements. After describing the whole procedure from the instant an accusation is levelled to court judgements, he said:

> You see, this is a foolproof method already in place to prevent the misuse of blasphemy laws. With all the safeguards against false reporting, there is no space left for the misuse of blasphemy laws in the legal procedures.

He emphasised several times that there was no misuse of the blasphemy laws and any such claims were mere propaganda from those who wanted to undermine the laws protecting Islam. He was referring here to the state law and Western legal principles in which he and his fellow lawyers had been trained. Nevertheless, this sense of legality (which remained present in their discussions throughout the course of my study) was not the only frame of moral reference on which they drew. They qualified their understanding of the law and legality with alternative ideas of legality derived from their religious and personal beliefs. One of the narratives they employed to qualify their understanding of the 'rule of law' and the legality of state law was based on the idea of 'exceptional circumstances'.

Exceptional circumstances, ineffective state laws and helpless victims

Having praised Pakistan's existing blasphemy laws, and after emphasising the importance of the 'rule of law', Chaudhry qualified his opinion:

> There may be exceptional circumstances when somebody is helpless. For example, let us look at the case of Salman Taseer … There were many applications to register a case against him. Petitions were made, but the court ruled that, as a governor, he was afforded protection by the Constitution. So, a case could not be registered against him. Both Lahore and Islamabad high courts dismissed petitions against him. There were protests from religious organisations all across the country. Mumtaz Qadri himself took an application to a police station to register the case. The police reproached him, calling him a *moulvi* [in this instance, a derogatory term for a person with a beard] and asked him to leave.[1] Despite all these protests and petitions against him, no apology or statement was issued by the governor or his spokesperson. He not only stood by his [blasphemous] words and [transgressive] actions, he further said on TV that he keeps the *moulvis* at the tip of his shoe. In such circumstances, there had to be an ultimate reaction. If the government had upheld the law created by the state, there would not have been the need for any Qadri to be born. So, in such a situation, exceptional circumstances have to be taken into account.

The 'exceptional circumstances' to which Chaudhry refers are imagined in relation to the state's inability to and ineffectiveness in carrying out desired punishments. Chaudhry explained:

> The nonstate punishment takes place when people feel that justice will not be served, and the blasphemer will be able to get away with it, as happened in the case of Salman Taseer. If the government had asked Taseer to resign and made him face the charges in the court, this would not have happened. Whenever there is mistrust between a person and the government, such incidents [of nonstate punishment] will take place.

Therefore, we see that an emphasis on the authenticity of legal claims (according to state law) and the ineffectiveness of the existing law, inducing a sense of helplessness, go hand in hand. This tension between the legality of state law and an extended legality of nonstate violence due to the ineffectiveness of state law remained a pertinent theme of my discussions with the members of KNLF. The sense of helplessness in Chaudhry's account rests on the image of lovers of the Prophet—

---

1   This story does not exist on the official legal record. Despite being Qadri's defence lawyer, Chaudhry did not bring it up in his legal arguments in the court.

true Muslims—as victims due to the ineffectiveness of the law and the government in delivering justice by punishing alleged blasphemers. It is derived from a feeling of being attacked, since they perceive themselves as peaceful Muslims who are attacked (by a blasphemer) and forced to act in a certain way. One day, while at Chaudhry's office, I met one of his clients, a Sunni Barelwi man. He wanted to register a complaint about disrespect of the 'holy personages' against an Ahmadi publisher who had published allegedly disrespectful material against prophets (Muhammad and Jesus) and Imam Hussain (the grandson of Prophet Muhammad). In explaining this particular case to me, the KNLF lawyers said:

> These people [the Ahmadis] are very powerful. Due to their influence and contacts, it is very difficult to get a complaint registered against them. Many people have tried to register a FIR [first information report] against them but the police refuse. We have *fatwas* from religious organisations and orders from some government authorities as well. We even had an order issued from the Lahore High Court that a police case should be registered, despite which no action has been taken by the police so far.

After showing me several documents with orders and *fatwas* from religious scholars and organisations against the accused publisher, they continued:

> These people publish such derogatory material that any Muslim who reads it will be severely hurt. There is no way to rectify the hurt. It is as if someone cuts the main artery of an animal and leaves it to bleed, to die a slow and painful death, and does not even offer water. Disrespect of the Prophet is like cutting our main artery ... They tie our hands and feet and leave us agonised. In such a situation, if some devout Muslim resorts to the desperate measure of killing a blasphemer, the whole world will reproach us for taking the law into our own hands and present us as violent people.

The perception is therefore that the first instance of attack or violence is perpetrated by the blasphemer; the reaction of killing the blasphemer is merely self-defence by the helpless victims of their attacks. These narratives of helplessness and injustice serve as an alternative point of reference for ideas of legality. They also induce sentiments of victimhood that fuel the passion for hero-worship—that is, the glorification of those who retaliate and are able to deliver punishment to the blasphemers. The more powerful the alleged blasphemer is perceived to be, the higher is the reverence accorded to her/his killer. Qadri is seen not only as the killer of an alleged blasphemer, but also as a symbol of resistance to power as it was the governor of Punjab he took down. He faced a much higher degree of helplessness with the highest of odds stacked against him. The number of people who came on to the streets at Qadri's funeral, the enormous amount of funds that were collected by the Qadri Foundation after his execution by the state, the construction of a shrine on his grave and the flocking of devotees to it (Pasha 2016)—all are signs of the reverence bestowed on the killer of a blasphemer, amplified in accordance with the narrative of helplessness and victimhood.

While the narrative of helplessness and injustice provides the lawyers with a compelling reason-based argument to justify their extended framework of moral legality, it is not the complete story. The explanation of nonstate violence as a consequence of 'exceptional circumstances' does not hold true if we look at my later interactions with the lawyers. The KNLF lawyers proudly supported those who punished blasphemers outside the law even when there were no exceptional circumstances and when the law was already in action. In such cases, they relied on ideas of devotion and passionate love—yet another narrative they used to construct their arguments. I will now discuss the narrative of devotion, passionate love and intuitive knowledge that drives the lawyers' judgements.

Devotion, passionate love and intuitive knowledge of the heart

One morning, after a hearing in the Lahore High Court that I attended with the KNLF team, Chaudhry suggested that we go to his office where a woman was waiting for him. She was the mother of a 23-year-old, Ahmed, who was sentenced to death in 2012 and imprisoned for killing a man accused of burning the Quran. I accompanied Chaudhry to his office and met this woman and another of her sons, who was accompanying her. She was a thin elderly woman, in very simple clothes and a white *chaadar* (large piece of cloth covering the head and body); her son was also a very plain village man. As per their account, one winter night during Ramzan (the Islamic month of fasting) a man burnt a Quran in their village, near a local shrine. This man was aged in his thirties and was a person of 'bad reputation'. He was known to be a thief and used to tease women in the community. He was also a drug addict. There were no witnesses to the act, but people who lived nearby found a burnt copy of the Quran and accused him of having burnt it. Ahmed, who was 15 years old and a student in the ninth grade at the time, lived in the same neighbourhood. He was a passionate boy. On learning about the incident, he went to the man accused of burning the Quran and asked him why he had done so. The man said: 'Yes, I have burnt the Quran, what can you do now?' Ahmed stabbed him with a knife and killed him on the spot.

After Ahmed's mother told us the story, with tears in her eyes, Chaudhry asked her whether she believed her son had committed the right deed. She said she thought he did the right thing because the dead man was 'a nuisance to the community anyway'. Chaudhry again asked her, in an assertive tone, whether it was due to the deceased being a blasphemer by burning a Quran that she thought her son's action was right. She said, more thoughtfully this time: 'Of course, burning the Quran was the prime reason and the foremost concern for us is the gracious Prophet'. Chaudhry declared that only if she was happy with and proud of her son's act would he take up the case for no charge and fight for Ahmed's freedom. He told her and her other son that Ahmed was a *ghazi* ('a successful warrior') and she was lucky to have such a brave, *naik aur kismet wala* ('pious and chosen') son. He said only lucky and blessed people were given such opportunities for spiritual fulfilment. He reassured Ahmed's agonised mother not to worry and to be thankful for the path (of love) on which her son had set his foot.

Ahmed's family was poor and lived in a small village. His father had died about 15 years earlier. Ahmed's three brothers worked as manual labourers in building and construction. They did not own land but had their own house. Chaudhry had written a letter to ask Ahmed's mother and brother to come to visit him in Lahore to appeal Ahmed's death sentence. He paid for their travel to and from the city. He had also bought some women's and children's clothes (in various sizes) and gave them to Ahmed's mother. He asked me to open the bag and show the clothes to her and her son before giving them away. Chaudhry proudly told me after this episode that he was fighting for many other *ghazis* who had killed blasphemers. In Ahmed's case, there were no 'exceptional circumstances' that would have made punishing the accused blasphemer through the state legal system unachievable. Ahmed acted solely on a whim and did not try to access the law in this matter. Nevertheless, Chaudhry not only supported him wholeheartedly, but also proactively reached out to his family to provide them with free legal services to save Ahmed from his death sentence. He told me that it was through these 'selfless' deeds (of helping the *ghazis* of Allah and his Prophet) that he hoped to receive salvation and success in the afterlife.

There were many other cases in which the KNLF lawyers were advocating for *ghazis* who had committed acts of violence against alleged blasphemers despite legal action being taken against them by the state. I will discuss in detail one example, that of Yousaf Ali, who had been sentenced to death for blasphemy, and Tariq, who was on death row for murder. They were both in jail in Lahore when, in 2002, Tariq killed Yousaf, for which he was later acquitted in court; Chaudhry was his defence lawyer. Tariq has since been revered as a hero, a *ghazi*, with movies and literature created around his character. This case also highlights how the performance of violent action is experienced and construed as well as how it is narrated and glorified.

One December afternoon, while sitting with the KNLF lawyers at their bench in the Lahore Sessions Court, Chaudhry and his close companion Tahir Sultan started telling me about Tariq. They have a close relationship with Tariq and think of him as a saintly figure. According to them, Tariq was chosen by Allah to perform the very special task of killing the blasphemer and false claimant of prophethood, Yousaf, who is popularly called 'Yousaf Kazzab', meaning 'Yousaf the Liar'. Yousaf allegedly claimed to be a prophet and was sentenced to death in 2000 by a lower court. Chaudhry appeared as the prosecuting lawyer against Yousaf and also defended his murderer, Tariq, in court. The following account of Yousaf and Tariq highlights how Chaudhry and other members of the KNLF support the nonstate killing of blasphemers regardless of whether legal action has been taken against them by the state.

According to Chaudhry and his team, Yousaf was a leader of a self-proclaimed religious group and used to preach false beliefs in the name of Islam. He would lure people into coming to his special room with a promise of *ziarat* ('seeing') the Prophet; and, after going through some ritual procedures, he proclaimed himself the Prophet. He allegedly played this trick with several people, who testified against him in court. He also proclaimed in his sermons that certain verses of the Quran were narrated in reference to him. Thus, he was accused of preaching false beliefs and of indirectly committing blasphemy by posing as a prophet. The court sentenced him to death for insulting the Prophet and posing as a prophet, among other charges.

Tariq was in the same prison as Yousaf on charges of murder. Another prisoner, who was Tariq's friend, had planned to kill Yousaf, but his plans were discovered and he was shifted to another jail. Before leaving, he told Tariq that it was now his duty to carry out the sacred task of killing Yousaf. Chaudhry and his team narrated the incident of that murder to me:

> Tariq had smuggled the gun into the jail through a friend. He had a conversation with the gun while sitting in his prison cell and told it that he planned to kill a *gustaakh-e-rasool* ['blasphemer']. He begged the gun: 'Please be on my side and support me in this sacred endeavour.' After that, events turned out such that Allah Himself provided the perfect opportunity for the act of killing to take place. Yousaf walked past Tariq's cell as he was being shifted to another cell. Right at that time, Tariq was outside his cell for the regular walk that was allowed for 30 minutes every morning and 30 minutes every evening to all the prisoners. When he saw Yousaf coming, he ran back into his cell and brought the gun. He emptied all six bullets into Yousaf's body. Yousaf was a black magician so he tried to ward off the attack by reciting some verses and moving his hand in a particular way [a gesture of magic]. However, Allah made even his magic ineffective/void. At the same time, a whirl of wind blew in such a direction that the garbage from the ground started rising up and sticking to Yousaf's body under the pressure of the wind. Yousaf fell on the ground and died. Tariq handed the gun over to the police superintendent, rushed back to his cell and offered prayers of gratitude.

The lawyers emphasised repeatedly that the sequence of events was made possible and facilitated by Allah Himself. They believe Allah then favoured Tariq so that he was acquitted by the court despite having three charges of murder against him. They insisted that Tariq was not a very pious or practising Muslim; rather, he was chosen by Allah to perform this highly spiritual act. I asked Chaudhry whether I could meet Tariq and other *ghazis* he had been talking about. A friend of his, a journalist and self-proclaimed *aashiq-e-rasool* ('lover of the Prophet') who was sitting next to him, asked whether I would like to meet *Ghazi* Qadri, too. I was surprised as Qadri had been executed months before this conversation took place. Seeing confusion on my face, he said: 'Forget it, you won't understand, these are ideas of *maarifat*'. They all exchanged glances and secretive smiles. I asked them to explain and, on my insistence, they agreed. Chaudhry asked whether I had listened to the *qawwali* ('devotional song') 'Oh disdaa meray peer wala werha' (lit.: 'There I See My Master's Courtyard'). I had not, so he went on to explain:

> The *qawwali* begins with the story of a man who had been sentenced to death by a king. However, whenever he was taken to the gallows, the rope broke mysteriously, safely landing him on to the ground. After several of these episodes, the king asked him to explain the matter. He smiled and said: '*Yeh meray pir ki karaamat hai* [This is the miracle of my spiritual master].' When the king demanded to see his spiritual master, he replied that the only way to see his *pir* ['spiritual master'] was to change positions with him. He said: 'Come in my place [on the gallows] and then you will be able to see my *pir*.'

Chaudhry and his journalist friend explained to me that Qadri is a *pir* to them and, to be able to see him, one must be at an advanced stage of love called *maarifat*. They told me that *maarifat* is not for everyone; only *chosen people* experience this intense form of love and devotion.

Maarifat, karamat, pir and the notion of being *chosen* are specific concepts within the mystical tradition of Sufism in South Asian Islam (see, for example, Schimmel 1975; Werbner and Basu 1998). Here I will only briefly describe the meanings associated with these ideas in the Sufi mystic tradition. Sufis are mystics on a path or journey to the *absolute truth*—that is, God (Schimmel 1975: 130–35). *Ishq* ('intense love') and *maarifat* ('inner knowledge or gnosis') are described as the last stations on this mystical path (Schimmel 1975). First, *ishq* has been praised as the highest possible state of a mystic (Schimmel 1975) because hearts that love God will receive a vision of him. However, such a station of love cannot be achieved without the will of Allah—that is, by being chosen by him. Schimmel (1975: 138) describes this:

> The mystics felt that the love they experienced was not their own work but was called into existence by God's activity … God's love precedes human love. Only when God loves His servant can he love Him, and on the other hand, he cannot refuse to love God, since the initiative comes from God.

Second, gnosis or *maarifat* is the light of certainty gained through intuitive knowledge that is the only possible way of approaching the mystery of love. This is the kind of knowledge that is opposed to knowledge gained by reason. Sufi mystics have often shown disdain for intellect or knowledge gained by worldly discursive reason, as described by Schimmel (1975: 140): 'On the way of love, intellect is like the donkey that carries books; it is a lame ass'.

The *pir* can thus be any spiritual leader who has been chosen by God to be in love with him. However, love of God is not possible without love of the Prophet Muhammad. Love of the Prophet is indeed seen as an essential stage leading to love of God. It was often termed *fanaa-fi-rasul* ('annihilation in the Prophet'). Hence, the Prophet is the ultimate spiritual leader or *pir* as all *pirs* enshrine his love (Schimmel 1975: 211–16). The Prophet Muhammad is the centre of devotion for mystics in Islam, as demonstrated by various forms of veneration including poetry, literature and performance. In fact, as Asani et al. (1995: 1) wrote in their book *Celebrating Muhammad*, no-one can estimate the power of Islam as a religion without first considering that at the heart of the tradition is love for the Prophet Muhammad.

Understanding the significance of these Sufi concepts and how they are employed in the discourse about nonstate violence against alleged blasphemers highlights the shift between reason-based and devotion-based discourses. *Ghazis* such as Tariq and Qadri are the chosen ones; they have been picked to love Allah and his Prophet by being given the opportunity (and spiritual powers) to punish alleged blasphemers. Their sense of right and wrong is thus derived not from discursive reason or state law. State law is merely an instrument to serve the ultimate truth—a truth that can only be gained by love and devotion. Their source of certainty and knowledge is the *maarifat*, the intuitive inner knowledge of the heart. They are also considered *pirs* because they have love of the ultimate *pir*—that is, the Prophet Muhammad—in their hearts. The KNLF lawyers themselves claim to be lovers of the Prophet and of those who are at a higher stage of loving the Prophet, the *ghazis*.

Another important concept that shapes their personal journeys on the 'path of love' is that of being sinners who pin their hopes of salvation to the love of the Prophet in their hearts. Throughout my research, I came across Pakistani Muslims who consider themselves sinful and in need of redemption and purification. In the story of Tariq, too, the lawyers told me he was not a pious practising Muslim. Rather, he was a sinner. But they rely on the mystical conception of the Prophet Muhammad as the intercessor for doomsday, who will intercede even for the greatest sinners of the Muslim community (Schimmel 1975: 10–11). The lawyers also have a sense of *maarifat* as they feel their understanding of the matters of the heart, or their inner knowledge, will be incomprehensible to outsiders who base their understanding on discursive reason. That is why they did not talk to me of these ideas until much later. The initial responses they gave were more inclined towards reason-based understandings of law, justice and exceptional circumstances. This implies that they are themselves conscious of the conflicts and contradictions between the matters of the heart and the matters of the mind with which they must deal every day. However, their reason-based responses also demonstrate an attempt to reconcile the two paradigms. It shows how they want the legal framework of the state to recognise matters of the heart. Intuitive knowledge or *maarifat* is the principle of decision-making for them, in terms of who is right and who is wrong, who should be punished and how, and they want this deeper sense of moral justice to prevail over the law of the state. By advocating against punishing those who carry out punishments of alleged blasphemers outside the law, they claim that the intuitive convictions of the heart should be acknowledged within the legal framework of the state.

The lawyers' arguments inside the court

So far, I have discussed two major narratives that the lawyers of KNLF employ to justify their support of nonstate violence against alleged blasphemers. First, they rely on reason-based arguments in which they blame the ineffectiveness of the legal system and exceptional circumstances for the occurrence of nonstate violence. Second, at a deeper level, they engage with narratives of devotion and passionate love as higher sources of morality. I also followed them into the courtroom, where they used a third set of arguments based on textual interpretations of Islamic law. They used some references to the Quran and *hadith* outside the courts as well, but they engaged with these sources in much greater detail inside the courtroom, where they used at least three sets of arguments: reason-based, passion-based and textual interpretations of religious sources. In terms of reason-based arguments, they relied on the concept of 'sudden and grave provocation'—a Western legal concept—to argue that those who kill blasphemers outside the law should not be held culpable as they act in self-defence against the attacks by blasphemers. They further argued that those who punish blasphemers outside the legal system are driven by their devotion and passionate love for the Prophet and hence should be absolved of any charges. Finally, they used references to the Quran and *hadith* to make their point and support their arguments through textual interpretations of Islamic law.

Their references to Quranic verses and prophetic traditions demonstrated that Allah and the Prophet Muhammad had not only allowed, but also encouraged, the individuals who killed those who insulted the Prophet.[2] Nonetheless, it is important to note that the lawyers' engagement with religious sources incorporated both reason and passion. Through discursive reasoning, they proved that the nonstate punishment of blasphemers is both rational and emotive, and that both aspects are valid provisions as per state law as well as Islamic law. I have argued throughout this book against the dichotomy of reason and passion in understanding the issue of blasphemy in Pakistan. The discourse of the KNLF lawyers further demonstrates that reason and passion are not only simultaneously present, but also mutually constitutive elements in the popular consciousness concerning the punishment of blasphemy. In the KNLF lawyers' worldview, it is completely reasonable for passionate lovers of the Prophet to kill alleged blasphemers outside the law based on their devotion and the provisions of Islamic law.

The lawyers' shifting narratives: Strategic argumentation

The discussion so far has shown multiple narratives on which the lawyers rely to justify their simultaneous support of state and nonstate punishments of blasphemy. Before moving on, I would like to emphasise that none of these narratives should be seen as either more or less valid than the other. The purpose of discussing these narratives is to highlight the multiple ways in which the lawyers as agents make meaning out of their work and strategically use those meanings to achieve certain ends. In interactions with outsiders (such as researchers like me, journalists and the media), they want to achieve acceptance as both professional lawyers and good Muslims who love the Prophet. They are uncertain as to whether or not these people share their devotional worldview, so they hesitate to bring up the narratives of passionate love and intuition. Hence, they are more likely to use reason-based arguments on the ineffectiveness of existing laws, which fosters a sense of injustice and helplessness. The narrative of victimhood of Muslims who are facing 'vile attacks against Islam and their beloved Prophet' is also more likely to be used in these

---

2   Most of these references were the same as quoted in Chapter 2 when describing the dominant religious discourse concerning blasphemy in Pakistan.

circumstances as it portrays a clearer *us versus them* picture, establishes the existence of a threat to society and justifies blasphemy-related violence as a mechanism of self-defence.

In interactions with other forum members who are also seen as the 'circle of lovers of the Prophet', and within the wider community of lawyers, their aim is to project their piety and spirituality as being higher than that of other lawyers, to gain political and social influence (for example, in the legal associations) and legitimise their cause. Hence, they fall back on Sufi-mystic concepts of love, devotion and passion when talking to each other. Talking of these ideas also brings them respect within the larger community of lawyers for whom these ideas resonate with their own religious beliefs. In the courts, the aim is to win the argument by bringing in sources that cannot be denied. Therefore, they use references to sources of Islamic law in addition to their reason-based and passion-based arguments. Using religious texts and sources also asserts a certain pressure on the judges, which is very much an intended effect. Therefore, in addition to Western legal concepts, they rely on religious texts and scholarly works to strengthen not only their arguments but also their position vis-a-vis the opposing parties by siding with Allah and his Prophet. It must also be noted that the shift between narratives also coincides with a shift in the use of language. When discussing reason-based justifications—such as self-defence, sudden provocation and other modern Western legal concepts—the lawyers use English words and terms. However, when talking about passion-based explanations and mystic ideas of love, devotion and intuitive knowledge, they usually use Urdu (the national language) or, even more so, Punjabi (the local language in Lahore). Thus, they not only shift between different arguments and narratives but also between different ontologies when speaking of different explanations for nonstate killings of blasphemers.

Nevertheless, these narratives should not be seen as mere means to certain ends; rather, they are meaningful and significant in their own right. They are both the motive and the means at the same time. They are actual belief systems and worldviews as well as carefully chosen arguments within specific circumstances. In fact, one of the main points I would like to assert is the continuity of what seems dissonant and discontinuous on the surface. The lawyers' discourse indeed presents a continuity and a coherent worldview constructed through various narratives and arguments. They are conscious of some of the contradictions and actively try to reconcile their worldview with the legal system. However, the different narratives they use—exceptional circumstances, devotion and religious law—are all components of a coherent ideology and way of life for them.

The discourse of judges: The law and popular justice

The judges deciding on cases of blasphemy also draw on multiple sources in their official judgements. They refer to modern legal principles and the sovereignty of the state as per the Constitution, religious sources and wider popular narratives. Their references to the sovereignty of the state and the Constitution distinguish between state and nonstate punishments. However, in the same judgements, they may refer to religious sources and other popular narratives that not only allow but also glorify nonstate punishment of alleged blasphemers. The judges' discourse also demonstrates that they find some discrepancies between 'the law of the land' and the legal ideal based on religious sources and popular justice. Let us first consider how the judges try to establish the state's monopoly over violence through references to the law. I will then discuss how they use religious sources and popular narratives in their judgements, through which they transcend the state's legality.

The law and the state's monopoly over violent punishment

In the recent Supreme Court judgement in *Asia Bibi vs The State* (2018: 13–14), the judges referred to Pakistan's Constitution:

> It is worth mentioning that it is a matter of great pride and satisfaction that we are governed by a written Constitution and Statutory Laws. The Constitution, as per Article 4 thereof mandates that 'to enjoy the protection of law and to be treated in accordance with the law is an inalienable right of every citizen, wherever he may be, and of every other person for the time being within Pakistan. In particular (a) no action detrimental to the life, liberty, body, reputation or property of any person shall be taken except in accordance with law (b) no person shall be prevented from or be hindered in doing that which is not prohibited by law; and no person shall be compelled to do that which the law does not require him to do.' ... Thus, under the authority and

> command of the Constitution and the Law, it is the duty of the State to ensure that no incident of blasphemy shall take place in the country. In case of the commission of such [a] crime, only the State has the authority to bring the machinery of law into operation, bringing the accused before a Court of competent jurisdiction for trial in accordance with [the] law. However, it is not for the individuals, or a gathering [the mob], to decide as to whether any act falling within the purview of Section 295-C has been committed or not, because as stated earlier, it is the mandate of the Court to make such decision[s] after conducting a fully qualified trial and on the basis of credible evidence brought before it. No such parallel authority could in any circumstances be bestowed upon any individual or a group of persons.

In the above excerpt, the judges assert the state's authority by arguing that it is the only legitimate deliverer of punishment and nonstate actors cannot punish alleged blasphemers themselves. Similarly, in the case of *Mumtaz Qadri vs The State* (2015: 37–38), the Supreme Court judges argued the following while rejecting his appeal against his sentence for killing Salman Taseer:

> The law of the land does not permit an individual to arrogate unto himself the roles of a complainant, prosecutor, judge and executioner. The appellant was a trained police officer who knew the importance of recourse to the law … If the appellant had suspected Mr. Salman Taseer to have committed the offence of blasphemy, then he should also have adopted the legal course.

In these examples, we see the judges representing the state and trying to establish the authority and legitimacy of the state (and of their own judgements) based on the law. The law is thus called on as a source of legitimacy, but at the same time, the judges use it to excuse themselves for making decisions that may not be in line with popular ideas of justice. For example, in the same judgement in the case of *Mumtaz Qadri vs The State* (2015: 3), the judges provide the following disclaimer:

> Without prejudice to the strong religious and philosophical views expressed before us we must state at the outset that we, in terms of our calling and vocation and in accord with the oath of our office, are obligated to decide this case in accordance with the law of the land as it exists and not in accordance with what the law should be.

Hence, the law is presented as both a source of legitimacy and a limitation imposed on the judges by the state. The apparent rift between the 'law of the land' and 'what the law should be', as mentioned by the judges in the above excerpt, is also a space in which the judges exercise their own discretion in interpreting the law through discursive reasoning. I will now discuss how judges employ the religious discourse and popular narratives in their attempts to reconcile the rift between the law and popular justice, as well as in providing alternative sources of higher legality.

Religious discourse and popular justice

While the KNLF lawyers used religious sources to establish that alleged blasphemers must be punished violently (inside or outside the law), judges sometimes use religious sources to counter these arguments and acquit those accused of blasphemy. Lower court judges usually use the religious sources in the same way as do the KNLF lawyers. The higher-court judges, however, may take liberties more frequently to offer their own interpretations or use alternative religious sources. Nevertheless, the judges' authority to interpret Islamic law is not fully established or universally accepted. Their authority is challenged when they go against the established interpretations of religious sources concerning the punishment of blasphemy, based on various factors—including their Westernised outlook, the fact they are not 'religious scholars' and the suspicion that they are colluding with Western powers to undermine Islam. Consequently, judges have to appeal to popular sentiment by testifying their own faith and drawing on narratives of popular justice, especially when deciding in favour of those accused of blasphemy. In so doing, they not only coopt popular narratives and ideals of religiosity, but also give them legal approval. The following discussion will elaborate how judges employ religious sources and popular narratives in constructing their arguments and the impact on the overall understanding of justice and punishment for blasphemy in Pakistan.

Those accused of blasphemy are rarely acquitted by the trial courts due to external pressure from mobs and religious organisations on the decisions of the sessions courts. As a result, most cases of blasphemy are decided in favour of the accusers. The sessions court judges rely on religious sources to convict the accused, sometimes despite a lack of convincing evidence to prove the offence. For example, in the case of *The State vs Liaqat Ali and Umar Draz*,³ in which the accused allegedly denied the existence of Allah, the sessions court judge remarked:

> There is no provision in the penal law of the country to take into task the person who used derogatory remarks in respect of the creator of this universe (The Almighty Allah), who is also creator of Hazrat Muhammad (PBUH). The lawmakers should give attention to this elapse [sic]. In this case, both the accused have made remarks more loudly regarding the Almighty Allah rather than the Holy Prophet Muhammad (PBUH). It chills the marrow of my bones that there is no law to set right such like people.

After having noted the discrepancy in the existing legal injunctions and his own sense of moral legality, he goes on, for three pages, quoting verses from the Quran and *hadith* to establish that insulting Allah is indeed an insult to the Prophet Muhammad as well. He writes conclusively:

> In the light of above Quranic injunctions as well as from Ayati Mubarka and the prevailing law of the country on the subject, in the peculiar circumstances of this case, I feel no hesitation, keeping in view the conduct of the accused, that they deserve no leniency. (*The State vs Liaqat Ali and Umar Draz* 2009: 11)

Similarly, in *The State vs Shafqat Masih and Mst. Shagufta Kousar* (2014),⁴ the presiding sessions court judge quotes Quranic verses and narrations from prophetic tradition for more than five pages to establish the offence of the accused and sentence both to death for insulting the Prophet Muhammad and the Quran. Furthermore, there are a number of cases in which the judges have relied on Quranic and *hadith* material to convict the accused, even in the absence of convincing legal evidence against them. In such instances, the judges have often relied on an earlier statement by a High Court judge that witnesses are not required to repeat offensive or derogatory words allegedly uttered by the accused to establish their claims under Section 295-C of the PPC. Many judges have referred to this judgement to justify bypassing the necessity of producing evidence in court and to convict the accused on the basis of religious arguments alone:

---

3   *The State vs Liaqat Ali and Umar Draz* (2009) FIR No. 166 dated 21 March 2006, Sessions Court Jhang: 8.
4   *The State vs Shafqat Masih and Mst. Shagufta Kousar* (2014) Sessions Trial No. 5-14 of 2014, Sessions Court Toba Tek Singh.

> To constitute [an] offence under section 295-C, PPC [Pakistan Penal Code,] [a] number witnesses are not required and it is not necessary that such abusive language should be made loudly in public or in a meeting or at some specific place, but [the] statement of [a] single witness that somebody had made [an] utterance for the contempt of the Holy Prophet (Peace be upon Him) even inside the house is sufficient to award [the] death penalty to such [a] contemnor.[5]

Thus, in the absence of the requirement for evidence, religious sources are used as both the logic and the content of the evidence to convict and punish people accused of blasphemy. On the other hand, judges (often in the higher courts) also use legal discourse to contest the dominant interpretations and offer alternative religious sources. For example, in a 2002 judgement, which was widely quoted in later judgements related to blasphemy, the Lahore High Court judge gave his own interpretation of blasphemy as follows:

> The greatest blasphemy of all is a child going hungry, a child condemned to the slow death of starvation. The miscarriage of justice is blasphemy. Misgovernment is blasphemy. An unconscionable gap between rich and poor is blasphemy. Denial of treatment to the sick, denial of education to the child, are alike examples of blasphemy.[6]

In a more recent judgement (in February 2017), the Lahore High Court asserted the need for followers of the Prophet Muhammad to adopt an attitude of forgiveness and mercy:

> Increase in the number of registration [sic] of blasphemy cases and [the] element of mischief involved therein calls for extra care at the end of the prosecution. Registration of such like cases cannot be allowed in a free and careless manner and ordinary citizens who have not much knowledge of religion must not be allowed to use the law in question to settle their scores. All this we are doing in the name of our Holy Prophet Hazrat Muhammad (Peace Be Upon Him), who is *'Rehmatu-lil-Aalmeen'* ['mercy for all the worlds'] and being *'Bashir'* ['one who brings good news'] has given assurance that even if [the] whole of ... [one's life is] spent in sins,

---

5 *Haji Bashir Ahmad vs The State* (2005) YLR 985, Lahore High Court.
6 *Muhammad Mahboob alias Booba vs The State* (2002) PLD Lahore 587. Available from: cite.pakcaselaw.com/pld-lahore-high-court-lahore/2002/587/.

but before a person breathes his last, [he] has recited '*Kalma Pak*' ['declaration of faith'], [he] is entitled to be relieved from all his sins by Allah Almighty on the day of judgment.[7]

Hence, references to religious sources are used not only to convict the accused but also to make opposing arguments. The alternative interpretations may also become precedents that are called on in future judgements. However, appealing to religious sources even in the most progressive of judgements may also set precedents that justify nonstate punishment of blasphemers. I have already mentioned the Supreme Court judgement in the case of *Mumtaz Qadri vs The State* (2015) in which the judges argued that Qadri was not justified in taking 'the law' into his own hands. This is seen as one of the most 'progressive' judgements to come out of the courts of Pakistan on the matter of the nonstate killing of blasphemers as it upheld the death penalty for Mumtaz Qadri. However, even in this judgement, the judges allowed for the possibility of a legitimate killing of a blasphemer by nonstate actors. I will quote from the judgement at some length to illustrate this point:

> We as Muslims are fully aware and convinced of the most exalted position held by the Holy Prophet Muhammad (peace be upon Him) in the eyes of Almighty Allah as well as in the hearts and minds of the Ummah and the followers of the Islamic faith. It goes without saying that deepest respect and profound reverence for the Holy Prophet Muhammad (peace be upon Him) is an article of faith with all of us. Be that as it may the issue involved in this case is not as to whether anybody is allowed to commit blasphemy by defiling the sacred name of the Holy Prophet Muhammad (peace be upon him) or not or as to whether a person committing blasphemy can be killed by another person on his own or not but the real question involved in the present case is as to whether or not a person can be said to be justified in killing another person on his own on the basis of an *unverified impression or an unestablished perception* that such other person has committed blasphemy. (*Mumtaz Qadri vs The State* 2015: 22; emphasis added)

There are two important points to note in the above excerpt. First, the judges had to make a declaration of their own faith and attest to the sanctity of Allah and his Prophet before making their judgement. Second, the judges did not condemn the nonstate killing of a blasphemer

---

7   *Muhammad Ishaq vs The State* (2017) HCJDA 38, Lahore High Court: 19.

in principle; they only denounced the fact that the said killing was carried out on the basis of *unverified* and *unestablished* evidence. Further on in the same judgement, the judges appear to accept the religious sources presented to them by the lawyers with regard to the legality and legitimacy of killing a blasphemer outside the law. The following passage from the judgement demonstrates the judges' position on the religious sources:

> A close and careful examination of all the references made and the religious material produced in this case by the appellant and his learned counsel shows, and shows quite clearly and unmistakably, that such references and material pertain to cases where commission of blasphemy stands established as a fact and then the discussion is about how the apostate may be treated and not a single reference made or instance referred to in the material produced permits killing of a person on the basis only of an unverified impression or an unestablished perception regarding commission of blasphemy. (*Mumtaz Qadri vs The State* 2015: 22)

Hence, it is clear that the blasphemer or apostate (both words are used interchangeably by the judges) *may* be killed by nonstate actors if the offence is established. While the judges may have exercised strategic discretion in this case to avoid controversy by dismissing the religious sources submitted to them, they did set a precedent that may be referred to in future judgements on the matter. Moreover, in making their argument that Mumtaz Qadri was not justified in the killing because he did not have sufficient evidence to establish that the offence was committed, they did not simply use the modern legal concepts concerning offence and evidence. They referred to the Quran to assert the correctness of their argument:

> As mentioned above, in the Holy Qur'an Almighty Allah has repeatedly warned those who start believing in hearsay without getting it ascertained, verified or investigated or conduct themselves on the basis of such hearsay. The appellant, therefore, would have done better if, notwithstanding his professed religious motivation in the matter, he had paid heed to those warnings of Almighty Allah as well before an unjustified killing of another on the sole basis of hearsay. An unjustified killing of a human being has been declared by Almighty Allah as murder of the entire mankind. (*Mumtaz Qadri vs The State* 2015: 22–23)

Here we see the judges offering their own interpretation of a religious source to make their argument—in this case, against an individual who killed an alleged blasphemer. As seen in other, earlier cases, judges engage with the religious sources in multiple ways, accepting some and offering their own interpretations of others. Regardless, it is through this discursive reasoning drawing on the law as well as religious sources that they construct their arguments both in favour of and against the punishment of alleged blasphemers. In so doing, they also set precedents—that may be positive or negative—for future cases. For example, the following passage written by the Supreme Court judges in the *Mumtaz Qadri vs The State* (2015) judgement was recently used by the judges in the case of *Asia Bibi vs The State* (2018: 28):

> Commission of blasphemy is abhorrent and immoral besides being a manifestation of intolerance but at the same time a false allegation regarding commission of such an offence is equally detestable besides being culpable. If our religion of Islam comes down heavily upon commission of blasphemy, then Islam is also very tough against those who level false allegations of a crime. It is, therefore, for the State of the Islamic Republic of Pakistan to ensure that no innocent person is compelled or constrained to face an investigation or a trial on the basis of false or trumped up allegations regarding commission of such an offence.

The above passage was used by the Supreme Court judges in 2018 to acquit Asia Bibi. Thus, in this case, we see the judges' intervention led to a positive precedent that may be drawn on in future. However, as noted in earlier cases, the judges in the case of Asia Bibi also made appeals to popular sentiment to establish the legitimacy of their judgement. They started the judgement with the following proclamation:

> 'I bear witness that there is no God worthy to be worshiped but Allah, and I bear witness that Muhammad is the Last Messenger of Allah.' The *Qalimah-e-Shahadat* ['profession of faith'] as shown above, is deemed to be the essence of Islam and the recitation of which makes us Muslims, is self-explanatory and testifies that there is no God but Allah and our Prophet Muhammad [صلى الله عليه وسلم] is the Last Messenger of Allah. It is our declaration of faith in the unseen and belief, to bow down our heads before our Lord Allah, admitting the fact that there is none like Him. The sanctity of our Prophet Muhammad [صلى الله عليه وسلم] is further evident from the *Qalimah-e-Shahadat*, as His name is being

> read together with Allah, thus ultimate care and great importance should be drawn while taking this Holy name. (*Asia Bibi vs The State* 2018: 1)

Once again, giving the affirmation of faith before deciding in favour of a person accused of blasphemy may very well be a strategic move by the judges to establish their authority and claim legitimacy on the basis of their faith. However, they did not stop there. They went on to refer not only to the religious sources (Quran and *hadith*) but also to popular narratives that legitimise and glorify the killing of blasphemers outside the law. In Chapter 2, I mentioned a couplet by Muhammad Iqbal—a poet celebrated as the ideological father of Pakistan—used by almost all religious groups campaigning for strict punishment for blasphemers. The couplet talks about love of the Prophet Muhammad as a guaranteed way to command Allah's 'pen of destiny'. The Supreme Court judges also referred to the same couplet in their judgement in the case of Asia Bibi. They wrote:

> As it is enunciated in the above verse of *Allama* Muhammad Iqbal, a well renowned activist and the 'Spiritual Father of Pakistan', from his poem *Jawab-e-Shikwa*, the veneration and adulation of Our Beloved Holy Prophet [صلى الله عليه وسلم] is evident and is reckoned as the foundational principle on which the religion Islam is based. There is no denial whatsoever of the fact that Prophet Muhammad [صلى الله عليه وسلم] holds the utmost respect, prestige and dignity amongst the Muslim Ummah and possesses the highest rank and status compared to all Creatures shaped by Allah Almighty, even the Messengers of Allah who came before him. (*Asia Bibi vs The State* 2018: 3)

They further referred to the popular narratives concerning Ghazi Ilmuddin, giving credence to the idea of nonstate killings of alleged blasphemers. They write:

> Reference may be made to an incident which occurred in 1923, when one said person, Rajpal, published a pamphlet/book containing derogatory remarks against Prophet Muhammad [صلى الله عليه وسلم]. A movement was launched by the Muslims of the sub-continent demanding a ban on the book. As a result, in 1927 the British Government was forced to enact a law prohibiting insults aimed at founders and leaders of religious communities, as such, section 295-A was inserted in the Pakistan Penal Code in the year 1927. However, the Muslims were not

satisfied with it and one Ghazi Ilm-ud-Din Shaheed succeeded in murdering Rajpal. After the trial, Ilm-ud-Din was convicted and was given [the] death penalty. He is considered by the Muslims to be a great lover of the Prophet. (*Asia Bibi vs The State* 2018: 9)

The judges called Ilmuddin a martyr, despite noting that he went against the law at the time to kill an alleged blasphemer. They further affirmed that he is accepted by Muslims as a hero and a great lover of the Prophet. It must be noted that the state in power at the time, Britain, is considered less legitimate than the current state of Pakistan in the eyes of the people. So, the judges could have been implying that Ilmuddin's act was justified in the context of British rule but would not be in the present context of Pakistan, an Islamic state. Nevertheless, as already discussed, the proponents of nonstate killings of blasphemers do not fully accept the legitimacy of the current state of Pakistan either. Within this context, a reference to Ilmuddin as an accepted lover of the Prophet sends a message to those who use Ilmuddin's story to carry out similar acts of nonstate punishment in the present day that their acts are justified.

Hence, to establish their legitimacy and credibility, the judges refer not only to the religious sources (Quran and *hadith*), but also to popular narratives concerning nonstate punishment of alleged blasphemers. There are clearly external pressures—including threats to their lives—under which the judges operate and decide on cases of blasphemy. Therefore, their appeal to religious sources and popular narratives may simply be a tactic to ensure their own safety. The judges may also be doing so to establish themselves as good Muslims and lovers of the Prophet to avert criticism of their judgements as anti-religious. In some instances, the judges may also truly believe in the narratives they are employing and appealing to in their judgements. Nevertheless, the fact that judges have to draw on ideas of popular justice highlights the symbolic power of these narratives. It also reiterates the fact that the legal system is not the only source of legality and legitimacy. In fact, the law is constantly held accountable to higher sources of morality and justice, and judges must appeal to those sources—religious texts and popular narratives—even when they are deciding in accordance with state law. References to the law are therefore not sufficient in establishing the legitimacy of their decisions. The state, despite its claim to represent Islamic law, does not hold a monopoly over the interpretation and implementation of what is thought to be Islamic law. The 'law of the land' is hence subservient to 'what the law should be' and, through their discursive reasoning within their judgements, the judges constantly attempt to reconcile the two. Despite the apparent incongruities, the discourse of judges also demonstrates a continuity between the law, religious sources and popular narratives.

Conclusion

In discussing the discourses of the lawyers and the judges, I have focused mainly on the microlevel continuities between the different narratives and arguments they employ. However, the implications of my analysis must be understood at two different levels: individual and structural. At the individual level, I argue that reason and passion are both present and mutually constitutive in constructing the worldviews and strategic arguments of the lawyers and the judges. I have demonstrated that both groups draw on multiple sources of legitimacy to establish the legality of their judgements concerning the appropriate punishment of blasphemy. The law is therefore not a sufficient source of legitimacy despite the state's claim to represent Islamic law. There is in fact a constant dialogue between the ideals of Islamic law—as per various actors in society—and the existing laws of the state. The lawyers and the judges, being at the nexus of the state and society, deal with the dilemmas concerning the appropriate punishment of blasphemers on an everyday basis. Both groups construct meaningful and strategic arguments drawing on multiple sources of morality and legality within the specific contexts and circumstances of the cases with which they are dealing. I argue that the shifting narratives and multiple arguments of the judges and lawyers should not be seen as either solely motivated by their belief systems or entirely tactical in nature. Instead, their arguments provide them with meaning and strategic benefits at the same time. The meaning is not static; rather, it is constantly constructed within specific circumstances and is derived from the process of contestation itself. It is within this process of meaning creation that the strategic arguments are also constructed. Hence, the multiple sources of legitimacy and morality are both means and motives at the same time. Moreover, the multiple narratives used by the lawyers and the judges bring reason-based and passion-based arguments together in constructing a coherent worldview.

6. AT THE NEXUS OF STATE AND SOCIETY

At the structural level, I argue that state and nonstate ideals of the appropriate punishment for an alleged blasphemer are extensions of each other rather than opposing forces. The state of Pakistan not only claims to be an Islamic state but is also itself an embodiment of the popular narratives concerning religious symbols. I mentioned in Chapter 1 that the Ilmuddin controversy was one of the major events involving mobilisation around religious symbols in the leadup to the creation of Pakistan. I have also mentioned that Jinnah, the main architect of Pakistan, represented Ilmuddin in the British courts, and Muhammad Iqbal, the ideological father of Pakistan, led Ilmuddin's funeral prayers. The popular narratives glorifying the nonstate punishment of alleged blasphemers are therefore embedded within the foundation of Pakistan. Pakistan's anti-blasphemy laws have further strengthened this foundation within the existing structure of the state. The *foundational* and *structural* violence of the state in Pakistan is, then, not very different from the nonstate violence carried out against those accused of blasphemy. I argue that the state and nonstate punishments of alleged blasphemers, and their sources of legitimacy, are indeed extensions of each other. From a state-centric perspective, the nonstate punishment of blasphemers has often been described as anti-state and delinquent. On the other hand, the modern state has been demonised as the sole culprit of structural and foundational violence. I argue that any useful understanding of blasphemy-related violence in Pakistan must look at state and nonstate violence as mutually constitutive.

Conclusion

I have demonstrated in this book that blasphemy accusations and subsequent violence in Pakistan arise from moral anxiety, escalation of interpersonal conflict into collective religious passions, contestation between (and among) state and nonstate actors over the authority to deliver legitimate punishment, and wider narratives of exclusivity and homogeneity engendered by the state. The violence related to blasphemy accusations is thus produced at multiple levels within society, ranging from interpersonal relationships to state policies. Individual and communal sensibilities are cultivated through wider religious and national narratives peddled by religious leaders, politicians and governments over time. State policies and narratives, on the other hand, reflect public concerns about the issue of blasphemy. It is this multiplicity of factors, locales of power and narratives that enflames blasphemy accusations and related violence in Pakistan.

Blasphemy accusations arise within interpersonal relationships disrupted by perceived transgressions of religious-cultural symbolic boundaries. These symbolic boundaries enthrone specific behaviours with respect to social hierarchies of caste, gender, socioeconomic status, religious identity and authority. Micro-transgressions of these symbolic boundaries within everyday interactions can be perceived and framed as blasphemy, but not all transgressions of religious, cultural and social norms lead to an accusation of blasphemy. Instead, familiar but vulnerable people are the ones against whom an accusation of transgressive behaviour gains public support. The accusers are motivated not only by personal rivalries, but also by their concern for displaying and maintaining personal purity. The purity of caste, ancestry, sexual behaviour and religious identity is central to the imagination and articulation of the offence of transgressive behaviour powerfully labelled as blasphemy. In most instances, several notions of purity are superimposed on to one another in perceptions of the offence of blasphemy.

In Pakistan, a nation defined by its religious devotion, the concern for purity is central to the lives of Muslims. This concern is inculcated by the imagining of Pakistan as the 'land of the pure'. While the imagining of an Islamic ideal is central to national identity, in practice, the ideals of religiosity are embedded within local conceptions of purity. Thus, the transgression of local ideals of purity is deemed morally deviant and perceived as a religious offence. Moral deviance can be based on religious difference or other forms of social nonconformity. Hence, it is the moral anxiety concerning individual and communal purity inculcated by national ideals and lived within the local sociocultural context that leads to blasphemy accusations. Blasphemy accusations are, therefore, neither a result of purely instrumental motives (as presented by, among others, Forte 1994; Gregory 2012; Jahangir and Jilani 2003; Julius 2016), nor grounded in a uniquely Islamic ethos (Mahmood 2009). Blasphemy accusations in Pakistan are also not simply the result of an exercise of freedom of speech by the accused to criticise religion, as proposed by Dobras (2009), Hayee (2012) and Khan (2015), among others. Instead, this book demonstrates that accusations of blasphemy are motivated by deep sociocultural understandings of offence and have both strategic and passionate drivers.

Accusations of blasphemy, however, do not automatically or inevitably lead to violent punishment. A certain congruity has to be established between the immediate offence (which may not be exclusively religious in nature) and broader religious symbols and identities. Religious leaders are usually the ones who convert interpersonal conflicts into communal and collective religious issues. Religious leaders are concerned with enhancing their own religious authority and/or the desire to purify their society. They strip the initial accusations of their immediate details and imbue them with wider religious symbolism and meaning. Once the interpersonal dimension of an accusation has been removed and figures of religious authority have established it as a religious offence, crowds are mobilised against the symbolic figure of the blasphemer, who represents the moral threat, the sin and the evil in society. Those who form the crowd are driven by their own moral anxieties about collective and national religious identities. The figure of a blasphemer is the impurity that has to be removed to realise the imagined community of 'the land of the pure'. It is the inherent impossibility of the imagined purity of the religious-national identity that further flames passions against the alleged blasphemer.

Ordinary Muslims who participate in violence are inspired by the dominant religious discourse that presents love for the Prophet as the key to rising in the religious ranks. Most significantly, it is the discourse of Sunni Barelwi religious scholars, who present love for the Prophet and the ability to defend his honour as central to Muslim identity. Loving the Prophet is understood as the only way to salvation by Muslims who are living with the guilt of being sinful. The religious discourse assures them that they will be absolved of their sins if they demonstrate passionate love for the Prophet, which is imagined in terms of physical reverence and bodily performances. This discourse glorifies the acts of killing and/or getting killed for the Prophet as the highest form of attachment to Him. Hence, ordinary Muslims living with a sense of guilt and insufficiency—a modern condition—are the ones who respond to the calls to defend the honour of the Prophet.

Nevertheless, despite the threat the alleged blasphemer poses to the collective identity, and despite the glorification of the act of killing a blasphemer, the implementation of violent punishment is contingent on the decisions of many other actors. Local powerholders, police, government officials, NGOs and the media all play a role in determining whether or not an accusation will lead to violent punishment of the blasphemer. These actors also have their own strategic and emotional interests in the issue. It is a culmination of decisions made by multiple actors with complex motivations that leads to anti-blasphemy violence. This book demonstrates the significance in the making of violence of religious leaders and other key actors (Brass 2003b), symbolic resources and metanarratives (Das 1990; Tambiah 1996), roused passions (Blom and Jaoul 2008; Kakar 1990) and anxieties about identity (Sidel 2006).

The violent punishment of alleged blasphemers can be carried out by state or nonstate actors, both claiming to represent the sovereign will of Allah. Pakistan's existing anti-blasphemy legislation claims to represent Islamic law and popular sentiment by prescribing punishments for those accused of blasphemy. However, owing to the perceived ineffectiveness of the state legal system in delivering abrupt and harsh punishments, and the perceived corruption of the ruling elite, the public does not always accept the state's right to deliver punishment. Alleged blasphemers can therefore be punished by nonstate actors who thus contest the state's claim to a monopoly over legitimate violence. A state of dispersed authority and multiple sovereignties is thus created (Comaroff and Comaroff 2006; Hansen 2005; Hansen and Stepputat 2006). This is best understood as an instance of legal pluralism (Benda-Beckmann 2009; Fitzpatrick 1983; Griffiths 1986; Pirie 2013) in which the multiple systems of moral regulation not only contest but also coopt each other. State and nonstate punishments of blasphemers thus draw on the same sources of legitimacy, embedded in the dominant religious discourse and narratives of popular justice.

Within this context, religious leaders, politicians and government officials compete with one another to claim their own authority through support for the violent punishment of alleged blasphemers. Religious leaders-cum-politicians have been at the forefront of campaigns to present the problem of blasphemy as an existential threat to the identity of Pakistan, an avowed Islamic state. Consequently, every politician—religious or secular, conservative or progressive—has to deal with the question of blasphemy in one way or another. It is clear from numerous cases that supporting punishment for alleged blasphemers helps politicians, other public figures and even judges gain legitimacy and authority. It is no wonder that successive governments in Pakistan have spearheaded anti-blasphemy campaigns not only at the national but also at the international level in their efforts to establish themselves as the true guardians of Islam, protecting the honour of the Prophet Muhammad.

The political battles over the issue of blasphemy are enabled by the very foundation of the state of Pakistan on an exclusivist narrative. By claiming to represent the Muslims of South Asia, the will of Allah and Islamic law, the state has opened up a space for the contestation of what these claims mean. The state's attempts to define these ideals to achieve a homogeneous, uniform Muslim community have produced competing claims and widespread anxieties among the people. Within this context, blasphemy becomes one among many expressions of deep concern for the religious-political identity of Pakistan. The competing religious and political narratives about Pakistan's identity have established the issue of blasphemy as an indispensable focus for the state and anyone vying for state power. This contestation engenders greater anxiety among the common people who then engage in blasphemy accusations and violence against those who fall out of line and do not conform to their idealised standards of religiosity and purity. Hence, anti-blasphemy violence is produced at the individual, communal and national levels, interconnected in a complex network of mutually enforcing narratives, ideals and practices. The pervasiveness of the concern about blasphemy is a consequence of interrelated processes of self-making, community-making and state-making.

CONCLUSION

This study of blasphemy in Pakistan offers insights for broader questions of violence and moral conflict in societies. In particular, I contribute to the discussion in the anthropology of violence (for example, Blom and Jaoul 2008; Das 1990; Hinton 2002; Scheper-Hughes and Bourgois 2004; Schinkel 2013; Sidel 2006; Tambiah 1996) and in the field of legal pluralism (for example, Benda-Beckmann 2009; Fitzpatrick 1983; Griffiths 1986; Pirie 2013; Rouland and Planel 1994; Tamanaha 2001). Anthropologists of violence have been mostly concerned with the violence inherent to states and imperialist forces (structural violence), the motivations of actors (subjective violence), and the cultural idioms and symbolic resources on which both the immediate agents of violence and the institutions of power draw. This book contributes to this body of literature by providing ethnographic examples of how the subjective and the structural forms of violence are enmeshed and how various systems of meaning (religion, culture, nationalism) offer symbolic resources to the production of violence. I suggest that we look at these systems of meaning as interconnected and mutually reinforcing instead of as separate categories. Thus, instead of asking whether a particular instance of violence is religious, cultural or a result of modern nationalism, we should understand it as grounded in a complex, multilayered system of meaning in which religion, culture and nationalism are inseparable.

The field of legal pluralism has been concerned with the possibilities of the coexistence of multiple systems of moral regulation and legality in societies. I contribute to this body of literature by providing an example not only of coexistence but also of simultaneous contestation and cooptation of multiple systems of morality and justice. Moreover, my study highlights that multiple systems of legality (traditional or indigenous systems, Western legal systems) are not fixed entities. Instead, as in the case of Pakistan, the traditional and the modern/Western legal systems may influence each other in such a way that they both draw on the same sources and are built on similar assumptions. By bringing together the theoretical frameworks of the anthropology of violence and legal pluralism, this book provides an integrative approach to understanding violence and moral conflict in a society. I suggest that we move beyond the dichotomies of emotion/reason, legal/extralegal, traditional/Western and cultural/religious to gain a more nuanced understanding of violent conflict in societies. These dichotomies have dominated the literature for far too long and prevent us from understanding the complexity of motivations and meanings in people's lives.

Appendix: Text of offences relating to religion (Pakistan Penal Code, 1860)

295 Injuring or defiling place of worship, with intent to insult the religion of any class:

Whoever destroys, damages or defiles any place of worship, or any object held sacred by any class of persons with the intention of thereby insulting the religion of any class of persons or with the knowledge that any class of persons is likely to consider such destruction, damage or defilement as an insult to their religion shall be punished with imprisonment of either description for a term which may extend to two years, or with fine, or with both.

295-A Deliberate and malicious acts intended to outrage religious feelings of any class by insulting its religion or religious beliefs:

Whoever, with deliberate and malicious intention of outraging the religious feelings of any class of the citizens of Pakistan, by words, either spoken or written, or by visible representations insults the religion or the religious beliefs of that class, shall be punished with imprisonment of either description for a term which may extend to ten years, or with fine, or with both.

295-B Defiling, etc., of copy of Holy Quran:

Whoever wilfully defiles, damages or desecrates a copy of the Holy Quran or of an extract therefrom or uses it in any derogatory manner or for any unlawful purpose shall be punishable by imprisonment for life.

295-C Use of derogatory remarks, etc., in respect of the Holy Prophet:

Whoever by words, either spoken or written, or by visible representation, or by any imputation, innuendo, or insinuation, directly or indirectly, defiles the sacred name of the Holy Prophet Mohammed (PBUH) shall be punished with death, or imprisonment for life, and shall also be liable to fine.

298-A Use of derogatory remarks, etc., in respect of holy personages:

Whoever by words, either spoken or written, or by visible representation, or by any imputation, innuendo or insinuation, directly or indirectly defiles a sacred name of any wife (Ummul Mumineen), or members of the family (Ahle-bait), of the Holy Prophet (PBUH), or any of the righteous caliphs (Khulafa-e-Rashideen) or companions (Sahaaba) of the Holy Prophet (PBUH) shall be punished with imprisonment of either description for a term which may extend to three years, or with fine, or with both.

298-B Misuse of epithet, descriptions and titles, etc., reserved for certain holy personages or places:

1. Any person of the Qadiani group or the Lahori group (who call themselves Ahmadis or by any other name) who by words, either spoken or written, or by visible representation:
    a. refers to or addresses any person, other than a Caliph or companion of the Holy Prophet Mohammad (PBUH), as 'Ameerul Momneen', 'Khalifat-ul-Momneen', 'Khalifat-ul-Muslimeen', 'Sahaabi' or 'Razi Allah Anho';
    b. refers to or addresses, any person, other than a wife of the Holy Prophet Mohammed (PBUH), as Ummul-Mumineen;
    c. refers to, or addresses, any person, other than a member of the family (Ahle-Bait) of the Holy Prophet Mohammed (PBUH), as Ahle-Bait; or
    d. refers to, or names, or calls, his place of worship as Masjid shall be punished with imprisonment of either description for a term which may extend to three years, and shall also be liable to fine.

2. Any person of the Qadiani group or Lahore group (who call themselves Ahmadis or by any other names), who by words, either spoken or written, or by visible representations, refers to the mode or form of call to prayers followed by his faith as 'Azan' or recites Azan as used by the Muslims, shall be punished with imprisonment of either description for a term which may extend to three years and shall also be liable to fine.

298-C Persons of Qadiani group, etc., calling himself a Muslim or preaching or propagating his faith:

Any person of the Qadiani group or the Lahori group (who call themselves Ahmadis or any other name), who directly or indirectly, poses himself as a Muslim, or calls, or refers to, his faith as Islam, or preaches or propagates his faith, or invites others to accept his faith, by words, either spoken or written, or by visible representation or in any manner whatsoever outrages the religious feelings of Muslims, shall be punished with imprisonment of either description for a term which may extend to three years and shall also be liable to fine.

Bibliography

Adamec, Ludwig. 2009. *Historical Dictionary of Islam*. 2nd edn. Lanham, MD: Scarecrow Press.

Agamben, Giorgio. 1998. *Sovereign Power and Bare Life*. Stanford, CA: Stanford University Press.

Ahmad, Mumtaz. 1998. 'Islamization and Sectarian Violence in Pakistan.' *Intellectual Discourse* 6(1): 11–37.

Ahmed, Asad Ali. 2009. 'Specters of Macaulay: Blasphemy, the Indian Penal Code and Pakistan's Postcolonial Predicament.' In *Censorship in South Asia: Cultural Regulation from Sedition to Seduction*, edited by Raminder Kaur and William Mazzarella, 172–205. Bloomington, IN: Indiana University Press.

Ahmed, Asad. 2018. 'A Brief History of the Anti-Blasphemy Laws.' *Herald by Dawn*, 31 October. Available from: herald.dawn.com/news/1154036.

Akbar, Ali. 2017a. 'Mardan University Takes Action against Victims; Launches Probe into "Blasphemous Activity".' *Dawn News*, 14 April. Available from: www.dawn.com/news/1326944/mardan-university-takes-action-against-victims-launches-probe-into-blasphemous-activity.

Akbar, Ali. 2017b. 'Mashal Murder Case: JIT Finds Group in University Incited Mob against Student on Pretext of Blasphemy.' *Dawn News*, 4 June. Available from: www.dawn.com/news/1337373/mashal-murder-case-jit-finds-group-in-university-incited-mob-against-student-on-pretext-of-blasphemy.

Akhtar, Aasim Sajjad, Asha Amirali, and Muhammad Ali Raza. 2006. 'Reading between the Lines: The Mullah–Military Alliance in Pakistan.' *Contemporary South Asia* 15(4): 383–97. doi.org/10.1080/09584930701329982.

Ali, Nosheen. 2008. 'Outrageous State, Sectarianized Citizens: Deconstructing the "Textbook Controversy" in the Northern Areas, Pakistan.' *South Asia Multidisciplinary Academic Journal* [Online], (2). doi.org/10.4000/samaj.1172.

Althusser, Louis. 1971. 'Ideology and Ideological State Apparatuses.' In *'Lenin and Philosophy' and Other Essays*. New York: Monthly Review Press.

Alvi, Sarah. 2015. 'Campaigning to Reform Pakistan's Deadly Blasphemy Law.' *Al Jazeera*, 28 April. Available from: www.aljazeera.com/indepth/features/2015/03/campaigning-reform-pakistan-deadly-blasphemy-law-150310053331313.html.

Amnesty International. 2016. *As Good as Dead: The Impact of the Blasphemy Laws in Pakistan*. Report. New York: Amnesty International USA. Available from: www.amnestyusa.org/reports/as-good-as-dead-the-impact-of-the-blasphemy-laws-in-pakistan/.

Anderson, Benedict. 1991. 'Imagined Communities: Reflections on the Origin and Spread of Nationalism.' In *Nationalism*. London: Verso.

Anderson, Clare. 2015. 'Execution and Its Aftermath in the Nineteenth-Century British Empire.' In *A Global History of Execution and the Criminal Corpse*, edited by Richard Ward, 170–98. London: Palgrave Macmillan. doi.org/10.1057/9781137444011_7.

Anderson, Michael R. 1993. 'Islamic Law and the Colonial Encounter in British India.' In *Institutions and Ideologies: A SOAS South Asia Reader*, edited by David Arnold, Peter Robb, and Peter G. Robb, 165–85. London: Curzon Press.

Appadurai, Arjun. 1990. 'Disjuncture and Difference in the Global Cultural Economy.' *Theory, Culture & Society* 7(1): 295–310. doi.org/10.1177/026327690007002017.

Appadurai, Arjun. 1998. 'Dead Certainty: Ethnic Violence in the Era of Globalization.' *Public Culture* 10(2): 225–47. doi.org/10.1215/08992363-10-2-225.

Arzt, Donna E. 2002. 'The Role of Compulsion in Islamic Conversion: Jihad, Dhimma and Ridda.' *Buffalo Human Rights Law Review* 8(15): 15–44.

Asad, Talal. 1983. 'Anthropological Conceptions of Religion: Reflections on Geertz.' *MAN* 18(2): 237–59. doi.org/10.2307/2801433.

Asad, Talal. 2003. *Formations of the Secular: Christianity, Islam, Modernity*. Stanford, CA: Stanford University Press.

Asad, Talal. 2009. 'Free Speech, Blasphemy, and Secular Criticism.' In *Is Critique Secular? Blasphemy, Injury, and Free Speech*, edited by Talal Asad, Wendy Brown, Judith Butler, and Saba Mahmood, 20–63. Berkeley, CA: Townsend Center for the Humanities, University of California. escholarship.org/uc/item/84q9c6ft.

Asani, Ali S., Kamal Abdel-Malek, and Annemarie Schimmel. 1995. *Celebrating Muhammad: Images of the Prophet in Popular Muslim Poetry*. Columbia: University of South Carolina Press.

Ashraf, S. 2018. 'Honour, Purity and Transgression: Understanding Blasphemy Accusations and Consequent Violent Action in Punjab, Pakistan.' *Contemporary South Asia* 26(1): 51–68. doi.org/10.1080/09584935.2018.1430745.

Bail, Christopher A. 2008. 'The Configuration of Symbolic Boundaries against Immigrants in Europe.' *American Sociological Review* 73(1): 37–59. doi.org/10.1177/000312240807300103.

Barker, Memphis. 2018. 'Imran Khan Criticised for Defence of Pakistan Blasphemy Laws.' *The Guardian*, 10 July. Available from: www.theguardian.com/world/2018/jul/09/imran-kahn-accused-over-defence-of-pakistan-blasphemy-laws.

Basit, Abdul. 2020. 'Barelvi Political Activism and Religious Mobilization in Pakistan: The Case of Tehreek-e-Labaik Pakistan (TLP).' *Politics, Religion and Ideology* 21(3): 374–89. doi.org/10.1080/21567689.2020.1812395.

Bauman, Zygmunt. 1990. 'Modernity and Ambivalence.' *Theory, Culture & Society* 7(2): 143–69. doi.org/10.1177/026327690007002010.

Bauman, Zygmunt. 2000. *Liquid Modernity*. Cambridge, UK: Polity Press. doi.org/10.2307/3089803.

BBC News. 2014. 'Pakistan "Blasphemy Lawyer" Shot Dead in Multan Office.' *BBC News*, 7 May. Available from: www.bbc.com/news/world-asia-27319433.

BBC News. 2015. 'What Is Behind Pakistan's Dramatic Rise in Executions?' *BBC News*, 16 December. Available from: www.bbc.com/news/world-asia-33033333.

BBC News. 2017. 'Pakistan Activist Waqass Goraya: The State Tortured Me.' *BBC News*, 9 March. Available from: www.bbc.com/news/world-asia-39219307.

Behuria, Ashok K. 2008. 'Sects Within Sect: The Case of Deobandi–Barelvi Encounter in Pakistan.' *Strategic Analysis* 32(1): 57–80. doi.org/10.1080/09700160801886330.

Benda-Beckmann, Franz von. 2009. 'Legal Pluralism and Social Justice in Economic and Political Development.' *IDS Bulletin* 32(1): 46–56. doi.org/10.1111/j.1759-5436.2001.mp32001006.x.

Berg, Manfred and Simon Wendt. 2011. 'Introduction: Lynching from an International Perspective.' In *Globalizing Lynching History: Vigilantism and Extralegal Punishment from an International Perspective*, edited by Manfred Berg and Simon Wendt, 1–18. New York: Palgrave Macmillan. doi.org/10.1057/9781137001245_1.

Berman, Marshall. 2010. *All That Is Solid Melts into Air: The Experience of Modernity*. London: Verso.

Berry, Maya, Claudia Chávez Argüelles, Shanya Cordis, Sarah Ihmoud, and Elizabeth Velásquez Estrada. 2017. 'Toward a Fugitive Anthropology: Gender, Race, and Violence in the Field.' *Cultural Anthropology* 32(4): 537–65. doi.org/10.14506/ca32.4.05.

Bhatti, Haseeb. 2018. 'If There Is No Proof Against Someone, How Can We Punish Them: CJP.' *Dawn News*, 1 November. Available from: www.dawn.com/news/1442831.

Bibi, Ayesha. 2018. 'Suspects Acquitted in Mashal Khan's Murder Termed "Ghazis" by JI and JUI-F.' *Pakistan Today*, 9 February. Available from: www.pakistantoday.com.pk/2018/02/08/suspects-acquitted-in-mashal-khans-murder-termed-ghazis-by-ji-and-jui-f/.

Bilal, Rana. 2018. 'Government, TLP Reach Agreement: State to Take Legal Measures to Place Asia Bibi's Name on ECL.' *Dawn News*, 2 November. Available from: www.dawn.com/news/1443123/government-tlp-reach-agreement-state-to-take-legal-measures-to-place-asia-bibis-name-on-ecl.

Blom, Amélie. 2008. 'The 2006 Anti–"Danish Cartoons" Riot in Lahore: Outrage and the Emotional Landscape of Pakistani Politics.' *South Asia Multidisciplinary Academic Journal* [Online] 2(2): 1–32. doi.org/10.4000/samaj.1652.

Blom, Amélie and Nicolas Jaoul. 2008. 'Introduction: The Moral and Affectual Dimension of Collective Action in South Asia.' *South Asia Multidisciplinary Academic Journal* [Online] 2(2): 1–25. doi.org/10.4000/samaj.1912.

Bohlander, Michael. 2012. 'There Is No Compulsion in Religion: Freedom of Religion, Responsibility to Protect (R2P) and Crimes against Humanity at the Example of the Islamic Blasphemy Laws of Pakistan.' *Journal of Islamic State Practices in International Law* 8: 36–66.

Boone, Jon. 2014. 'Pakistan Hangs Four More Prisoners as Execution Campaign Widens.' *The Guardian*, 22 December. Available from: www.theguardian.com/world/2014/dec/21/pakistan-hangs-four-prisoners-terrorism-school-attack-peshawar.

Bourdieu, Pierre. 1973. 'Cultural Reproduction and Social Reproduction.' In *Knowledge, Education, and Cultural Change*, edited by Richard Brown, 71–112. London: Routledge. doi.org/10.4324/9781351018142-3.

Bowman, Glenn. 2001. 'The Violence in Identity.' In *Anthropology of Violence and Conflict*, edited by Bettina E. Schmidt and Ingo W. Schröder, 25–46. London: Routledge.

Brass, Paul R. 1991. *Ethnicity and Nationalism: Theory and Comparison*. New Delhi: SAGE Publications. doi.org/10.2307/2546808.

Brass, Paul R. 2003a. 'The Partition of India and Retributive Genocide in the Punjab, 1946–47: Means, Methods, and Purposes 1.' *Journal of Genocide Research* 5(1): 71–101. doi.org/10.1080/14623520305657.

Brass, Paul R. 2003b. *The Production of Hindu–Muslim Violence in Contemporary India*. Seattle: University of Washington Press.

Butler, Judith. 1999. 'Performativity's Social Magic.' In *Bourdieu: A Critical Reader*, edited by Richard Shusterman, 113–28. Oxford: Blackwell Publishers.

Butt, Ahsan I. 2016. 'Street Power: Friday Prayers, Islamist Protests, and Islamization in Pakistan.' *Politics and Religion* (9): 1–28. doi.org/10.1017/S1755048316000031.

Ceja-Zamarripa, Tanya L. 2007. 'Casting Out Demons: The Native Anthropologist and Healing in the Homeland.' *Journal for the Anthropology of North America* 10(1): 11–14. doi.org/10.1525/nad.2007.10.1.11.

Chatterjee, Partha. 1993. *The Nation and Its Fragments: Colonial and Postcolonial Histories*. Princeton Studies in Culture/Power/History Vol. 4. Princeton, NJ: Princeton University Press. doi.org/10.2307/j.ctvzgb88s.

Clifford, James. 1997. *Routes: Travel and Translation in the Late Twentieth Century*. Cambridge, MA: Harvard University Press.

Clifford, James and George E. Marcus, eds. 1986. *Writing Culture: The Poetics and Politics of Ethnography*. Berkeley, CA: University of California Press.

Coakley, John. 2018. '"Primordialism" in Nationalism Studies: Theory or Ideology?' *Nations and Nationalism* 24(2): 327–47. doi.org/10.1111/nana.12349.

Cohen, Stephen P. 2004. *The Idea of Pakistan*. Washington, DC: Brookings Institution Press.

Comaroff, John L. and Jean Comaroff. 2006. 'Law and Disorder in the Postcolony: An Introduction.' In *Law and Disorder in the Postcolony*, edited by Jean Comaroff and John L. Comaroff, 1–56. Chicago: University of Chicago Press. doi.org/10.7208/chicago/9780226114101.001.0001.

Copland, Ian. 2010. 'The Production and Containment of Communal Violence: Scenarios from Modern India.' *South Asia: Journal of South Asia Studies* 33(1): 122–50. doi.org/10.1080/00856401003592503.

Corbin, J.R. 1976. 'An Anthropological Perspective on Violence.' *International Journal of Environmental Studies* 10(1): 107–11. doi.org/10.1080/00207237608737300.

Cottle, Simon. 2008. *Global Crisis Reporting: Journalism in the Global Age*. Berkshire, UK: McGraw Hill Open University Press.

Coulson, N. 1964. *A History of Islamic Law*. London: Routledge. doi.org/10.4324/9781315083506.

Crisp, James and Ben Farmer. 2018. 'Geert Wilders Cancels Muhammad Cartoon Contest after Pakistan Protests.' *Telegraph*, 31 August. Available from: www.telegraph.co.uk/news/2018/08/31/geert-wilders-cancels-muhammad-cartoon-contest-pakistan-protests/.

Das, Veena. 1990. 'Introduction: Communities, Riots, Survivors—The South Asian Experience.' In *Mirrors of Violence: Communities, Riots, and Survivors in South Asia*, edited by Veena Das, 1–36. Oxford: Oxford University Press.

Das, Veena. 1996. *Critical Events: An Anthropological Perspective on Contemporary India*. New Delhi: Oxford University Press.

Das, Veena. 1998. 'Specificities: Official Narratives, Rumour, and the Social Production of Hate.' *Social Identities: Journal for the Study of Race, Nation, and Culture* 4(1): 109–30. doi.org/10.1080/13504639851915.

Das, Veena. 2007. *Life and Words: Violence and the Descent into the Ordinary*. Berkeley, CA: University of California Press. doi.org/10.1525/9780520939530.

Das, Veena and Arthur Kleinman. 2000. 'Introduction.' In *Violence and Subjectivity*, edited by Veena Das, Arthur Kleinman, Mamphela Ramphele, and Pamela Reynolds, 1–18. Berkeley, CA: University of California Press.

Das, Veena and Arthur Kleinman. 2001. 'Introduction.' In *Remaking A World: Violence, Social Suffering, and Recovery*, edited by Veena Das, Arthur Kleinman, Margaret Lock, Mamphela Ramphele, and Pamela Reynolds, 1–30. Berkeley, CA: University of California Press. doi.org/10.1525/california/9780520223295.003.0001.

Das, Veena and Deborah Poole. 2004. 'State and Its Margins: Comparative Ethnographies.' In *Anthropology in the Margins of the State*, edited by Veena Das and Deborah Poole, 3–34. New Delhi: Oxford University Press.

Dawn News. 2010. 'Blasphemy Laws: A Fact Sheet.' *Dawn News*, 15 April. Available from: www.dawn.com/news/845129/blasphemy-laws-a-fact-sheet.

Dawn News. 2011a. 'Minorities Minister Shahbaz Bhatti Assassinated in Islamabad.' *Dawn News*, 2 March. Available from: www.dawn.com/news/610105.

Dawn News. 2011b. 'Seven Sentenced to Death for Sialkot Lynching.' *Dawn News*, 21 September. Available from: www.dawn.com/news/660548.

Dawn News. 2017. '"No One Was Prepared to Come to the Funeral".' *Dawn News*, 24 April. Available from: www.dawn.com/news/1328938.

Dawn News. 2018. 'Zainab's Father Moves LHC for Public Hanging of Convict.' *Dawn News*, 24 June. Available from: www.dawn.com/news/1415709.

Delanty, Gerard. 2007. 'Modernity.' In *The Blackwell Encyclopedia of Sociology*. Oxford, UK: John Wiley & Sons. doi.org/10.1002/9781405165518.wbeosm117.

Devji, Faisal. 2013. *Muslim Zion: Pakistan as a Political Idea*. Cambridge, MA: Harvard University Press. doi.org/10.4159/harvard.9780674074163.

Dobras, Rebbeca J. 2009. 'Is the United Nations Endorsing Human Rights Violations? An Analysis of the United Nations' Combating Defamation of Religions Resolutions and Pakistan's Blasphemy Laws.' *Georgia Journal of International & Comparative Law* 37(2): 341–80. digitalcommons.law.uga.edu/gjicl/vol37/iss2/5.

Douglas, Mary. 1966. *Purity and Danger: An Analysis of Concepts of Pollution and Taboo*. London: Routledge.

Dumont, Louis. 1980. *Homo Hierarchicus: The Caste System and Its Implications*. Chicago: University of Chicago Press.

Duschinsky, Robbie. 2013. 'The Politics of Purity: When, Actually, Is Dirt Matter Out of Place?' *Thesis Eleven* 119(1): 63–77. doi.org/10.1177/0725513 613511321.

DW. 2011. 'Pakistani Judge Flees Country after Receiving Death Threats.' *DW*, 26 October. Available from: www.dw.com/en/pakistani-judge-flees-country-after-receiving-death-threats/a-6646576.

Eisenstadt, S.N. 2000. 'Multiple Modernities.' *Daedalus* 129(1): 1–29. Available from: www.jstor.org/stable/20027613.

Election Commission of Pakistan (ECP). 2018. *Party Wise Vote Bank: National Assembly*. Statistical Report. Islamabad: ECP. Available from: www.ecp.gov.pk/frmVotebank.aspx.

Emon, Anver M. 2012. *Religious Pluralism and Islamic Law: Dhimmis and Others in the Empire of Law*. Oxford, UK: Oxford University Press. doi.org/10.1093/acprof:oso/9780199661633.001.0001.

Epping, Ethan. 2013. 'Politics and Pirs: The Nature of Sufi Political Engagement in 20th and 21st Century Pakistan.' *Pakistaniaat: A Journal of Pakistan Studies* 5(3): 1–25. Available from: pakistaniaat.org/index.php/pak/article/view/221.

Fazal, Tanweer. 2015. *'Nation-State' and Minority Rights in India*. New York: Routledge. doi.org/10.4324/9781315796857.

Firdous, Iftikhar. 2017. 'Mardan Lynching: JIT Says Mashal's Murder Was Premeditated.' *The Express Tribune*, 4 June. Available from: tribune.com.pk/story/1427069/plot-get-rid-mashal-khan-hatched-month-murder-concludes-jit/.

Fitzpatrick, Peter. 1983. 'Marxism and Legal Pluralism.' *Australian Journal of Law and Society* 1(2): 45–59. Available from: www5.austlii.edu.au/au/journals/AUJlLawSoc/1983/9.html.

Forte, David F. 1994. 'Apostasy and Blasphemy in Pakistan.' *Connecticut Journal of International Law* 10: 27–68.

Foucault, Michel. 1971. 'Orders of Discourse.' *Social Science Information* 10(2): 7–30. doi.org/10.1177/053901847101000201.

Foucault, Michel. 1982. 'The Subject and Power.' *Critical Inquiry* 8(4): 777–95. doi.org/10.1086/448181.

Foucault, Michel. 1988. *Technologies of the Self: A Seminar with Michel Foucault*. Edited by Luther H. Martin, Huck Gutman, and Patrick H. Hutton. Amherst, MA: University of Massachusetts Press.

Foucault, Michel. 2002. *The Archaeology of Knowledge*. Routledge Classics. New York: Routledge.

Fox, Jonathan. 2000. 'The Ethnic–Religious Nexus: The Impact of Religion on Ethnic Conflict.' *Civil Wars* 3(3): 1–22. doi.org/10.1080/13698240008402444.

Free and Fair Election Network (FAFEN). 2018. *FAFEN General Election Observation 2018: Result Assessment and Analysis*. Islamabad: FAFEN. Available from: www.fafen.org/fafen-general-election-observation-2018-result-assessment-and-analysis/.

Friedmann, Yohanan. 2003. *Tolerance and Coercion in Islam: Interfaith Relations in the Muslim Tradition*. New York: Cambridge University Press. doi.org/10.1017/CBO9780511497568.

Fuller, C.J. 1976. 'Kerala Christians and the Caste System.' *MAN* 11(1)(NS): 53–70. doi.org/10.2307/2800388.

Geertz, Clifford. 1993. *The Interpretation of Cultures: Selected Essays*. London: Fontana Press. doi.org/10.4324/9781315017570.

Gellner, Ernest. 1983. *Nations and Nationalism*. Ithaca, NY: Cornell University Press.

Giddens, Anthony. 1991. *The Consequences of Modernity*. Stanford, CA: Stanford University Press.

Gilmartin, David. 1991. 'Democracy, Nationalism and the Public: A Speculation on Colonial Muslim Politics.' *South Asia: Journal of South Asian Studies* 14(1): 123–40. doi.org/10.1080/00856409108723150.

Gilmartin, David. 2014. *Civilization and Modernity: Narrating the Creation of Pakistan*. New Delhi: Yoda Press.

Girard, René. 1977. *Violence and the Sacred*. Baltimore: Johns Hopkins University Press.

Goldstein, Daniel M. 2003. '"In Our Own Hands": Lynching, Justice, and the Law in Bolivia.' *American Ethnologist* 30(1): 22–43. doi.org/10.1525/ae.2003.30.1.22.

Gregory, Shaun. 2012. 'Under the Shadow of Islam: The Plight of the Christian Minority in Pakistan.' *Contemporary South Asia* 20(2): 195–212. doi.org/10.1080/09584935.2012.670201.

Griffiths, John. 1986. 'What Is Legal Pluralism?' *The Journal of Legal Pluralism and Unofficial Law* 18(24): 1–55. doi.org/10.1080/07329113.1986.10756 387.

Gross, Jan T. 2001. *Neighbors: The Destruction of the Jewish Community in Jedwabne, Poland.* Princeton, NJ: Princeton University Press. doi.org/10.1515/ 9781400843251.

Gupta, Akhil and James Ferguson. 1997. 'Discipline and Practice: "The Field" as Site, Method, and Location in Anthropology.' In *Anthropological Locations: Boundaries and Grounds of a Field Science*, edited by Akhil Gupta and James Ferguson, 1–46. Berkeley, CA: University of California Press.

Hallaq, Wael B. 2004. *Authority, Continuity and Change in Islamic Law.* Cambridge, UK: Cambridge University Press.

Hansen, Thomas Blom. 2005. 'Sovereigns Beyond the State: On Legality and Authority in Urban India.' In *Sovereign Bodies: Citizens, Migrants, and States in the Postcolonial World*, edited by Thomas Blom Hansen and Finn Stepputat, 169–91. Princeton, NJ: Princeton University Press. doi.org/10.1515/97814 00826698.169.

Hansen, Thomas Blom and Finn Stepputat. 2006. 'Sovereignty Revisited.' *Annual Review of Anthropology* 35: 295–315. doi.org/10.1146/annurev.anthro.35. 081705.123317.

Haq, Farhat. 2019. *Sharia and the State in Pakistan: Blasphemy Politics.* New York: Routledge. doi.org/10.4324/9780429054778.

Harris, Olivia. 1996. 'Introduction: Inside and Outside the Law.' In *Inside and Outside the Law: Anthropological Studies of Authority and Ambiguity*, edited by Olivia Harris, 1–15. London: Routledge.

Hartmann, Eddie. 2015. 'Symbolic Boundaries and Collective Violence: A New Theoretical Argument for an Explanatory Sociology of Collective Violent Action.' *Journal for the Theory of Social Behaviour* 46(2): 165–86. doi.org/ 10.1111/jtsb.12093.

Hasan, Fawad. 2017. 'Faizabad Sit-In: The Trail of 21 Days.' *The Express Tribune*, 27 November. Available from: tribune.com.pk/story/1569778/1-faizabad-sit-trail-21-days/.

Hashim, Asad. 2017a. 'Disappeared: Silencing Pakistan's Activists.' *Al Jazeera*, 21 January. Available from: www.aljazeera.com/indepth/features/2017/01/ disappeared-silencing-pakistan-activists-170121074139848.html.

Hashim, Asad. 2017b. 'In Pakistan, a Shrine to Murder for "Blasphemy".' *Al Jazeera*, 11 February. Available from: www.aljazeera.com/indepth/features/2017/02/pakistan-shrine-murder-blasphemy-170206103344830.html.

Hashim, Asad. 2018. 'Pakistan PM Calls for Calm after Aasia Bibi Cleared of Blasphemy.' *Al Jazeera*, 1 November. Available from: www.aljazeera.com/news/2018/10/pakistan-pm-calls-calm-aasia-bibi-cleared-blasphemy-181031173052989.html.

Hassner, Ron E. 2011. 'Blasphemy and Violence.' *International Studies Quarterly* 55(1): 23–45. doi.org/10.1111/j.1468-2478.2010.00634.x.

Hayee, Bilal. 2012. 'Blasphemy Laws and Pakistan's Human Rights Obligations.' *University of Notre Dame Australia Law Review* (3): 25–53. Available from: www.austlii.edu.au/au/journals/UNDAULawRw/2012/3.html.

Herriman, Nicholas. 2006. 'Fear and Uncertainty: Local Perceptions of the Sorcerer and the State in an Indonesian Witch-Hunt.' *Asian Journal of Social Science* 34(3): 360–87. doi.org/10.1163/156853106778048669.

Hervieu-Léger, Danièle. 1990. 'Religion and Modernity in the French Context: For a New Approach to Secularization.' *Sociological Analysis* 51: 15–25. doi.org/10.2307/3711671.

Hinton, Alex. 1998. 'Why Did the Nazis Kill? Anthropology, Genocide and the Goldhagen Controversy.' *Anthropology Today* 14(5): 9–15. doi.org/10.2307/2783388.

Hinton, Alexander Laban. 2002. 'The Dark Side of Modernity: Toward an Anthropology of Genocide.' In *Annihilating Difference: The Anthropology of Genocide*, edited by Alexander Laban Hinton, 1–42. Berkeley, CA: University of California Press. doi.org/10.1525/california/9780520230286.003.0001.

Hinton, Alexander Laban. 2005. *Why Did They Kill? Cambodia in the Shadow of Genocide*. Berkeley, CA: University of California Press. doi.org/10.1525/9780520937949.

Hobsbawm, Eric J. 1983. 'Introduction: Inventing Traditions.' In *The Invention of Tradition*, edited by Eric J. Hobsbawm and Terence Ranger, 1–14. Cambridge, UK: Cambridge University Press. doi.org/10.1017/CBO9781107295636.001.

Hoebel, Edward Adamson. 1954. *The Law of Primitive Man: A Study in Comparative Legal Dynamics*. Cambridge, MA: Harvard University Press.

Hoffman, Matt. 2014. 'Modern Blasphemy Laws in Pakistan and the Rimsha Masih Case: What Effect—If Any—The Case Will Have on Their Future Reform.' *Washington University Global Studies Law Review* 13(2): 371–92. Available from: openscholarship.wustl.edu/law_globalstudies/vol13/iss2/9.

Horowitz, Donald L. 2001. *The Deadly Ethnic Riot*. Berkeley, CA: University of California Press.

Human Rights Watch (HRW). 2017. 'Pakistan: Escalating Crackdown on Internet Dissent.' *News*, 16 May. New York: Human Rights Watch. Available from: www.hrw.org/news/2017/05/16/pakistan-escalating-crackdown-internet-dissent.

Human Rights Watch (HRW). 2018. *Pakistan: Events of 2017*. World Report 2018. New York: Human Rights Watch. Available from: www.hrw.org/world-report/2018/country-chapters/pakistan.

International Commission of Jurists (ICJ). 2015. *On Trial: The Implementation of Pakistan's Blasphemy Laws*. November. Geneva: ICJ. Available from: www.refworld.org/pdfid/565da4824.pdf.

Iqtidar, Humeira. 2012. 'State Management of Religion in Pakistan and Dilemmas of Citizenship.' *Citizenship Studies* 16(8): 1013–28. doi.org/10.1080/13621025.2012.735026.

Jacob, Peter. 2018. 'Someone's Crying Lahore.' *The Express Tribune*, 5 March. Available from: tribune.com.pk/story/1651335/6-someones-crying-lahore/.

Jahangir, Asma and Hina Jilani. 2003. *The Hudood Ordinances: A Divine Sanction?* Lahore, Pakistan: Sang-e-Meel Publications.

Jalal, Ayesha. 2000. *Self and Sovereignty: Individual and Community in South Asian Islam Since 1850*. London: Routledge.

Jalal, Ayesha. 2014. *The Struggle for Pakistan: A Muslim Homeland and Global Politics*. Cambridge, MA: Harvard University Press.

Johansson, Leanne. 2015. 'Dangerous Liaisons: Risk, Positionality and Power in Women's Anthropological Fieldwork.' *Journal of the Anthropological Society of Oxford* 7(1): 55–63. Available from: www.anthro.ox.ac.uk/sites/default/files/anthro/documents/media/jaso7_1_2015_55_63.pdf.

Jordan, David A. 2003. 'The Dark Ages of Islam: Ijtihad, Apostasy, and Human Rights in Contemporary Islamic Jurisprudence.' *Washington and Lee Race and Ethnic Ancestry Law Journal* 9: 55–71.

Julius, Qaiser. 2016. 'The Experience of Minorities under Pakistan's Blasphemy Laws.' *Islam and Christian–Muslim Relations* 27(1): 95–115. doi.org/10.1080/09596410.2015.1108639.

Kakar, Sudhir. 1990. 'Some Unconscious Aspects of Ethnic Violence in India.' In *Mirrors of Violence: Communities, Riots, and Survivors in South Asia*, edited by Veena Das, 135–45. Oxford, UK: Oxford University Press.

Kakar, Sudhir. 1996. *The Colors of Violence: Cultural Identities, Religion, and Conflict*. Chicago: University of Chicago Press.

Kamali, Mohammad Hashim. 1997. *Freedom of Expression in Islam*. Cambridge, UK: Islamic Texts Society.

Khan, Amjad Mahmood. 2015. 'Pakistan's Anti-Blasphemy Laws and the Illegitimate Use of the "Law, Public Order, and Morality" Limitation on Constitutional Rights.' *The Review of Faith and International Affairs* 13(1): 13–22. doi.org/10.1080/15570274.2015.1005918.

Khan, Haq Nawaz and Pamela Constable. 2018. 'Religious Groups Protest Guilty Verdicts in Slaying of Pakistani Student.' *The Washington Post*, 10 February. Available from: www.washingtonpost.com/world/religious-groups-protest-guilty-verdicts-in-slaying-of-pakistani-student/2018/02/10/4ae90d4a-0da0-11e8-998c-96deb18cca19_story.html?noredirect=on&utm_term=.b12b94dd5b0e.

Khan, Ismail. 2011. 'The Assertion of Barelvi Extremism.' *Current Trends in Islamist Ideology* 12(1): 51–72.

Khan, Naveeda Ahmed. 2012. *Muslim Becoming: Aspiration and Skepticism in Pakistan*. Durham, NC: Duke University Press. doi.org/10.1215/9780822395256.

Khan, Siraj. 2014. 'Blasphemy Against the Prophet.' In *Muhammad in History, Thought and Culture: An Encyclopedia of the Prophet of God. Volume 1*, edited by Coeli Fitzpatrick and Adam Hani Walker, 59–67. Santa Barbara, CA: ABC-CLIO.

Kloß, Sinah Theres. 2017. 'Sexual(ized) Harassment and Ethnographic Fieldwork: A Silenced Aspect of Social Research.' *Ethnography* 18(3): 396–414. doi.org/10.1177/1466138116641958.

Korom, Frank J. 2000. 'Holy Cow! The Apotheosis of Zebu, or Why the Cow is Sacred in Hinduism.' *Asian Folklore Studies* 59(2): 181–203. doi.org/10.2307/1178915.

Krohn-Hansen, Christian. 1994. 'The Anthropology of Violent Interaction.' *Journal of Anthropological Research* 50(4): 367–81. doi.org/10.1086/jar.50.4.3630559.

Lambert, Yves. 1999. 'Religion in Modernity as a New Axial Age: Secularization or New Religious Forms?' *Sociology of Religion* 60(3): 303. doi.org/10.2307/3711939.

Leys, Ruth. 2011. 'The Turn to Affect: A Critique.' *Critical Inquiry* 37(3): 434–72. doi.org/10.1086/659353.

Mahmood, Saba. 2009. 'Religious Reason and Secular Affect: An Incommensurable Divide?' In *Is Critique Secular? Blasphemy, Injury, and Free Speech*, edited by Talal Asad, Wendy Brown, Judith Butler, and Saba Mahmood, 64–100. Berkeley, CA: Townsend Center for the Humanities, University of California. Available from: escholarship.org/uc/item/84q9c6ft.

Malik, Jamal. 2008. *Islam in South Asia: A Short History*. Themes in Islamic Studies Vol. 4. Leiden: Brill. doi.org/10.1163/ej.9789004168596.i-520.

Malkki, Liisa Helena. 1995. *Purity and Exile: Violence, Memory, and National Cosmology among Hutu Refugees in Tanzania*. Chicago: University of Chicago Press. doi.org/10.7208/chicago/9780226190969.001.0001.

Marcus, George E. 1995. 'Ethnography in/of the World System: The Emergence of Multi-Sited Ethnography.' *Annual Review of Anthropology* 24(1): 95–117. doi.org/10.1146/annurev.an.24.100195.000523.

Marcus, George E., ed. 1996. *Connected: Engagements with Media*. Chicago: University of Chicago Press.

Marglin, Frédérique Apffel. 1977. 'Power, Purity and Pollution.' *Contributions to Indian Sociology* 11(2): 245–70. doi.org/10.1177/006996677701100201.

Marmon, Shaun Elizabeth. 1995. *Eunuchs and Sacred Boundaries in Islamic Society*. Oxford, UK: Oxford University Press.

Massumi, Brian. 2002. *Parables for the Virtual: Movement, Affect, Sensation*. Durham, NC: Duke University Press. doi.org/10.1215/9780822383574.

Mateen Khalid, Muhammad, ed. 2007. *Shaheedan-e-Namoos-e-Risaalat* [*Martyrs of the Honour of the Prophet*]. [In Urdu.] Lahore, Pakistan: Faateh Publishers.

Mazhar, Arafat. 2015. 'The Fatwas That Can Change Pakistan's Blasphemy Narrative.' *Dawn News*, 4 January. Available from: www.dawn.com/news/1154856.

Mazhar, Arafat. 2018. *The Untold Truth of Pakistan's Blasphemy Law: A Reconciliation with the Past and a Way Forward*. Pakistan: Engage Foundation for Research and Dialogue. Available from: engagepakistan.com/engage/.

Maznab, Rehman. 2007. 'Ghazi Ilmuddin Shaheed.' [In Urdu.] In *Shaheedan-e-Namoos-e-Risaalat* [*Martyrs of the Honour of the Prophet*], edited by Muhammad Mateen Khalid, 25–43. Lahore, Pakistan: Faateh Publishers.

Mehdi, Tahir. 2013. 'Hanging in Shame: Pedophilia, Masculinity and the Media.' *Dawn News*, 18 September. [Updated 14 January 2018.] Available from: www.dawn.com/news/1043753.

Melchert, Christopher. 1997. *The Formation of the Sunni Schools of Law, 9th–10th Centuries C.E.* Studies in Islamic Law and Society Vol. 4. Leiden: Brill.

Metcalf, Barbara Daly. 1982. *Islamic Revival in British India: Deoband, 1860–1900*. Princeton Legacy Library, 778. Princeton, NJ: Princeton University Press. doi.org/10.1515/9781400856107.

Metcalf, Barbara Daly. 2004. *Islamic Contestations: Essays on Muslims in India and Pakistan*. Oxford, UK: Oxford University Press.

Micheelsen, Arun. 2002. '"I Don't Do Systems": An Interview with Clifford Geertz.' *Method and Theory in the Study of Religion* 14(1): 2–20. doi.org/10.1163/157006802760198749.

Mosse, David. 1996. 'South Indian Christians, Purity/Impurity, and the Caste System: Death Ritual in a Tamil Roman Catholic Community.' *The Journal of the Royal Anthropological Institute* 2(3): 461–83. doi.org/10.2307/3034898.

Nair, Neeti. 2013. 'Beyond the "Communal" 1920s: The Problem of Intention, Legislative Pragmatism, and the Making of Section 295A of the Indian Penal Code.' *The Indian Economic & Social History Review* 50(3): 317–40. doi.org/10.1177/0019464613494622.

Narayan, Kirin. 1993. 'How Native Is a "Native" Anthropologist?' *American Anthropologist* 95(3): 671–86. doi.org/10.1525/aa.1993.95.3.02a00070.

Nasir, Mohammad Jibran. 2016. 'Mumtaz Qadri: From Ghazi to Shaheed.' *The Express Tribune*, 1 March. Available from: tribune.com.pk/article/32676/mumtaz-qadri-from-ghazi-to-shaheed.

Nasr, Vali R. 2000a. 'International Politics, Domestic Imperatives, and Identity Mobilization: Sectarianism in Pakistan 1979–1998.' *Comparative Politics* 32(2): 171–90. doi.org/10.2307/422396.

Nasr, Vali R. 2000b. 'The Rise of Sunni Militancy in Pakistan: The Changing Role of Islamism and the Ulama in Society and Politics.' *Modern Asian Studies* 34(1): 139–80. doi.org/10.1017/S0026749X00003565.

Nelson, Matthew J. 2009. 'Dealing with Difference: Religious Education and the Challenge of Democracy in Pakistan.' *Modern Asian Studies* 43(3): 591–618. doi.org/10.1017/S0026749X07003423.

The News International. 2016. 'Jamaat-e-Islami's Anti-Corruption Train March Begins Today.' *The News International*, 25 May. Available from: www.thenews.com.pk/latest/122412-Jamaat-e-Islamis-anti-corruption-train-march-begins-today+com%2FYEor+.

Olivelle, Patrick. 1998. 'Caste and Purity: A Study in the Language of the Dharma Literature.' *Contributions to Indian Sociology* 32(2): 189–216. doi.org/10.1177/006996679803200203.

Olwig, Karen Fog and Kirsten Hastrup. 1997. 'Introduction.' In *Siting Culture: The Shifting Anthropological Object*, edited by Karen Fog Olwig and Kirsten Hastrup, 1–14. New York: Routledge.

Osella, Filippo and Caroline Osella. 2008. 'Introduction: Islamic Reformism in South Asia.' *Modern Asian Studies* 42(2): 247–57. doi.org/10.1017/S0026749X07003186.

O'Sullivan, Declan. 2001. 'The Interpretation of Qur'anic Text to Promote or Negate the Death Penalty for Apostates and Blasphemers.' *Journal of Qur'anic Studies* 3(2): 63–93. doi.org/10.3366/jqs.2001.3.2.63.

Otunnu, Ogenga. 2016. *Crisis of Legitimacy and Political Violence in Uganda, 1890 to 1979*. [eBook.] African Histories and Modernities series. London: Palgrave Macmillan. doi.org/10.1007/978-3-319-33156-0.

Pakistan Bureau of Statistics (PBS). 2017. *Province Wise Provisional Results of Census 2017*. Islamabad: Pakistan Bureau of Statistics. Available from: www.pbs.gov.pk/sites/default/files/PAKISTAN%20TEHSIL%20WISE%20FOR%20WEB%20CENSUS_2017.pdf.

Pakistan Today. 2018a. 'CM Opens Ghazi Block, Liver Clinic at Services Hospital.' *Pakistan Today*, 15 January. Available from: www.pakistantoday.com.pk/2018/01/15/cm-opens-ghazi-block-liver-clinic-at-services-hospital/.

Pakistan Today. 2018b. 'NA Body Rejects Bill Seeking Public Hanging of Child Rapists, Murderers.' *Pakistan Today*, 1 February. Available from: www.pakistantoday.com.pk/2018/02/01/na-body-rejects-bill-seeking-public-hanging-of-child-rapists-murderers/.

Pakistan Today. 2018c. 'Video: Aasiya Case Judgement Resonates in British Parliament.' *Pakistan Today*, 1 November. Available from: www.pakistan today.com.pk/2018/11/01/video-aasiya-case-judgement-resonates-in-british-parliament/.

Pandey, Gyanendra. 2003. *Remembering Partition: Violence, Nationalism and History in India*. Cambridge, UK: Cambridge University Press. doi.org/10.2307/3518329.

Paracha, Nadeem F. 2013. 'Pinning Jinnah.' *Journal of the Pakistan Historical Society* 61(4). Available from: www.questia.com/library/journal/1P3-3178363931/pinning-jinnah.

Pasha, Adil. 2016. 'Mumtaz Qadri's Shrine: In Memory of Salmaan Taseer's Assassin.' *Dawn News*, 27 December. Available from: www.dawn.com/news/1302289.

Pennycook, Alastair. 2004. 'Performativity and Language Studies.' *Critical Inquiry in Language Studies* 1(1): 1–19. doi.org/10.1207/s15427595cils0101_1.

Philippon, Alix. 2014. 'A Sublime, Yet Disputed, Object of Political Ideology? Sufism in Pakistan at the Crossroads.' *Commonwealth & Comparative Politics* 52(2): 271–92. doi.org/10.1080/14662043.2014.894284.

Pirie, Fernanda. 2013. *The Anthropology of Law*. Clarendon Law Series. Oxford, UK: Oxford University Press. doi.org/10.1093/acprof:oso/9780199696840.001.0001.

Pratt Ewing, Katherine. 1997. *Arguing Sainthood: Modernity, Psychoanalysis, and Islam*. Durham, NC: Duke University Press. doi.org/10.2307/j.ctv11vc7dt.

The Punjab Disturbances Court of Inquiry. 1954. *Report on Punjab Disturbances of 1953*. 10 April 1954. Lahore, Pakistan: The Punjab Disturbances Court of Inquiry. Available from: www.thepersecution.org/archive/munir/intro.html.

Qasmi, Ali Usman. 2011. *Questioning the Authority of the Past: The Ahl Al-Qur'an Movements in the Punjab*. Karachi, Pakistan: Oxford University Press.

Qasmi, Ali Usman and Megan Eaton Robb. 2017. 'Introduction.' In *Muslims against the Muslim League: Critiques of the Idea of Pakistan*, edited by Ali Usman Qasmi and Megan Eaton Robb, 1–34. New York: Cambridge University Press. doi.org/10.1017/9781316711224.001.

Qureshi, Mufti Muhammad Hanif. 2012. *Ghazi Mumtaz Hussain Qadri*. [In Urdu.] Pakistan: Shabab Islami Pakistan.

Ramzan, Muhammad. 2015. 'Sectarian Landscape, Madrasas and Militancy in Punjab.' *Journal of Political Studies* 22(421): 421–36.

Riches, David. 1986. 'The Phenomenon of Violence.' In *The Anthropology of Violence*, edited by David Riches, 1–27. New York: Blackwell.

Robbins, Joel. 2004. *Becoming Sinners: Christianity and Moral Torment in a Papua New Guinea Society*. Berkeley, CA: University of California Press. doi.org/10.1525/9780520937086.

Robinson, Francis. 1998. 'The British Empire and Muslim Identity in South Asia.' *Transactions of the Royal Historical Society* 8: 271–89. doi.org/10.2307/3679298.

Robinson, Francis. 2008. 'Islamic Reform and Modernities in South Asia.' *Modern Asian Studies* 42(2): 259–81. doi.org/10.1017/S0026749X07002922.

Rouland, Norbert and Philippe G. Planel. 1994. *Legal Anthropology*. London: Athlone Press.

Roy, Olivier. 1994. *The Failure of Political Islam*. Cambridge, MA: Harvard University Press.

Rumi, Raza. 2018. 'Unpacking the Blasphemy Laws of Pakistan.' *Asian Affairs* 49(2): 319–39. doi.org/10.1080/03068374.2018.1469338.

Saeed, Abdullah. 2011. 'Ambiguities of Apostasy and the Repression of Muslim Dissent.' *The Review of Faith & International Affairs* 9(2): 31–38. doi.org/10.1080/15570274.2011.571421.

Saeed, Raza. 2013. 'Metamorphosis of the Ideals and the Actuals: Blasphemy Laws in Pakistan and the Transplantation of Justice in British India.' *Pólemos: Journal of Law, Literature and Culture* 7(2): 235–47. doi.org/10.1515/pol-2013-0012.

Saiya, Nilay. 2016. 'Blasphemy and Terrorism in the Muslim World.' *Terrorism and Political Violence* 29(6): 1087–105. doi.org/10.1080/09546553.2015.1115759.

Scheper-Hughes, Nancy. 2002. 'Coming to Our Senses: Anthropology and Genocide.' In *Annihilating Difference: The Anthropology of Genocide*, edited by Kenneth Roth and Alexander Laban Hinton, 348–81. Berkeley, CA: University of California Press. doi.org/10.1525/california/9780520230286.003.0014.

Scheper-Hughes, Nancy and Philippe I. Bourgois, eds. 2004. *Violence in War and Peace: An Anthology*. Malden, MA: Blackwell.

Schick, İrvin Cemil. 2010. 'The Harem as Gendered Space and the Spatial Reproduction of Gender.' In *Harem Histories: Envisioning Places and Living Spaces*, edited by Marilyn Booth, 69–86. Durham, NC: Duke University Press. doi.org/10.1215/9780822393467-005.

Schimmel, Annemarie. 1975. *Mystical Dimensions of Islam*. Chapel Hill, NC: University of North Carolina Press.

Schimmel, Annemarie. 2004. *The Empire of the Great Mughals: History, Art and Culture*. London: Reaktion Books.

Schinkel, Willem. 2013. 'Regimes of Violence and the Trias Violentiae.' *European Journal of Social Theory* 16(3): 310–25. doi.org/10.1177/1368431013476537.

Schröder, Ingo W. and Bettina E. Schmidt. 2001. 'Introduction: Violent Imaginaries and Violent Practices.' In *Anthropology of Violence and Conflict*, edited by Bettina Schmidt and Ingo Schroeder, 1–24. London: Routledge.

Shakir, Naeem. 2015. 'Islamic Shariah and Blasphemy Laws in Pakistan.' *The Round Table* 104(3): 307–17. doi.org/10.1080/00358533.2015.1053235.

Siddique, Osama and Zahra Hayat. 2008. 'Unholy Laws and Holy Speech: Blasphemy Laws in Pakistan—Controversial Origins, Design Defects and Free Speech Implications.' *Minnesota Journal of International Law* 17(2): 303–85.

Sidel, John T. 2006. *Riots, Pogroms, Jihad: Religious Violence in Indonesia*. Ithaca, NY: Cornell University Press. doi.org/10.7591/9781501729898.

Siegel, James T. 2006. *Naming the Witch*. Stanford, CA: Stanford University Press.

Sirajuddin. 2017. 'Mob Attacks Man in Chitral Accused of Making "Blasphemous Remarks".' *Dawn News*, 21 April. www.dawn.com/news/1328360.

Skoggard, Ian and Alisse Waterston. 2015. 'Introduction: Toward an Anthropology of Affect and Evocative Ethnography.' *Anthropology of Consciousness* 26(2): 109–20. doi.org/10.1111/anoc.12041.

Smith, Daniel Jordan. 2004. 'The Bakassi Boys: Vigilantism, Violence, and Political Imagination in Nigeria.' *Cultural Anthropology* 19(3): 429–55. doi.org/10.1525/can.2004.19.3.429.

Spradley, James P. 1980. *Participant Observation*. New York: Holt, Rinehart & Winston.

Stephens, Julia. 2014. 'The Politics of Muslim Rage: Secular Law and Religious Sentiment in Late Colonial India.' *History Workshop Journal* 77(1)(Spring): 45–64. doi.org/10.1093/hwj/dbt032.

Suleman, Muhammad. 2018. 'Institutionalisation of Sufi Islam After 9/11 and the Rise of Barelvi Extremism in Pakistan.' *Counter Terrorist Trends and Analyses* 10(2): 6–10. doi.org/10.2307/26358994.

Sundar, Nandini. 2010. 'Vigilantism, Culpability and Moral Dilemmas.' *Critique of Anthropology* 30(1): 113–21. doi.org/10.1177/0308275X09360140.

Tahir-ul-Qadri, Muhammad. 2013. *Protection of the Honour of the Prophet*. [In Urdu.] Lahore, Pakistan: Minhaj-ul-Quran Publications.

Tamanaha, Brian Z. 2001. *A General Jurisprudence of Law and Society*. New York: Oxford University Press. doi.org/10.1093/acprof:oso/9780199244676.001.0001.

Tambiah, Stanley J. 1996. *Leveling Crowds: Ethnonationalist Conflicts and Collective Violence in South Asia*. Berkeley, CA: University of California Press. doi.org/10.1525/9780520918191.

Tanveer, Rana. 2017. 'Over 100 Clerics Arrested in Lahore for Trying to "Celebrate" Salmaan Taseer's Assassination.' *The Express Tribune*, 4 January. Available from: tribune.com.pk/story/1284399/100-clerics-arrested-lahore-trying-celebrate-salmaan-taseers-assassination/.

Thurston, Robert W. 2011. 'Lynching and Legitimacy: Toward a Global Description of Mob Murder.' In *Globalizing Lynching History: Vigilantism and Extralegal Punishment from an International Perspective*, edited by Manfred Berg and Simon Wendt, 69–86. New York: Palgrave Macmillan. doi.org/10.1057/9781137001245_5.

Tilly, Charles. 1986. *The Contentious French*. Cambridge, MA: Belknap Press.

Tomkins, Silvan S. 2009. 'Affect Theory.' In *Approaches to Emotion*, edited by Klaus R. Scherer and Paul Ekman. London: Psychology Press. doi.org/10.4324/9781315798806.

Toor, Saadia. 2011. *The State of Islam: Culture and Cold War Politics in Pakistan*. London: Pluto Press.

Turner, Victor. 1980. 'Social Dramas and Stories about Them.' *Critical Inquiry* 7(1)(Autumn): 141–68. doi.org/10.1086/448092.

Uddin, Asma T. 2011. 'Blasphemy Laws in Muslim-Majority Countries.' *The Review of Faith & International Affairs* 9(2): 47–55. doi.org/10.1080/15570274.2011.571423.

van der Veer, Peter. 2001. *Imperial Encounters: Religion and Modernity in India and Britain*. Princeton, NJ: Princeton University Press.

van der Veer, Peter. 2002. 'Religion in South Asia.' *Annual Review of Anthropology* 31: 173–87. doi.org/10.1146/annurev.anthro.31.040402.085347.

Verkaaik, Oskar. 2004. 'Purity and Transgression: Sacred Violence and the Quest for Authenticity.' *Etnofoor* 17(1–2): 44–57. doi.org/10.2307/25758068.

Walsh, Declan. 2011. 'Pakistan's Blasphemy Laws Have Left Even Judges in Fear of Their Lives.' *The Guardian*, 4 October. Available from: www.theguardian.com/commentisfree/belief/2011/oct/03/pakistan-blasphemy-laws.

Wasim, Amir and Munawer Azeem. 2017. 'Faizabad Sit-In Ends as Army Brokers Deal.' *Dawn News*, 28 November. Available from: www.dawn.com/news/1373274.

Wasti, Tahir. 2009. *The Application of Islamic Criminal Law in Pakistan: Sharia in Practice*. Leiden: Brill. doi.org/10.1163/ej.9789004172258.i-408.

Weber, Max. 1946. 'Politics as a Vocation.' In *Max Weber: Essays in Sociology*, edited by H.H. Gerth and C. Wright Mills, 77–128. New York: Oxford University Press. [From Wikisource.] Available from: fs2.american.edu/dfagel/www/class%20readings/weber/politicsasavocation.pdf.

Weiss, Kenneth J. and Robert Garfield. 2017. 'The Elephant in the Courtroom.' *Journal of the American Academy of Psychiatry and the Law Online* 45(2): 218–20.

Werbner, Pnina and Helene Basu. 1998. 'The Embodiment of Charisma.' In *Embodying Charisma: Modernity, Locality and the Performance of Emotion in Sufi Cults*, edited by Pnina Werbner and Helene Basu, 3–30. London: Routledge. doi.org/10.4324/9780203025208.

Wielderhold, Lutz. 1997. 'Blasphemy against the Prophet Muhammad and His Companions (Sabb Al-Rasul, Sabb Al-Sahabah): The Introduction of the Topic into Shafi'i Legal Literature and Its Relevance for Legal Practice under Mamluk Rule.' *Journal of Semitic Studies* 42(1): 39–70. doi.org/10.1093/jss/42.1.39.

Wood, Amy. 2009. *Lynching and Spectacle: Witnessing Racial Violence in America, 1890–1940*. Chapel Hill, NC: University of North Carolina Press. doi.org/10.5149/9780807878118_wood.

Woodman, Gordon R. 1998. 'Ideological Combat and Social Observation: Recent Debate about Legal Pluralism.' *The Journal of Legal Pluralism and Unofficial Law* 30(42): 21–59. doi.org/10.1080/07329113.1998.10756513.

Zaidi, Hassan Belal. 2017. 'NA Body to Probe Blasphemous Content Online.' *Dawn News*, 15 March. Available from: www.dawn.com/news/1320622.

Zaman, Muhammad Qasim. 1999. 'Religious Education and the Rhetoric of Reform: The Madrasa in British India and Pakistan.' *Comparative Studies in Society and History* 41(2): 294–323. doi.org/10.1017/S0010417599002091.

Zaman, Muhammad Qasim. 2002. *The Ulama in Contemporary Islam: Custodians of Change*. Princeton, NJ: Princeton University Press.

Žižek, Slavoj. 2008. *Violence*. New York: Pergamon.

Žižek, Slavoj. 2013. 'Neighbors and Other Monsters: A Plea for Ethical Violence.' In *The Neighbor: Three Inquiries in Political Theology*, edited by Slavoj Žižek, Eric L. Santner, and Kenneth Reinhard, 134–90. Chicago: University of Chicago Press.

Index

A page number containing 'n.' indicates a reference appearing in a footnote on that page.

9/11 attacks 33, 58, 60, 62
Ahl-e-Hadith 14, 40, 41, 71
Ahmadi 5, 14, 15, 55, 83, 100, 109, 110, 113, 129, 139, 178, 208–9
Al-Khidmat Foundation 90
All India Muslim League (AIML) 47, 48, 49, 51
Allah xv, 39, 40, 62, 87, 132, 191, 193, 195
   and killing of blasphemers 181, 182, 184, 186, 203
   house of (*Kaaba*) 8n.4, 9, 78
   insulting of 7, 75, 191
   invocation in court judgements 194, 195–6
   law of 75, 76
   lawyers' invocation of 173, 174, 181
   love for 183, 194
   Muhammad as prophet of 71, 191, 193, 195
   prescriptions of 76, 77, 187, 194
   relations with 69, 136, 162, 183
   revelations from 72, 101
   sovereignty of commands 148–9, 150, 151, 158, 159, 167, 203
   will of 149, 150, 158, 159, 167, 183, 204
   see also Muhammad, the Prophet
Anderson, Benedict 44, 45, 161n.4
apostasy 77, 80, 81, 83

Arabia 40
Arabic 8, 9, 65, 76, 90
Asia Bibi vs The State (2018) 148, 174, 188, 195–7
   see also Bibi, Asia

Baluchistan 56
Bangladesh 51, 53n.14, 56
   see also East Pakistan
Barelwi, Ahmed Raza Khan 42, 86
Barelwis xvii, 14, 42, 61, 82
   activism 61–2
   and politics 48, 61, 62, 68, 70, 72, 86, 93
   anti-blasphemy activities xvii, 14, 42, 59, 62, 63, 93, 178
   criticism of xxv, 89, 175
   practices and beliefs xxv, 40–2, 69–73, 74, 84, 175, 203
   reformists 40, 42, 61, 84, 86
   rivalry with other sects 14, 48, 61–2, 69
Bengal 111
bey-hurmati (sacrilege) 6, 7, 8, 9
Bhatti, Shahbaz 148
Bibi, Asia 138n.3, 147–8, 151, 152, 157, 159, 168, 195, 196
   see also *Asia Bibi vs The State*
blasphemy law 5–6, 13, 68, 113, 175, 176, 199, 203
   abuse of 15–16, 97

233

and international law 16, 17, 19
criticism of 32n.1, 62n.1, 75, 174
extralegal enforcement of 20, 151, 152, 153, 157–8, 168, 173, 178, 179, 185, 186, 190, 193, 194, 196, 197, 199
flaws in 15, 32
instrumental use of 2, 15–16, 19, 97, 103, 138n.3, 192
misuse of 16, 75, 97, 154, 176
perceived failure of 153, 154, 157, 158, 167, 168, 177–8, 186
use of 154, 180
see also Islamic law; law; legislation
Brass, Paul 44, 46, 119, 120, 121, 144
Britain 140, 197
British
and modernisation 34, 35, 36, 60
and secularisation 35n.3, 36
colonial justice 31, 160, 161, 165, 199
colonial legislation 5, 13, 35, 36n.5, 196
colonisation 34, 35, 60, 197
education policy 35, 36n.4
religious history 35
British India 5, 13, 31, 32, 35, 36n.5, 39n.7, 42–3, 46–7, 48, 49, 50, 61, 86, 160, 161, 165, 196, 199
see also colonial India
Buddhist 99

caste xvi, 105, 106, 110, 134, 141, 201
caste system
Hindu 34, 46, 106
in India 74n.6, 107
Chaudhry, Mustafa 173, 174, 175–7, 178, 179–81, 182, 183
Cheema, Amir 73
Christianity 35n.3, 36n.4, 39n.7, 40n.8, 70n.4, 84, 114
Christians xxv, 14, 15, 128, 129, 130
accused of blasphemy 14, 15, 100, 103–7, 113–14, 124–38, 141, 142, 143, 147–8, 151, 152, 155, 157, 159, 168, 174
killing of 14, 15, 117
missionaries 36n.4, 41
perceived as impure 105, 106, 107, 108
place in Pakistani society 14, 106, 141
relations with Muslims 104, 105, 133–6, 138, 141–3
segregation from Muslims 104, 105, 106
violence against 117, 129, 134, 135
colonial India 35n.3, 165
impact of colonisation 35, 39n.7
justice 31, 160, 161, 165, 199
legislation 5, 13, 35, 36n.5, 196
Muslim activism in 42–3, 47, 61, 86
Muslim identity in 42–3, 46, 50
Muslims as minority in 32, 47, 49
nationalism 46–7, 48, 49, 50
see also British India; India; Partition
courts
application of death sentence 13, 147, 148, 156, 157, 179, 180–1, 191, 193, 197
British 31, 161, 199
district 156
high 1, 156, 191
high, Lahore xvii, 175, 177, 178, 179, 192
higher 157, 172, 190, 192
imperial 35, 36
legitimacy of 149, 151, 152, 174
lower 156–7, 172, 181, 190
sessions xvii, 155, 156, 157, 172, 190–1
sessions, Lahore 59, 173, 174, 181
see also judges; justice; Supreme Court of Pakistan

INDEX

Danish cartoon 17, 19, 23, 70
death penalty 6, 13, 62, 75, 82, 108, 138n.3, 148, 156, 157, 158, 165, 179, 180, 181, 183, 192, 193, 197
  see also legitimate violence
defilement 6, 99, 166
  of name of the Prophet 193, 208
  of places of worship 5, 207
  of Quran 5, 207
  see also derogatory remarks; desecrating; sacrilege
Deobandis xxv, 14, 47, 48, 82, 113, 175
  beliefs 40–1, 71, 84
  militancy 56, 61, 62
  sectarian rivalry 14, 48–9
derogatory remarks 5, 6, 31, 78, 124, 178, 191, 196, 207–8
  see also defilement; hate speech; insulting; moral—injury
desecrating 6, 99, 125, 154, 155, 207
  see also defilement
dishonour 8, 9, 11
  see also honour
disrespect 9, 11, 178
  of Islam 8, 114
  of the Prophet xxiv, 9, 31, 42, 178, 191
  terms for 8, 9, 11
  see also defilement; derogatory remarks; desecrating; insulting; moral—injury; respect; sacrilege

East Pakistan (Bangladesh) 51, 53n.14
  see also Bangladesh
elections 12, 86, 88, 92
English language 4, 6, 8, 11, 80, 152, 187
extralegal enforcement of blasphemy law 20, 151, 152, 153, 157–8, 168, 173, 178, 179, 185, 186, 190, 193, 194, 196, 197, 199

extralegal system 20, 124
  legitimacy of 21, 152, 166
  state discontinuities with 171–99, 205

Facebook 1, 91, 165
  see also social media
fiqh (Islamic jurisprudence) 40, 80
  see also Islamic law
freedom of speech 16–17, 202

Gellner, Ernest 44, 45
ghairatmand (honourable) 6, 7, 10
ghayoor (honourable) 6, 7, 10
ghazi (successful warrior) 180, 181, 182, 184
Gilgit 54, 56
God, *see* Allah

hadith (transmitted knowledge of the Prophet) 42, 75, 82, 172, 185, 191, 196, 197
  see also Quran
Hanafi 41, 80, 81, 82
Hanbali 41n.9, 80, 81, 82
Harkat-ul-Ansar 56
hate speech 31, 70
  see also derogatory remarks
hierarchical relations 8, 59, 97, 115, 118
hierarchy 7, 152
  see also social hierarchy
high court, *see* courts—high
Hindus 5, 36–7, 41
  and colonisation 35, 36–7
  and identity 34, 35, 37n.6
  and Muslims 34, 41, 46, 47
  as lesser than Muslims 49, 53, 55
  caste system 34, 46, 106
  in India 49, 50, 99
  practices 42n.10, 49, 74
  –Sikh violence 99
  violence against 15, 31, 32, 160
Hobsbawm, Eric 44, 54

235

honour 7–10, 11, 61, 107
  see also dishonour; respect
honour of the Prophet xxv, 61, 103, 173
  attacks on 7, 91
  defending xvii, 8, 10, 31–2, 43, 62, 63, 73, 80, 87, 89, 90, 91, 92, 160, 162, 173, 203, 204
  discourse on 9–10, 11, 63, 80, 92, 160
  martyrs for 31, 148, 160, 162, 163, 197
  organisations to defend 87, 89, 90, 91, 92, 204
  protecting xvii, 10, 32–3, 43, 62, 63, 73, 75, 89, 168, 203
  terms for 7, 9–10
  see also Muhammad, the Prophet; *namoos-e-risaalat*
human rights 2, 4, 16, 17, 57, 128, 130, 138

Ilmuddin Shaheed, Ghazi 31, 160, 161, 162, 172, 176, 196–7
India 34, 52, 58, 113, 165
  caste system 74n.6, 107
  communal violence xxvii, 99, 119
  Sikh militancy 107
  see also British India; colonial India; Indian Punjab; Mughal Empire; Partition; Subcontinent
Indian National Congress 50
Indian Punjab 107, 111
injury, see moral—injury
injustice 178, 179, 186
  see also justice; justice, state— perceived ineffectiveness of
insulting
  Allah 7, 75, 191
  images 1, 73, 124
  Islam 1, 8, 70, 75, 76, 77, 104, 114, 125, 175

Muhammad 5, 6, 59, 70, 71, 75, 76, 77, 78, 81, 83, 174, 175, 181, 186, 191
  publications 5, 31, 32, 160, 178, 196
  terms for 6, 7, 8, 9, 10, 67, 75, 83, 173
  words 42, 78, 125
  see also defilement; derogatory remarks; desecrating; moral— injury; sacrilege
Iqbal, Allama Muhammad 43n.11, 47, 68, 69, 161, 196, 199
Islam 5, 17, 33, 72, 81–2, 113, 132, 181, 193
  adherence and the self 39, 40, 43
  anti-Islam xxvii, 58, 68, 165
  attacks on 32, 58, 159, 186
  conceptions of 53, 55, 57, 183, 184, 195
  concepts of the Prophet in 70, 71, 76, 196
  conversion to 105, 109, 125n.1, 138
  insulting 1, 8, 70, 75, 76, 77, 104, 114, 125, 175
  Islamisation 56
  legal protection of 176, 204
  martyrs 160, 162
  pan-Islamism 47, 59, 86
  reform of 37, 38, 86, 87, 116
  revival of 36–7, 38
  symbols of 42, 43, 56
  'true' 36, 38, 41
  un-Islamic 54, 159
  see also individual sects
Islamabad xviii, 1, 90, 93, 162, 177
Islamic 37, 47, 53, 56, 85
  governance 43n.12, 56
  ideals 4, 40, 108, 202
  ideology 84, 87
  jurisprudence (*fiqh*) 40, 80
  juristic literature 68, 79–82, 84, 85
  justice 151, 152, 167, 174

Pakistan as Islamic state 16, 49, 51, 52, 53, 55, 59, 60, 88, 150, 167, 197, 199, 202, 204
  policies 86, 88
  practices 5, 34, 52, 76–7
  principles 4, 8, 19, 151
  scholarship 42, 47, 67, 68, 77, 79, 82, 87
  universalism 47, 48, 50
Islamic law 8, 36, 79–81, 149, 153, 167, 175, 176, 188, 203, 204
  and international law 17
  and killing of blasphemers 79, 186
  authority of 79, 84, 148, 149, 150, 152, 174, 197, 198
  influence on state law 149, 153, 175, 197, 198, 203, 204
  interpretation of 35, 167, 185, 186, 188, 190, 195, 196, 197
  schools of 40, 82
  sources of 79, 82, 172, 187
  see also justice—Islamic
Islamophobia 33, 58, 60

Jaafari 80, 81, 82
Jamaat-e-Islami (JI) xxi, 46, 53, 56, 86, 87, 89, 90
  and blasphemy 76, 77
  formation of 68, 86, 92
  politics of 86, 88, 91
Jamiat Ulama-i-Hind 47, 48
JI, *see* Jamaat-e-Islami
Jinnah, Muhammad Ali 48, 49, 50, 51, 161, 199
Joseph Colony 117, 139
judges 156, 157, 159, 167, 187, 188
  acquittals by 147, 157, 159, 168, 181, 182, 190, 195
  and state's monopoly over violence 27, 188, 189
  appeal to popular sentiment 168, 172, 188, 189, 190, 195, 197–8
  appeal to religion 168, 196, 197
  as representatives of state 168, 171, 189
  British 161n.4
  criticism of 148, 152, 159, 163
  discourse on blasphemy 4, 27, 172, 188–98
  endorsement of nonstate punishment 27, 172, 193–4
  favouring accused 157, 172, 193
  favouring accusers 157, 190–1
  interpretation of Islamic law 172, 190, 192, 193, 194–5, 195
  legitimacy of 167, 168, 189, 195, 196, 197
  sources of legitimacy 172, 190, 204
  threats against 147, 156, 157, 197
  use of death penalty 156, 191, 193
  use of Quran 151, 191, 196, 197
  use of religious teaching 151, 172, 188, 190–1, 192, 194, 195, 197–8
justice 88, 176, 185, 192, 205
  Islamic 4, 151, 152, 167, 174
  understanding of 20, 25, 27, 53, 185, 190
  see also courts; injustice
justice, popular 4, 21, 149, 158, 168
  comparison with state justice 22, 27, 171
  execution of 2, 165
  ideals 22, 147, 149, 168, 188–90
  ideas of 4, 150, 153, 164, 167, 168, 169, 197
  legitimacy of 4, 20, 21, 147, 149, 150–1, 159–60, 164, 166, 167, 168
  narratives of 27, 149–50, 167, 190, 204
justice, state 4, 150, 152, 155, 156
  comparison with popular justice 22, 27, 171, 172

ideals 21, 22, 197
legitimacy of 4, 147, 148–53, 158, 168, 169
perceived ineffectiveness of 154, 157, 158, 159, 167, 168, 177–8

Karachi xvii, 87, 91
Khan, Mashal 1–2, 3, 20, 117, 124, 137, 139, 164
Khatm-e-Nabuwwat Lawyers' Forum (KNLF) xxii, 173, 174, 175, 177, 178, 179, 181, 184, 185, 186, 190
Köppel, Roger 73

Labbaik ya Rasool Allah 87
Lahore xvii, xviii, 14, 59, 86, 100, 125, 133, 173, 180, 187, 209
   activism in 23, 43
   high courts xvii, 175, 177, 178, 179, 192
   nonstate violence in 91, 181
   sessions courts 59, 173, 174, 181
   shrines in 161, 162
Lahore University of Management Sciences x, xxi
law 3, 18, 20–1, 22, 34, 35, 93, 149, 152
   and nonstate violence 4, 171, 186, 189, 192
   anthropology of 20–1, 22, 25
   as reflection of public morality 21, 22, 185, 189, 197
   authority for violence 20, 188–9
   centrism 20, 21, 97, 149
   challenge to 148, 149, 150, 152, 167, 176, 177, 189–91, 197
   challenge to authority of 150, 152, 153
   colonial influence on 5, 13, 36, 46, 196
   conflict with nonstate law 22, 148–50, 151, 152, 177, 184, 188–90, 204
   discourse on 19–22, 80, 81, 152, 154, 176, 185, 187–99
   enforcement 126, 132–3, 150, 158, 177
   extralegal enforcement 20, 151, 152, 153, 157–8, 168, 173, 178, 179, 185, 186, 190, 193, 194, 196, 197, 199
   influence of Islamic law on 149, 153, 175, 197, 198, 203, 204
   lack of primacy of 126, 148, 152, 197, 198
   legitimacy of 20, 21, 126, 148, 149, 150–1, 153, 172, 174, 175–7, 188–9, 197, 198
   modern 20, 21
   Pakistani 6, 109, 126, 148, 158
   rule of 22, 175, 176
   secular 36, 44
   state 2, 5, 19, 20–2, 118, 158, 175, 176, 177, 184, 186
   understanding of 176, 185, 189, 190, 191, 198
   Western 20, 149, 172, 175, 176, 185, 187, 205
   see also blasphemy law; Islamic law; Pakistan Penal Code
lawyers 109, 129, 154, 156
   at nexus of state and society 27, 171–2, 198
   condemnation of nonstate punishment 13, 27
   discourse on blasphemy 4, 27, 102, 172, 173–6, 179, 185–7, 190, 198
   engagement with religion 182, 187,
   religious motivation of 155, 172, 173, 184, 186–7,
   sources of legitimacy 27, 79, 187, 198
   support for nonstate punishment 27, 107, 109, 155, 157, 172, 179, 185

threats against 155, 156
use of religious sources 79, 190, 194
voluntary defence of nonstate punishers 171, 173, 181
voluntary prosecutions 155, 156, 171, 173
legal
anthropology 20–1, 22, 25
categorisation 21, 35
discourse 19–22, 80, 81, 152, 154, 176, 185, 187–99
framework 149, 150, 175, 179, 185
Islamic authority 84, 88, 149, 153
pluralism 20, 21, 22, 149, 204, 205
reform 35, 36, 44
sovereignty 153, 167
Western concepts 20, 149, 172, 175, 176, 185, 187, 205
see also blasphemy law; Islamic law; law; legislation
legal system, extralegal 20, 124
discontinuities with state legal system 171–99, 205
legitimacy of 21, 152, 166
legal system, state 18, 22, 132, 157
conceptions of legitimacy of 27, 148, 149, 150, 151, 166, 168, 177, 198
discontinuities with extralegal system 171–99, 205
effectiveness of 153–5, 156
lack of sole authority 20, 21, 148, 197
perceived failure of 147, 153–4, 157–9, 167, 177, 180, 185, 203
violence enshrined in 22, 25
legislation 4–6, 11, 15, 19, 32, 203
British colonial 5, 13, 36, 196
see also blasphemy law; Pakistan Penal Code

legitimacy
competition for 26, 86, 89, 90, 92–3, 133, 168, 187, 204
contestation of state 140, 148, 149–53, 158, 159, 164, 167–9, 198
of punishment forms 27, 44, 147–69, 172
of state law 20, 21, 126, 148, 149, 150–1, 153, 172, 174, 175–7, 188–9, 197, 198
of state punishment 27, 150–1, 158, 164, 167, 189, 195–6, 199, 201
politics of 63–94, 102, 140, 167–8, 197
social 103, 149
sources of 3, 4, 20, 21, 22, 27, 149, 150, 153, 160, 161, 164, 172, 189–90, 198, 199, 204
symbols of 56, 57, 63
understandings of 20, 21, 27, 55, 149
legitimate violence 24, 25, 193, 194, 196
nonstate authority over 20, 21, 103, 159–60, 163, 164, 166, 199
religious authority over 124, 126, 144, 152, 153
state authority over 4, 20, 27, 203
state monopoly over 22, 27, 150–2, 158, 159, 164, 167, 169, 188–90, 197, 203
see also death penalty

Madani, Husayn Ahmad 47
Malik Muhammad Mumtaz Qadri vs The State (2015) 148, 174, 189, 193, 194, 195
see also Qadri, Mumtaz
Maliki 41n.9, 80, 81, 82
Maududi, Abul A'la 47, 53, 86
Mazhar, Arafat 62n.1

media 4, 37, 54, 58, 59, 86, 123, 129, 130, 138, 140, 143, 186, 203
  see also social media
Minhaj Welfare Foundation 90
Minhaj-ul-Quran 70, 86, 90
moral xvii, xxvii, 8, 19, 48, 58, 59, 100, 142, 185, 205
  anxiety 26, 33, 40, 51, 59, 60, 94, 98, 100, 115, 133, 201, 202
  authority, competition for 26, 103, 121, 140
  character of women 100, 107
  code, transgression of 12, 99, 103, 106, 110, 115, 118, 142, 195, 202
  framework 18, 19, 98, 115, 176, 179
  individual reform 38, 39
  injury 5, 6, 16, 17, 18, 19–20, 71, 207
  narratives 121, 133, 191
  nonstate regulation 21, 205
  order xvi, 100, 103, 108, 118, 120
  outrage 19, 22, 23, 24, 42n.10, 71, 144
  policing xvii, xxvii, 108, 110, 112
  regulation 21, 54, 140, 205
  systems 20, 21, 204, 205
  'threat' 19, 20, 202
morality 17, 22, 23, 205
  individual 38, 39
  public 21, 22, 26, 27
  sources of 3, 21, 185, 197, 198
  state as authority over 21, 22, 25, 27, 149
  understanding 11, 25, 27
  universal 19, 43
Mughal Empire 34, 35, 36, 165
  see also India
Muhammad, the Prophet xxv, xxvii, 76, 78, 161, 180, 181, 192
  and blasphemy discourse 9, 10
  as human being 70, 71–2, 101
  as prophet of Allah 62, 70, 71, 184, 195

authority of 67–8, 71
blasphemy against 61, 63, 83, 101, 103, 107, 163, 181, 193
Christian attacks on 133, 134
conceptions of 70, 71, 184
defilement of name of 193, 208
disrespect of xxiv, 9, 31, 42, 178, 191
imitation of 42, 72–3, 74
insulting 5, 6, 59, 70, 71, 75, 76, 77, 78, 81, 83, 174, 175, 181, 186, 191
insulting images 1, 73, 124
insulting publications 5, 31, 32, 160, 178, 196
insulting words 42, 78, 125
killing for love of xx, 2, 31–2, 73, 148, 159, 160, 162, 164, 173, 185, 186, 197, 203
literature about 67, 68, 69, 72, 160, 184
love for 32, 43, 63, 67, 69–74, 76, 89, 90, 91–2, 93, 155, 160, 163, 168, 173, 174, 177–8, 182, 184, 186, 187, 196, 203
loyalty to 10, 69
personality of 18, 41, 42, 46, 69, 70, 76, 134, 160
physical appearance 41, 72, 104
place of in Islam 41, 42, 69, 71–2, 184, 196
respect for 9, 71, 73, 193, 196
status of 41, 70–1, 93, 193, 195, 196
terms for insulting 6, 7, 8, 9, 10, 67, 75, 83, 173
transmitted knowledge of (*hadith*) 42, 75, 82, 172, 185, 191, 196, 197
ways of relating to 17, 18, 42, 69, 70–4, 178
see also honour of the Prophet

namoos-e-risaalat (honour of the Prophet) 6, 7, 9, 10, 61, 173
see also honour of the Prophet
Namoos-e-Risaalat Convention (Honour of the Prophet Convention) 87
New Delhi 31, 113

outrage
  as offence 6, 126, 207, 209
  see also moral—outrage

Pakistan Awami Tehreek (PAT) 68, 70, 72, 86, 88, 90, 91, 92
Pakistan Muslim League (PMLN) 12
Pakistan Penal Code (PPC) 5, 6, 44, 77, 83, 155, 191, 192, 196, 207–9
Pakistan Tehreek-e-Insaf (PTI) 12
Partition 43, 47, 51, 52, 55, 62, 82, 111
  see also British India; colonial India; Subcontinent
Persian 34, 65
Peshawar 87, 88, 165
popular justice, see justice, popular
posing (as Muslim) 6, 109, 181, 209
Punjab xvii, xviii, 12, 13, 32, 43, 107, 111, 113, 124, 148, 161, 179
  see also Indian Punjab
Punjabi xv, 10, 87, 90, 107, 187

Qadri, Aftab 63
Qadri, Mumtaz xviii, 32–3, 73, 87, 89, 113, 138n.3, 148, 159, 162–3, 177, 178–9, 182–3, 184, 193, 194
  see also *Malik Muhammad Mumtaz Qadri vs The State*
Quran 5, 7, 40, 42, 47, 59, 79, 101, 106n.1, 181
  and killing of blasphemers 75–6, 77, 78–9, 186

and punishment of blasphemy 62n.1, 68, 191, 207
burning of 179–80
defilement of 5, 207
jurists' use of 82, 151, 172, 185–6, 191, 194, 196, 197
see also *hadith*
Quranic 37, 134
Qureshi, Hanif 162

Rajpal, Mahashe 31–2, 43, 44, 160, 161, 196–7
Renan, Ernest 48
respect 8, 9
  for the Prophet 9, 71, 73, 193, 196
  see also disrespect; honour
Rizvi, Allama Khadim Hussain 73, 87, 89, 90, 91–3, 152, 174

sacrilege (*bey-hurmati*) 6, 7, 8, 80
  see also defilement; desecrating; insulting
Salafi 56, 71
sessions courts, see courts—sessions
Shafi'i 41n.9, 80, 81–2
Shah, Bulleh xv, xvi
Shia xv, xxii, xxv, 14, 56, 59, 73n.5, 80, 113, 175
Sikhs 42n.10, 43, 99, 106, 107, 113
Sipah-e-Sahaba Pakistan (SSP) 56
social hierarchy 11, 18, 19, 100, 118, 143, 201
  transgression of 3, 9, 97, 98–110, 115
  see also hierarchy
social media xxii, 1, 78, 79, 87, 123, 135, 138, 165
  see also media; names of individual platforms
state justice, see justice, state
state law, see law—state
state legal system, see legal system, state

Subcontinent 69, 82, 111, 160, 165
  colonisation 5, 34, 35, 58
  modernisation 34, 35, 36
  nationalism 43, 46–7, 86
  reform movements 33, 37, 42n.10
  secularisation 35, 36
  see also Partition
Sufism xv, xvi, xxv, 43n.11, 73, 86, 161–2, 172, 183, 184, 187
Sunni xv, xvii, xxii, xxv, 56, 61, 62, 70, 125, 178
  beliefs 40–1, 56, 70, 71, 101
  identity 59, 113
  political parties 56, 68, 69–70, 86, 91, 93, 134
  reformists 40, 56, 61, 86
  schools of thought 41, 80, 84, 203
  sectoral conflict 16, 61, 69–70, 71, 175
  sects xvii, 14, 16, 56, 59, 61, 68, 69, 101
  versus Shia xv, 56, 59, 175
  see also individual sects
Sunni Tehreek 93, 134
Supreme Court of Pakistan 93n.15, 147–8, 152, 156, 157, 159, 163, 174, 188–9, 193, 195–6

Tahir-ul-Qadri, Muhammad 72, 73, 76, 77, 86–7, 90
Taseer, Salman 32, 75, 91, 113, 148, 162, 174, 177, 189
Tehreek-e-Labbaik Pakistan (TLP) 12, 68, 72, 73, 86, 87, 88, 89, 90, 91, 92, 93, 147, 152
Twitter xxii

Urdu xxii, 6, 7, 8, 43n.11, 45, 53n.14, 83, 125n.1, 152, 160, 187

violence
  against Christians 117, 129, 134, 135
  against Hindus 15, 31, 32, 160
  communal, in India xxvii, 99, 119
  enshrined in legal system 22, 25
  Hindu–Sikh 99
  nonstate and the law 4, 171, 186, 189, 192
  nonstate, in Lahore 91, 181
  see also legitimate violence

Wahabbis 71

Zia-ul-Haq, General 5, 13, 32, 55–6, 62n.2, 165

www.ingramcontent.com/pod-product-compliance
Lightning Source LLC
Chambersburg PA
CBHW042043240426
43667CB00048B/2963